Educational Strategies
and Services for
Exceptional Children

Educational Strategies and Services for Exceptional Children

By

GEORGE R. TAYLOR, Ph.D.

Director of Institutional Research
Coppin State College
Baltimore, Maryland

and

STANLEY E. JACKSON, Ed.D.

Assistant Executive Director
The Council for Exceptional Children
Reston, Virginia

CHARLES C THOMAS • **PUBLISHER**
Springfield • *Illinois* • *U.S.A.*

Published and Distributed Throughout the World by
CHARLES C THOMAS • PUBLISHER
Bannerstone House
301-327 East Lawrence Avenue, Springfield, Illinois, U.S.A.

© *1976, by* **CHARLES C THOMAS • PUBLISHER**
ISBN 0-398-03530-X
Library of Congress Catalog Card Number: 75-40046

With **THOMAS BOOKS** *careful attention is given to all details of
manufacturing and design. It is the Publisher's desire to present books that are
satisfactory as to their physical qualities and artistic possibilities and
appropriate for their particular use.* **THOMAS BOOKS** *will be true to those
laws of quality that assure a good name and good will.*

Printed in the United States of America
R-1

Library of Congress Cataloging in Publication Data

Taylor, George R
  Educational strategies and services for exceptional children.

  Bibliography: p.
  1. Exceptional children--Education--Addresses,
essays, lectures. I. Jackson, Stanley E., joint author.
II. Title.
LC3965.T37   371.9   75-40046
ISBN 0-398-03530-X

CONTRIBUTORS

PAUL J. AREND, Ed.D., is a school administrator with the Board of Education of Baltimore County, Maryland. He completed his undergraduate degree at Towson State College, Maryland, and his master's degree at Johns Hopkins University. His doctorate was earned in administration and supervision at the University of Virginia. He has administered teacher training programs and served as a consultant to various school districts in the State of Maryland. He is presently an adjunct professor of administration and supervision in the department of special education at Coppin State College, Baltimore, Maryland.

Dr. Arend has held faculty positions at the University of Virginia, Western Maryland College, and Dundalk Community College. He has published numerous articles in the realm of special education. He is also a film reviewer for the editor of *Exceptional Children,* and a consultant to Hallmark Films, the special education series.

STEPHANIE LAFOREST BROWN, M.Ed., is associate director of the Office of Institutional Research at Coppin State College, Baltimore, Maryland. Prior to this position, she was a research associate for four years in this office. She has administered tests in both an Early Childhood Research Program and a Contingency Management Project with special education students. Her other experiences have been in psychological services at the Westinghouse Electric Corporation, and a social worker with the Baltimore Department of Social Services. She is a member of the National Rehabilitation Association and the American Educational Research Association.

CATHERINE A. GROFF, Ed.D., is an associate professor of special education at Coppin State College, Baltimore, Maryland. She completed her undergraduate work at Monmouth College, West Long Branch, New Jersey. She received her master's degree in behavioral sciences from Kean College, Union City, New Jersey, and her education specialist degree from the University of Louisville, Louisville, Kentucky. Her doctorate was earned in 1968 from Indiana University, Bloomington, Indiana.

Dr. Groff was a teacher of gifted and learning-disabled children in the New Jersey school system. She has served on the faculty at the University of Miami, Coral Gables, Florida; Western Maryland College, Westminster, Maryland; Howard Community College, Columbia, Maryland; Morgan State College, Coppin State College, and Johns Hopkins University, Baltimore, Maryland. She has also served as consultant to many school districts, and is the editor of *Mental Retardation: A Book of Readings*. Dr. Groff is a member of Kappa Delta Pi National Honor Society in Education; Outstanding Young Women, 1973; and Distinguished Community Leaders, 1974.

JACK F. GROSMAN, M.A., is currently associate professor and coordinator of the undergraduate program in special education at Coppin State College. Mr. Grosman is presently pursuing his doctorate degree at Columbia University in the education of the exceptional. He has been a classroom teacher of regular and special classes, principal of a large state institutional school, director of a psychotherapeutic program for behaviorally disordered children, administrator of research centers for exceptional children, and an educational consultant. He is presently serving on advisory committees of a number of state agencies and parental groups concerned with the education and treatment of the handicapped.

COLONEL T. HAWKINS, M.S., is an assistant professor of special education at Coppin State College, Baltimore, Maryland. He completed his undergraduate and graduate degrees at Virginia State College in the area of special education. He is presently a doctoral candidate at the University of Pittsburgh. He has served as a teacher of exceptional children in the District of Columbia public schools, the Head Start Program, and St. Elizabeth's Hospital. He was the director of the day care center for retarded individuals at the Baltimore Association for Retarded Citizens. Mr. Hawkins is a former chairman of the CEC Committee on Minority Groups. He is also a member of several local and national organizations concerned with improving the welfare of exceptional individuals.

STANLEY E. JACKSON, Ed.D., is an assistant executive director at The Council for Exceptional Children. He completed his undergraduate work at the District of Columbia Teachers College and his graduate work at Columbia University in the areas of administration and supervision of the exceptional. He was a teacher and principal of exceptional children in the District of Columbia public schools. He served as the director of special education for a number of years in the same system. Dr. Jackson has received numerous awards and citations from school and community groups.

He has held faculty positions at the Catholic University of America and the District of Columbia Teachers College. He has published widely in the field of special education. Dr. Jackson is a member of several local and national organizations and serves on numerous boards concerned with the education and training of the exceptional.

RAE LOUISE JONES, Ph.D., is an assistant professor of special education at Coppin State College. She completed her M.A. degree at George Washington University and her doctorate degree at the University of Pittsburgh in the areas of child development and special education. Dr. Jones has held positions as a counselor, instructor, and day care director in Allegheny County and the District of

Columbia public schools. She is a member of the American Personnel and Guidance Association, NEA, CEC, and the Alpha Kappa Alpha Sorority.

INEZ W. LATTIMORE, M.A., is an associate professor of special education at Coppin State College. She completed her undergraduate degree at D. C. Teachers College in Washington, D. C., where she also served as a part-time faculty member. Her master's degree was earned at the George Washington University where she participated in the pilot program of the Diagnostic-Prescriptive Teacher Model. She was an assistant principal at Sharpe Health School for Handicapped Children and director of special projects in Washington, D. C. She was also director of the Parent Participation Reading Program for Nonachieving Students and assistant director of the Reading Institute — a Model School Division Project in the District of Columbia public schools.

Mrs. Lattimore has written several unpublished documents: *Resource Materials for Parents and Teachers, Diagnostic Techniques for Classroom Teachers, Individualized Curriculum for Severely Retarded Students, Curriculum Guides for EMR and TMR Children.* She has served in a variety of consultative capacities for private and state consultative firms, and as a proposal writer and researcher for physically handicapped programs in the Washington metropolitan area.

LAFAYETTE MERCHANT, M.A., is associate director of the Instructional Media Center at Coppin State College. He received his undergraduate and graduate degrees in the area of educational technology. He has worked in several public school systems as a media specialist. Mr. Merchant has developed several instructional systems to instruct children. He instructs students at Coppin State College in the construction and use of hardware and software. Mr. Merchant is an active member of several educational agencies.

DR. HAROLD RUVIN, Ed.D., is an associate professor and acting chairman of special education at Coppin State College. He received his doctorate degree in special education at Yashiva University. Dr. Ruvin has coordinated programs and held administrative positions in special education at the University of Northern Colorado, Boston University, Jersey City State College, and Bird S. Coler Hospital.

He has had extensive experience in teaching exceptional individuals in the public schools of New York City. Dr. Ruvin has also made significant contributions to the field of special education through his scholarly publications. He is a consultant for several school districts in the Baltimore metropolitan area and is an active member of the CEC, AAMD, National Association for Retarded Citizens and other numerous organizations serving the exceptional.

LING SONG, M.Ed., is a research associate in the office of institutional research at Coppin State College. She completed her undergraduate work at National Taiwan University, and earned her M.Ed. degree in special education at Coppin State College. Ms. Ling Song has taught the retarded at Rosewood State Hospital in Baltimore, Maryland, and has also worked as a research assistant in the department of vocational rehabilitation at Coppin State College.

GEORGE R. TAYLOR, Ph.D., is the director of Institutional Research at Coppin State College, Baltimore, Maryland. He has taught both trainable and educable mentally retarded individuals in the District of Columbia public schools, and was a research analyst in the department of research and evaluation.

Dr. Taylor has served on the faculties of Coppin State College, Howard University, and the District of Columbia Teachers College. He has been a consultant to various school districts in the Washington and Baltimore Metro-

politan areas. Dr. Taylor has published numerous articles
in professional journals and textbooks concerned with the
education of the exceptional individual. He is an active
member of several local and national organizations, and in
1973 was listed in "Outstanding Educators of America."

PETER VALLETUTTI, Ed.D., is currently the dean of extension and experimental programs at Coppin State College,
Baltimore, Maryland. He is also a professor of special education at Coppin State College as well as a visiting professor at Johns Hopkins University and an assistant professor
in pediatrics at the Johns Hopkins Medical School.

He has been a classroom teacher of regular and special
classes, a principal, a speech and hearing therapist, and an
educational consultant. He has been listed in "Outstanding Educators of America," "Leaders In Education,"
"Who's Who In the East," and "Dictionary of International Biographies." He has published widely in professional
journals and has several textbooks to his credit.

PREFACE

PUBLIC reaction to labeling exceptional children has been propounded in several ways: through parent groups, federal and state legislation, and the courts. The present movement reflects that society recognizes that exceptional children, regardless of their handicaps, have a democratic right to a free public education. Combined, these factors have been responsible for advancing the concept of "mainstreaming the exceptional."

In keeping with this humanistic approach, *Educational Strategies and Services for Exceptional Children* is one of the first texts to advocate the discontinuance of etiological classification systems employed for grouping exceptional individuals. A proposed classification system is recommended based upon a developmental approach.

Each chapter in the text is based upon a noncategorical approach to the education of exceptional children with emphasis on the needs of individuals rather than upon categorical labels. Sound principles for implementing strategies within the regular classroom are highlighted. Chapters stress how these strategies may be successfully applied by the classroom teacher with little or no formal training and/or experience with techniques. The appendices provide an additional source for developing innovative approaches.

This text was written primarily for training junior and senior college students and those students in graduate programs majoring in education or related disciplines. It was also written as a guide to assist in-service teachers and school administrators concerned with providing quality education for the exceptional.

The first chapter gives an overview of trends and issues in the education of exceptional children, outlining some of the conventional systems used to classify exceptional individuals. The remaining chapters are addressed to the following topics: (1) new

xi

directions in classifying and labeling exceptional individuals, (2) individualized instruction, (3) behavior modification strategies, (4) perceptual remediation, (5) programmed instructional devices and materials, (6) nonprogrammed devices and materials, (7) organizational and instructional strategies, (8) college and university programs; and (9) the roles of the federal, state, and local agencies in their attempts to mainstream the exceptional.

This text is premised upon the idea that etiological labels have adverse effects on the total well-being of the exceptional. The schools can play a dominant role in eliminating the stigma associated with labels by accepting children with special needs into the mainstream of education. Instructional strategies for most exceptional individuals can be modified to meet their unique needs in the realm of regular education.

George R. Taylor
Stanley E. Jackson

CONTENTS

xiii

Educational Strategies
and Services for
Exceptional Children

CHAPTER I

TRENDS AND ISSUES IN THE EDUCATION OF EXCEPTIONAL CHILDREN

HAROLD RUVIN

DURING the past two decades, tremendous progress has been made in the field of special education. One of the major outgrowths of this thrust has been directed toward making special education a part, rather than a separate entity, of regular education.

Traditionally, special education programs were not initiated in response to the needs of exceptional individuals, but rather as expedient measures to resist a perceived threat to the existing goals for normal children.[1] The anticipated purpose of such classes was to develop within the pupil basic attitudes, habits, and skills which would enable his satisfactory adjustment to life in an increasingly complex society. Basic to the achievement of this goal was the ability of the pupils to use these attitudes, habits, and skills in securing and holding a job. Much controversy exists because many specialists agree that special education has not provided exceptional individuals with a viable education.

Today many organizational structures are being developed to maintain exceptional individuals in the mainstream of education. These structures do not appear to eliminate categorical labels that have plagued special education since its inception. In Chapter II, the authors have proposed a classification system which will focus on educational variables rather than on etiology. However, this first chapter is designed to review trends and issues

---

[1]M. C. Reynolds, "The Surge in Special Education," *National Education Association Journal*, 1967.

that have led special education to the crossroads.

HISTORICAL OVERVIEW

Prior to the early part of the nineteenth century, exceptional individuals were at the mercy of the societies in which they lived. Notions regarding handicapping conditions were closely linked with spirits and mysticism. Since there was no universal understanding of individual differences, some exceptional individuals were avoided, or placed in institutions and ignored. Inhuman treatment was rather pronounced for many of the mentally and physically handicapped. The gifted individual was usually exploited as his abilities were used to promote selfish interests within his society. Research concerning the exceptional individual was practically unheard of prior to the eighteenth century.

The early history of the United States was closely linked with a strong religious philosophy. The consensus generally held was that imperfect individuals were bedeviled. Consequently, exceptional individuals were considered to be outside the realm of religion. Since religion played a dominant role in the politics of the United States during this time frame, realistic planning and treatment for the exceptional individual was severely hampered.

During the early nineteenth century, improved attitudes toward exceptional individuals were expounded by such leaders as Horace Mann, Samuel Gridley Howe, Dorothea Dix, and Reverend Gallaudet. Horace Mann and Samuel Gridley Howe spoke out on behalf of the retarded; Dorothea Dix pleaded for the socially maladjusted; and Reverend Gallaudet was instrumental in promoting programs for the deaf. These leaders gave impetus to the movement establishing residential schools for the exceptional. It was proven that appropriate teaching procedures could be successful in helping exceptional individuals become useful citizens. Societal pressure, including numerous protests from the partents of exceptional children, led to the change from residential schools to day schools.

Classification of exceptional children was accelerated by Goddard. He brought the Binet-Simon Intelligence Test to this country in 1914, and it was standardized for American children by

Lewis Terman in 1916. This opened the era of mental testing in the United States. Mental testing revealed that distinct differences existed between individuals. Practices and attitudes began to change from concepts of custody, care, and treatment to creating programs of education and rehabilitation for exceptional individuals. The influence of World Wars I and II had far-reaching effects on the education of exceptional individuals. Many individuals who had gone into the services with no handicaps frequently returned with a disability; thus, public attention was focused more and more on disabilities. Combined, these factors caused public agencies, especially the schools, to give increasing attention to individuals who had exceptional differences.

Present Day Trends

The role of public schools in this country parallels the social and historical movements reflected in our culture. Education was viewed as such an important function that it was reserved as a right of the individual states. Since a democracy accepts the responsibility for the education of all youth, the constitution of each state provides for a system designed to provide educational opportunities for all children. Children who deviated in mental, physical, social, or emotional traits to such a degree that they could not reach their optimum growth in regular classes were not covered in most state constitutions until the beginning of the nineteenth century. Today, most states provide educational opportunities for all exceptional individuals.

Interest in special education has greatly increased because of the events of recent years. The influence of parent movement groups shows their deep concern for the future welfare of exceptional individuals. A significant factor is the social change in attitude toward the exceptional individual which was instilled into the minds of the general public by parents. Changes in attitude with regard to the education of the visually limited have led to their inclusion in the public school system. Advances in scientific fields have enabled many exceptional individuals to enter the mainstream of education. A case in point is the development of electronic devices which promoted the practicability of maintaining the hard of hearing in the schools. Another advance is the launching of the Russian Sputnik which, by spurring technology, renewed interest in the education of the gifted.

As a result of these developments, many reforms in educational philosophy and administration have been instituted.[2] Various trends have emerged that appear to be leading to significant changes in the education of the exceptional. President John F. Kennedy was the first president to introduce a national plan to combat mental retardation. Since then, federal, local, and state governments are financially supporting programs for exceptional individuals through several agencies. Therefore, special education is being presented with a new thrust, a thrust which stresses continuity and appropriateness of educational programs and also emphasizes effectiveness in delivering services to exceptional individuals.

Advancements have been made in knowledge, program development, remedial techniques, behavior modification, evaluation, and a variety of individualized techniques unparalleled in the history of special education. These various techniques will be dealt with in subsequent chapters. Significant advances have also been made during the past decade toward the economic and social integration of exceptional individuals into society, rectifying some of the ills resulting from segregating exceptional individuals. Unfortunately, modifications in instructional strategies are still based upon psychological or medical models as well as conventional classification systems.

CONVENTIONAL DEFINITIONS AND CLASSIFICATIONS OF EXCEPTIONAL CHILDREN

The conventional term "exceptional children" denotes many different degrees of disability. According to numerous authorities, that term is difficult to define because exceptionality represents a variety of medical and psychological categories. The

---

[2]Edgar A. Doll, "Adultation of the Special Child." *Exceptional Children, 29* (February, 1963). p. 280.

consensus, therefore, is that a general definition for an exceptional child is one who deviates mentally, physically, socially, or emotionally so markedly from what is considered normal growth and development that he cannot receive maximum benefit from a regular school program unless modifications are made in the instructional program, or special instruction and ancillary services are provided to enable him to achieve at a level commensurate with his respective abilities.[3, 4, 5]

Telford[6] outlined that many operational definitions of exceptionality are statistical and quantitative in nature. The mentally retarded can be defined as the intellectually lowest 2 or 3 percent of the population as indicated by intelligence tests; whereas, the intellectually gifted can be defined in terms of test scores at the upper 1 or 2 percent of the general population. The hard of hearing and the deaf can be identified in terms of hearing loss as measured in decibels by a standard audiometer. Blindness is typically defined legally as a visual acuity of 20/200 or less in the better eye after maximum correction, or as a possession of a visual field limited to 20 degrees or less. There are no conventional quantitative indices of most other types of deviant individuals, such as the orthopedically handicapped, the socially maladjusted, the emotionally disturbed, the epileptic, and the individual with speech defects. In most of these conditions, the diagnostic judgment of trained specialists replaces quantitative measurement. All of the above definitions appear to operate from medical or psychological terminology which has little relevancy for educational intervention.

Exceptional individuals are generally grouped on the basis of their major deviation or handicap, and may be classified as fol-

[3]Lloyd M. Dunn (Ed.), *Exceptional Children in the Schools* (New York: Holt, Rinehart and Winston, Inc., 1963), pp. 2-3.
[4]Samuel A. Kirk, *Educating Exceptional Children* (Boston: Houghton-Mifflin Company, 1972), p. 4.
[5]William A. Cruickshank (Ed.), *Psychology of Exceptional Children and Youth* (New Jersey: Prentice-Hall, 1963).
[6]Charles W. Telford and James M. Sawrey, *The Exceptional Individual* (New Jersey: Prentice-Hall, Inc., 1972), pp. 13-25.

lows: (1) the physically handicapped, (2) the mentally handicapped, (3) the intellectually gifted, (4) the emotionally unstable, (5) those with special health impairments, (6) the blind and hard of seeing, (7) the deaf and hard of hearing, (8) those with speech defects, (9) the socially maladjusted, and (10) the multiple handicapped.

Various authorities have advanced different categories for areas of deviations. Kirk[7] outlined the following areas: (1) communication disorders, including individuals with learning and speech handicaps, (2) mental deviations, including the gifted and the mentally retarded, (3) sensory handicaps, including individuals with auditory and visual handicaps, (4) neurologic, orthopedic, and other health impairments, and (5) behavior disorders, including the socially maladjusted and the emotionally disturbed. Similarly, Cruickshank[8] divided the areas of deviations into the following categories: (1) the intellectually exceptional individual, including the gifted and the mentally retarded, and (2) the physically handicapped, including visual and auditory handicaps, speech handicaps, orthopedic and neurological impairments.

INCIDENCE OF EXCEPTIONAL CHILDREN

It is estimated that exceptional children constitute approximately 7 percent to 12 percent of the general population. Part of the difficulty in determining the number of exceptional children is due to various definitions used by different disciplines in identifying the exceptional individual, and the lack of consensus concerning the classification and selection criteria. States differ in their classification systems, and to compound the problem, local school districts in various states also differ.

The number of children identified as retarded reflects certain political connotations. In the United States, the number of retarded individuals is generally accepted as approximately 3 percent of the total population. In some countries, such as the Soviet

---

[7]Kirk, *op. cit.*, p. 5.
[8]Cruickshank, *loc. cit.*

Union, there is a generally accepted figure of 1 percent. The difference in the Soviet figures reflects two basic concepts: first, that mental retardation is a condition caused by heredity or some central nervous system condition (approximately 1%); second, that the 2 percent additionally identified in the United States, according to Soviet authorities, were the direct result of social inadequacies reflecting the evils of capitalism and exploitation. There are growing numbers of scientists in the United States who are beginning to recognize that there are large numbers of individuals who function as though they are retarded due to factors in society. Factors such as social class, race, inappropriate use of tests, inadequate environments, attitude, health, diet, and quality of education modify performance as measured by intelligence tests. How many of these factors were the result of capitalism and exploitation, as suggested by the Russians, is difficult to assess. However, there is no question that changes in social policies and attitudes may alter the number of children classified as retarded.

A different way of looking at incidence is to identify the severity of the handicap. This is especially true when the need arises to provide school programs and services. The severely to profoundly handicapped, the totally deaf, the multiple-handicapped, the blind, the severely retarded, and the psychotic are such a comparatively small number (less than 1% of the population), and are usually identified long before they come to school.[9] Most children with severe handicaps are currently served outside of the regular public school, and require the efforts of many public and private programs in health, education, and welfare.

The larger number of exceptional children are those who have minimal kinds of deficiencies. These children are served within the public schools and usually are not identified until they have entered school. They can profit from school, providing that teachers receive supportive services.

U. S. Office of Education statistics appear to provide the best data on the number of exceptional children in the schools. The Office of Education has provided estimates since 1922. In 1964,

---

[9]David Kendall, *The Education of Visually Handicapped Children in the Atlantic Provinces: Critical Issues* (Halifax, Nova Scotia: Department of Education, Province of Nova Scotia, July, 1972).

Congress created the Bureau of Education for the Handicapped within the Office of Education. In order to provide more reliable data from the states, federal regulation in 1967 required all state departments of education to submit reports on the number of handicapped children the schools were serving. The office is presently engaged in providing updated, precise data for future use. In 1970, the Bureau of Education for the Handicapped estimated that 10 percent of the school population, from birth through nineteen years of age, was handicapped. The evaluation staff of the Bureau has estimated that by 1975, 13.2 percent of the school population will be handicapped. The difference between the 1970 estimates and the 1975 projected estimates can be attributed to the deletion of the gifted in the 1970 estimates, and a 1 percent increase for children classified as learning disabled.

The data in Table I are based on estimated 1965 population statistics as reported by the Bureau of Education for the Handicapped.

Table I indicates that the speech impaired constitute the largest grouping of exceptional children. Speech impairments cut across all areas of exceptional as well as physical, social, and mental traits. Thus, it would not be uncommon to find speech impairment among gifted children. Mental retardation has the next highest percentage, followed by learning disabilities, emotionally disturbed, and the gifted.

By way of review, classification and estimations of exceptional individuals have been based upon the total population within given age ranges. Educational institutions should be dedicated to providing the best opportunities possible for assisting exceptional individuals in reaching their optimum growth. In order to achieve this, the focus of special education must be radically shifted from a categorical model to one which stresses serving the needs of individuals. Remaining sections of this chapter will endeavor to provide information on similarities and relationships among exceptional individuals. Information discussed will be used in Chapter II to develop a proposed classification system based upon relevant educational variables.

ADJUSTMENT AND THE EXCEPTIONAL

The severity of the handicapping conditions of some excep-

TABLE I-I

PERCENT OF HANDICAPPED CHILDREN
PROJECTED ESTIMATES FOR 1975 (AGES 5-18)*

AREAS OF EXCEPTIONALITY	PERCENT OF THE POPULATION	NUMBER OF CHILDREN PROJECTED BY 1975
Mentally Retarded (Educable and Trainable)	2.5	1,375,000
Deaf	.1	55,000
Hard of Hearing	.5	275,000
Speech Impaired	3.5	1,925,000
Crippled and Other Health Impaired	.5	275,000
Visually Handicapped	.1	55,000
Learning Disabilities	2.0	1,100,000
Emotionally Disturbed	2.0	1,100,000
Gifted	2.0	1,100,000
TOTAL:	13.2	7,260,000

*Source: Bureau of Education for the Handicapped, 1975 Population Estimates

tional individuals may not be the critical factor in their adjustment. Although it would appear that individuals with nonambulatory handicaps would suffer more anguish than individuals with mild limps, some research results and reports clearly demonstrate that there is not a 100 percent positive relationship between severity of handicap and the resultant educational, social, and vocational adjustment. Enough examples exist to demonstrate this view — Helen Keller, Charles Steinmetz, Louis Braille. Such factors as school and community support, family concerns and initiatives, self-motivation, personality, and drives collectively affect the way individuals perform regardless of the severity of their handicaps.

One of the considerations that must be recognized when working with exceptional individuals is to discover what procedures or techniques can improve behaviors most effectively. Change in behavior may be the result of an altered or more favorable attitude by the teacher. Expectancy of good performance, comfortableness with the individual, and acceptance generate better performance on the part of exceptional individuals rather than attitudes of denigration, nonexpectancy of performance, uncomfortableness, and lack of acceptance.

One aspect is reflected in current concerns about labeling exceptional individuals. There is some evidence that when individuals are labeled, they develop feelings of negative self-worth. Labels also tend to encourage stereotyped ways of viewing exceptional individuals.[10] Special education should be less concerned with labels and more concerned with learning problems arising from negative concepts.

Another aspect involves feelings and attitudes relating to the segregation of exceptional individuals in special classes. When individuals are segregated, a two-way process is created. Not only are the exceptional cut off from the normal, but also the normal from the exceptional. This may have the effect of making it more difficult for the normal to accept the exceptional on more or less equal terms. Thus, the effect of segregated special classes tends to create social handicaps over and above the actual effect of the original handicap. It seems more realistic for disabled individuals to learn to live with their disabilities in normal surroundings.

---

[10]George Taylor, "Special Education at the Crossroad: Class Placement for the EMR," *Mental Retardation,* 2 (April, 1973), pp. 30-33.

COMMONALITY AMONG EXCEPTIONAL INDIVIDUALS

Characteristics attributed to most exceptional individuals seem to overlap. Regardless of how exceptional individuals are classified, they cannot really be described in neatly self-contained compartments without some overlapping. For example, impaired communication is recognized as a characteristic of individuals with sensory impairment or speech disorders. However, communication impairment is being increasingly recognized as a common element in the assessment and remediation of learning disabilities, emotional disturbance, and mental retardation.

Perceptual disorders are identified as important characteristics frequently attributed to individuals with learning disorders. The same characteristics of perceptual disorders are also seen among some individuals with cerebral palsy, mental retardation, hearing handicaps, and others. It thus seems reasonable to state that with few major exceptions most handicapped children have in common many similar characteristics.

Characteristics that differentiate exceptional individuals from each other are directly related to categorical classifications. Retardates have problems chiefly in the area of cognitive development; the crippled in motor development; the blind and deaf in sensory deficiencies. The majority of exceptional individuals not only have primary disabilities but also associated secondary disabilities that may contribute significantly to their handicapping conditions.

HANDICAPS VERSUS DISABILITIES

Exceptional individuals may have disabilities in several areas of functioning, such as hearing and speech. Most authorities agree that the impairment of structure or function is a disability. A disability does not necessarily denote a handicap. A handicap, according to Wright,[11] is a social phenomenon. Handicaps arise when standards instituted by society make a person stand out or draw attention to his disability.

---

[11]B. A. Wright, *Physical Disabilities: A Psychological Approach* (New York: Harper and Row Publishers, 1960).

Special education exists mainly because society chooses to treat exceptional individuals differently. Special classes, treatment, labeling, and attitudes displayed by society combine to single out individuals as exceptional. These factors operate to remove exceptional individuals further from the mainstream of society and pinpoint their disabilities. Minimal adaptations are usually enough to help some exceptional individuals overcome the negative effects of their disabilities.

A handicap should be defined in terms of the situation or condition. An exceptional individual who is crippled should not be classified as handicapped if he can perform a task that does not require excessive movement or locomotion. On the other hand, blindness should not constitute a handicap if vision is not required to perform the task. These examples may be generalized to most areas of exceptionality. If exceptional individuals can perform as normal under certain conditions, their disabilities should not be classified as handicapping conditions. In essence, simply because an individual is blind, his disability should not be equated with a global handicap. He might be able to operate within normal ranges on certain tasks if society provides the opportunities for him to demonstrate his skills.

LEARNING STYLES OF EXCEPTIONAL INDIVIDUALS

A review of the research indicated very few studies in the area of learning styles. The styles which are recognized as being acceptable in the classroom are limited. Similarly, Riessman[12] asserted that some pupils learn most readily by reading, some by listening, and others by means of physical doing. He also outlined that these styles are used in a variety of ways by individuals to suit their unique needs. Nations [13] classified learning styles as a combination of sensory orientation, responsive mode, and thinking pattern. Sensory orientation was described as whether the learner

[12]Frank Riessman, "Styles of Learning," *NEA Journal,* 55 (March, 1969), pp. 15-17.
[13]Jimmy Nations, Caring for Individual Differences in Reading Through Nongrading, (Address delivered to Seattle, Washington Teachers, May, 1967).

depends primarily on sensory contact with his environment; responsive mode was concerned with whether one works best alone or in a group; thinking pattern was referred to as whether one learns best by first getting many details and then organizing them into a pattern.

Children display diverse skills in learning. McCaslin[14] stated that this necessitates proven knowledge as well as sound theories for teaching. She further postulated that adults interested in the development of children often lack the necessary understanding of how children learn, what they are interested in, and how to put these two together. Due to wide individual differences among exceptional individuals, instructional techniques must vary. Individuals with special handicaps need special attention; their teachers need special orientation to meet their special needs. The teacher must know what can be expected of them, and then try to adapt the activities to their capabilities.

It has been voiced that no activity provides a greater variety of opportunities for learning than creative dramatics. Children are given a rationale for creative dramatics with specific objectives and values, exercises in pantomime, improvisation, play structure, and procedures involved in preparing a play.[15] Creative dramatics and play are not meant to be modes of learning styles, but rather, as more is discovered about learning and in particular the variety of ways certain exceptional individuals learn, they add immeasurable knowledge to the development of a theoretical construct for various types of learning styles. Equally important, these techniques may lead to the discovery of different learning styles at various developmental levels.

In spite of the paucity of research studies in the area of learning styles, it is generally recognized that individuals learn through a variety of sensory channels and have individual patterns of sensory strengths and weaknesses. It then becomes tantamount to discover techniques for assessing the individual's sensory strengths

---

[14]Nellie McCaslin, *Creative Dramatics in the Classroom* (New York: David McKay Company, Inc., 1968).
[15]Millie Almay, "Spontaneous Play: An Avenue for Intellectual Development," *The Bulletin of the Institute of Child Study*, University of Toronto, 28, (1966), p. 2.

and weaknesses, and to identify ways that materials can be presented to capitalize on sensory strengths and/or weaknesses. This does not mean that materials should be presented to the pupil via his preferred style, but it would mean that credit would be given for his strength (e.g., hearing) while he worked to overcome his weakness (e.g., vision). Basic to the concept of learning styles is the recognition that individuals differ with respect to what they require to initiate and sustain the learning process. Some exceptional individuals seem to have adequate sensory acuity, but are unable to utilize their sensory channels effectively.

A major concern of all education is to assist individuals in realizing their full learning potentialities. Educational services should be designed to take into account individual learning behavior and style. To be able to accomplish this task it will be required that we know something about the pupil as a learner. The Maryland State Department of Education, Division of Instructional Television[16] has listed several ways to characterize a pupil's learning style: (1) the speed at which a pupil learns, (2) the techniques the pupil uses to organize materials he hopes to learn, (3) the pupil's need for reinforcement and structure in the learning situation, (4) the channels of input through which the pupil's mind proceeds, and (5) the channels of output through which the pupil best shows us how much he has learned. Other techniques for assessing learning abilities and styles are reported in Chapters III and V.

The speed at which a pupil learns is important for individualizing instruction. Observations of the learner's characteristics will facilitate planning for his individual needs. A keen observer should be cognizant of the various ways an individual organizes materials. Some children learn best by proceeding from general to specific details, others from specific to general details. Knowing a pupil's style of organization can assist the teacher in individualizing his instruction. All learners need some structure and reinforcement in their learning. Pupils who have had successful experiences tend to repeat them. Proceeding from simple to com-

---

[16]Maryland State Department of Education, Teacher Manual, "Teaching Children with Special Needs," (Owings Mills, Maryland: Division of Instructional Television, 1973), p. 27.

plex, or from known to unknown principles provides opportunities for successful experiences for children.

The senses provide the only contact that any individual has with his environment. Sensory stimulations are received through the five sensory channels: auditory, visual, tactile, olfactory, and gustatory. These stimuli are organized into cognitive patterns called perceptions. The input channel through which the person readily processes stimuli is referred to as his preferred modality. The one through which he processes stimuli less readily is the weaker modality. Similar differences are also apparent in output which may be expressed verbally or nonverbally. Individuals usually prefer to express themselves through one of these channels.

A pupil's preferred mode of input is not necessarily related to his strongest acuity channel. Individuals with impaired vision may still process the vision stimuli they receive more efficiently than they do auditory stimuli. Sometimes a pupil will transfer information received through one channel into another with which he is more comfortable. This process is called intermodal transfer. An example of intermodal transfer might be the pupil who whispers each word as he reads it. The pupil is attempting to convert the visual stimuli (the printed word) into auditory stimuli (the whispering). Pupils differ in their ability to perform the intermodal transfer. For many exceptional individuals, failure to perform the intermodal transfer may hamper learning.

Many exceptional individuals might be using their preferred channels of input, which could be their weakest modality. Therefore, it is essential that the pupil's preferred mode of input and output be assessed. A variety of formal or informal techniques may be employed. Differentiation of instructional techniques based on assessment will improve the pupil's efficiency as a learner.[17]

The following tables have been prepared to provide some possible behaviors, assessment techniques, and instructional procedures to assist the teacher working with exceptional individuals.

These tables, Table II, III, and IV, describe three basic modalities: auditory, visual, and tactilekinesthetic. The olfactory and the

---

[17]*Ibid.*, p. 28.

TABLE I-II

THE AUDITORY MODALITY*

POSSIBLE BEHAVIORS		POSSIBLE TECHNIQUES		
Pupil Who is strong auditorily MAY:		The teacher may utilize these:		
SHOW THE FOLLOWING STRENGTHS	SHOW THE FOLLOWING WEAKNESSES	FORMAL ASSESSMENT TECHNIQUES	INFORMAL ASSESSMENT TECHNIQUES	INSTRUCTIONAL TECHNIQUES
Follow oral instructions very easily.	Lose place in visual activities.	Present statement verbally; ask pupil to repeat.	Observe pupil reading with the use of finger or pencil as a marker.	Reading: Stress phonetic analysis, avoid emphasis on sight vocabulary or fast reading. Allow pupils to use markers, fingers, etc., to keep their place.
Do well in tasks requiring phonetic analysis.	Read word by word.	Tap auditory pattern beyond pupil's point of vision. Ask pupil to repeat pattern.	Observe whether pupil whispers or barely produces sounds to correspond to his reading task.	Arithmetic: Provide audio tapes of story problems. Verbally explain arithmetic processes as well as demonstrate.
Appear brighter than tests show him to be.	Reverse words when reading			
Sequence speech sounds with facility.	Make visual discrimination errors.	Provide pupil with several words in a rhyming family. Ask pupil to add more.	Observe pupil who has difficulty following purely visual directions.	Spelling: Build on syllabication skills; utilize sound clues.
Perform well verbally.	Have difficulty with written work; poor motor skill.	Present pupil with sounds produced out of his field of vision. Ask him if they are the same or different.		Generally: Utilize worksheets with large unhampered areas. Use lined wide-spaced paper. Allow for verbal rather than written responses.
	Have difficulty copying from the chalkboard.			

*Reprinted with permission of Maryland State Department of Education, Division of Instructional Television.

TABLE I-III

THE VISUAL MODALITY*

| POSSIBLE BEHAVIORS | | POSSIBLE TECHNIQUES | | |
| Pupil who is strong visually MAY: | | The teacher may utilize these: | | |
SHOW THE FOLLOWING STRENGTHS	SHOW THE FOLLOWING WEAKNESSES	FORMAL ASSESSMENT TECHNIQUES	INFORMAL ASSESSMENT TECHNIQUES	INSTRUCTIONAL TECHNIQUES
Possess good sight vocabulary.	Have difficulty with oral directions.	Give lists of words which sound alike. Ask pupil to indicate if they are the same or different.	Observe pupil in tasks requiring sound discrimination, i.e., rhyming, sound blending.	Reading: Avoid phonetic emphasis; stress sight vocabulary, configuration clues, context clues.
Demonstrate rapid reading skills.	Ask "what are we supposed to do" immediately after oral instructions are given.	Ask pupil to follow specific instructions. Begin with one direction and continue with multiple instructions.	Observe pupil's sight vocabulary skills. Pupil should exhibit good sight vocabulary skills.	Arithmetic: Show examples of arithmetic function.
Skim reading material.	Appear confused with great deal of auditory stimuli.			Spelling: Avoid phonetic analysis; stress structural clues, configuration clues.
Read well from picture clues.	Have difficulty discriminating between words with similar sounds.	Show people visually similar pictures. Ask him to indicate whether they are the same or different.	Observe to determine if the pupil performs better when he can see the stimulus.	Generally: Allow a pupil with strong auditory skills to act as another child's partner. Allow for written rather than verbal responses.
Follow visual diagrams and other visual instructions well.				
Score well on group tests.		Show pupil a visual pattern, i.e., block design or pegboard design. Ask pupil to duplicate.		
Perform nonverbal tasks well.				

*Reprinted with permission of Maryland State Department of Education, Division of Instructional Television.

TABLE I-IV

THE TACTILEKINESTHETIC MODALITY*

| POSSIBLE BEHAVIORS | | POSSIBLE TECHNIQUES | | |
| Pupil who is strong tactile-kinesthetically MAY: | | The teacher may utilize these: | | |
SHOW THE FOLLOWING STRENGTHS	SHOW THE FOLLOWING WEAKNESSES	FORMAL ASSESSMENT TECHNIQUES	INFORMAL ASSESSMENT TECHNIQUES	INSTRUCTIONAL TECHNIQUES
Exhibit good fine and gross motor balance.	Depends on the "guiding" modality or preferred modality since tactile kinesthetic is usually a secondary modality. Weaknesses may be in either the visual or auditory mode.	Ask pupil to walk balance beam or along a painted line.	Observe pupil in athletic tasks.	Reading: Stress the shape and structure of a word; use configuration clues, sandpaper letters; have pupil trace the letters and/or words.
Exhibit good rhythmic movements.		Set up obstacle course involving gross motor manipulation.	Observe pupil maneuvering in classroom space.	Arithmetic: Utilize objects in performing the arithmetic functions, provide buttons, packages of sticks, etc.
Demonstrate neat handwriting skills.		Have pupil cut along straight, angled and curved lines.	Observe pupil's spacing of written work on a paper.	Spelling: Have pupil write the word in large movements, i.e., on chalkboard, on newsprint, utilize manipulative letters to spell the word. Call pupil's attention to the feel of the word. Have pupil write word in cursive to get feel of the whole word by flowing motion.
Demonstrate good cutting skills.		Ask child to color fine areas.	Observe pupil's selection of activities during free play, i.e., does he select puzzles or blocks as opposed to records or picture books.	
Manipulate puzzles and other materials well.				
Identify and match objects easily.				

*Reprinted with permission of Maryland Department of Education. Division of Instructional Television.

gustatory modalities are not included in the tables because they constitute detailed medical and psychological insight that are outside the realm of education. Specific behaviors that are characteristic for auditory, visual, and tactilekinesthetic modalities are given, with suggestions for possible techniques that might be employed.

It appears to be psychologically sound that exceptional individuals should be introduced to new tasks through their strongest input channels and review tasks presented to the weak channels. The concept of learning styles holds great promises for facilitating the achievement of exceptional individuals. As further investigations are conducted in relationship to specific exceptional individuals, more will be discovered about sensory acuity and the inability of some individuals to use their sense modalities effectively.

SUMMARY

As a practical guide to understanding and helping exceptional individuals, the following suggestions are made:

1. Individuals with handicaps, with rare exceptions, basically are more like other individuals than they are different, and areas of similarity and strengths should not be neglected.
2. Acceptance is of paramount importance to exceptional individuals. When acceptance is clearly communicated, exceptional individuals see themselves as important, unique, and useful.
3. Exceptional individuals are likely to have more difficulties than their normal peers, thus extra effort must be devoted to provide strategies, materials, adaptations, and assistance in overcoming their difficulties.
4. Individuals, regardless of their handicap, have highly individual learning and personality patterns. No two individuals learn in exactly the same manner or at the same speed. Therefore, lockstep methods are usually not desirable and are often ineffectual for exceptional individuals.

   The strengths and weaknesses of individuals, learning styles and modalities, task analyses, and other factors need to

be considered in planning learning activities and individualized instruction.

5. Some individuals considered as severely handicapped seem
to require specific instruction in highly structured settings.

6. Academic skills are only part of what exceptional individuals need to acquire. Developing adequate self-concept, a
sense of worth, coping with skills, and appropriate attitudes
are also essential for many exceptional individuals.

7. Research findings have consistently showed that categorical
labels have little significance for educational intervention.

8. The major task of special education should be focused on
providing services for individuals who have special needs, in
most instances, through innovative programs in the regular
classroom.

CHAPTER II

NEW DIRECTIONS IN CLASSIFYING AND LABELING EXCEPTIONAL INDIVIDUALS

GEORGE R. TAYLOR

CHAPTER I presented an overview of trends in special education. Some of the challenges facing special educators concerned with the education of exceptional individuals were indicated. Historically, many of these trends are responsible for special education programs in existence today. In the present chapter will be summarized the classification and labeling processes which have led special education to the crossroads. Views concerning alternative approaches for classifying exceptional individuals will also be discussed.

EFFECTS OF CLASSIFYING AND LABELING EXCEPTIONAL INDIVIDUALS

The traditional view of classifying handicapping conditions reflects the medical model.[1] Whereas the medical model has been successful in treating physical symptoms associated with disabilities, it has not been as successful when applied to psychological and educational behavior. That model does not permit special educators to develop appropriate strategies to cope with the various learning patterns of exceptional individuals. Strategies as outlined in this volume cannot be successfully implemented by using the medical model.

Baldwin[2] stated that each exceptional individual is a unique

---

[1]Clara Baldwin and Alfred Baldwin, "Personality and Social Development of Handicapped Children," *Psychology and the Handicapped Child* (Washington, D. C.: U. S. Office of Education, 1974), pp. 169-171.
[2]Baldwin, *loc. cit.*

person with his own spectrum of handicaps and his own problems in coping with the demands of the world; consequently, it has come to be recognized that many of the problems faced by exceptional individuals are not strikingly different among individuals with different handicaps. The prejudices faced and the sympathy received are not so fundamentally different whether the person is blind or walks with the aid of braces and crutches. Thus, the whole array of handicaps is seen as merging imperceptibly into one:

Dreikurs[3] indicated in 1952 that:

> Despite our best efforts, exceptional children will remain so until society stops considering them as such, and treats them as human beings who are respected and needed. Then it will become apparent that it is less important what we have, than what we do with what we have. There is no human being — with the exception of the complete imbecile — who cannot be useful and contribute to the welfare of others. Usefulness and contribution are the real bases for social integration, in contrast to our prevalent assumption that superiority gives social status and inferiority deprives. The emphasis on each child's ability to be useful and to participate is the only means to bring the best out in him. Judgmental evaluation, comparison, criticism and humiliation may be effective with a very few, but are damaging to almost all. Success and failure become insignificant if we stop measuring and comparing, judging and condemning. Then alone can we stimulate children in their development and function, not toward becoming a success, but toward becoming a useful social being, who has a secure place in the group regardless of what he is and how much he can do.

Gallagher's[4] remarks support those outlined by Dreikurs. He expressed the view that the problem with labeling a child educably mentally retarded, for example, and placing him in a special program is a current suspicion, backed by reliable research, that such a placement does not lead to effective treatment. He added

---

[3]Dreikurs, *Understanding the Exceptional — In Music Therapy* (Chicago: National Association for Music Therapy, 1952).
[4]J. Gallagher, "The Special Education Contract for Mildly Handicapped Children," *Exceptional Children*, 38 (March, 1972), pp. 527-535.

further that if it is true that the major adjustment problem facing exceptional individuals is the combination of other peoples' reaction to their handicaps, then special educators must consider whether the exceptional should be segregated into special homogeneous groups or should be kept in the regular class and integrated as much as possible with normal children.

There are ample research findings to answer the question concerning the integration of exceptional individuals as much as possible with normal children.[5, 6, 7, 8, 9, 10, 11, 12] In addition to the stated research, Baldwin[13] discussed the negative effects of placing the educable mentally retarded in special classes. He stated that the academic consequences of special class placement on educable retarded children have not been proven to be significant. At times, in a special class placement for academic skills emotional adjustment has been found; but a student did not achieve up to his academic optimum level. In support of this premise, a survey conducted under the auspices of the U. S. Office of Education[14] found no clear support for either regular or special placement in terms of academic achievement, motivation, or social-emotional adjustment. The only exceptions were found when personality variables were considered. The aforementioned research can be summarized by stating that special class placement has not signif-

[5]B. Blatt, "Public Policy and the Education of Children with Special Needs," *Exceptional Children*, 38 (March, 1972), pp. 537-543.

[6]Gallagher, *op. cit.*

[7]R. Jones, "Labels and Stigma in Special Education," *Exceptional Children*, 38 (March, 1972), pp. 553-564.

[8]M. Lilly, "Improving Social Acceptance of Low Sociometric Status, Low Achieving Students," *Exceptional Children*, 37 (January, 1971), pp. 341-347.

[9]Glen Foster, "I Wouldn't Have Seen It If I Hadn't Believed It." *Exceptional Children*, 41 (April, 1975), pp. 469-473.

[10]Christoplos and P. Renz, "A Critical Examination of Special Education Programs," *The Journal of Special Education*, 3 (Winter, 1969), pp. 371-379.

[11]Hardwick Harshman, "Toward A Differential Treatment of Curriculum," *The Journal of Special Education*, 3 (Winter, 1969), pp. 385-387.

[12]M. Reynolds and B. Balow, "Categories and Variables in Special Education." *Exceptional Children*, 38 (January, 1972), pp. 357-366.

[13]Baldwin, *op. cit.*, p. 182.

[14]J. Franseth and R. Doury, *Survey of Research on Grouping As Related to Pupil Learning* (Washington, D. C.: U. S. Government Printing Office, 1966).

icantly influenced the academic achievement of educable retardates.

The possibility of attitudinal effects on parents whose children have been given special class placement should not be minimized. Research findings revealed that parents of EMR children in special classes generally showed greater awareness of their child's retardation, but tended to devalue their child to a greater degree than did parents of EMR children in regular classes. It was concluded that special classes may lead, in the long run, to maladaptive behavior.[15]

HUMANIZING SPECIAL EDUCATION

Special educators must develop a humanistic approach when instructing exceptional individuals. A humanistic approach encompasses and at the same time deemphasizes categorical labels and focuses on personalized, individualized types of instruction. Strategies based upon the preceding research findings are designed in Chapter VIII to achieve these purposes.

Fairbank[16] illustrated three decades ago the importance of a teacher's personality as being the prime item in the success of exceptional individuals' education. One hundred and sixty-six subjects were identified as emotionally unstable; their prognosis as adults was that they would be dependent, delinquent, or would need the support of public agencies. Findings later revealed that ninety-two pupils in the original survey had never had contact with any agency, either welfare or legal. Fairbank attributed the adjustment of these pupils to highly capable and involved teachers.

Studies of teacher personality and pupil behavior have shown that teachers play a critical role in the behavior and interests of

[15]J. H. Meyerowitz, "Parental Awareness of Retardation," *American Journal of Mental Deficiency*, 71 (January, 1967), pp. 637-643.

[16]Ruth E. Fairbank, "The Subnormal Child — Seventeen Years After," *Mental Hygiene*, 17 (April, 1933), pp. 177-208.

pupils.[17, 18, 19, 20] In many instances, the influence of a teacher's personality persist long after his contact with pupils end. Teachers play a dominant role in the degree to which pupils accept differences in other children. As indicated by Rosenthal,[21] it should be recognized that when exceptional individuals are grouped and labeled according to some characteristic believed relative to their abilities to profit from education, that label becomes an explanation for their behavior. Such easy access to explanations for failure can serve to reduce efforts for improved educational practices. There is some evidence that such grouping and labeling not only influence the student's perception of his own abilities, but also affect his actual abilities.

Evidence presented by Rosenthal and Jacobson concerning the effects of grouping and labeling upon exceptional individuals are not new to the field of special education. As early as 1934, Laycock[22] stated that every teacher is a diagnostician capable of providing for the variety of learning and behavior problems presented by exceptional individuals without regard to separate etiological categories. Similarly, Lord's[23] approach supports Laycock's view. He remarked that rehabilitation does not begin its thinking with disability categories, rather it plans in terms of individual needs and establishes priorities for meeting those needs. There is a consensus of opinion between Lord's view and one posed by Hill.[24] He wrote that special education has devel-

[17]George Dennison, *The Lives of Children* (New York: Random House, 1969).

[18]Ned Flanders, *Teacher Influence, Pupil Attitudes, and Achievement* (Washington, D.C.: U. S. Government Printing Office, 1965).

[19]James Campbell and Cyrus Barnes, "Interaction Analysis — A Breakthrough?" *Phi Delta Kappan*, 50 (June, 1969), pp. 587-590.

[20]Jean Grambs, *Understanding Intergroup Relations, What Research Says to the Teacher* (Washington, D. C.: National Education Association, 1960).

[21]R. Rosenthal and L. Jacobson, "Teacher Expectancies: Determiners of Pupils' IQ Gains," *Psychological Reports*, 19 (August, 1966), pp. 115-118.

[22]S. R. Laycock, "Every Teacher A Diagnostician," *International Council for Exceptional Children*, 1 (October, 1934), p. 47.

[23]F. E. Lord, "A Realistic Look at Special Classes," *Exceptional Children*, 22 (May, 1956), pp. 321-325, 342.

[24]A. S. Hill, "The Status of Mental Retardation Today with Emphasis on Service," *Exceptional Children*, 25 (March, 1959), pp. 298-299.

oped around the isolation of supposedly discrete entities of disabilities rather than in terms of learning problems. In the same framework, Kirk and Batemen[25] stressed the need for special educators to diagnose learning problems based upon behavioral symptoms from which remediation can be provided irrespective of etiological factors.

In reviewing the many studies associated with conventional classification systems, it should be evident that most of the research is in conflict with the present model utilized for classifying exceptional individuals. Furthermore, findings clearly indicate a consensus among most authorities that changes in the widely accepted classification model are long overdue. The preponderance of research findings have clearly demonstrated that there is sufficient knowledge to effect change now in the present special education model which is responsible for many problems experienced today.

STRATEGIES FOR EFFECTING CHANGE

As stated in Chapter I, a viable system of classifying exceptional individuals should be based upon the behavioral characteristics of exceptional individuals, using the commonalities of learning styles among exceptional children regardless of their etiological categories. Special education should not place emphasis upon categories of handicaps, rather it should be a system designed to render services to children who have special needs. Additionally, classification methods based upon medical, social, or psychological dimensions should be refuted and replaced with a system that does not stigmatize the exceptional individual. From a humanistic point of view, special education should be concerned with supplanting the present classification system with one that is based upon the diverse learning and educational needs of each exceptional individual. This thinking is guided by Roos'[26] state-

---

[25]S. Kirk and Barbara Bateman, "Diagnosis and Remediation of Learning Disabilities," *Exceptional Children*, 29 (September, 1962), pp. 73-78.

[26]Phil Roos, "Present Day Management of the Individual with Mental Retardation Is No Longer Hamstrung by Horse and Buggy Philosophy," *Meeting the Needs of the Mentally Retarded*, Texas Department of Mental Health and Mental Retardation, 1972, p. 12.

ment: "Education is the process whereby an individual is helped to develop new behavior or to apply existing behavior so as to equip him to cope more effectively and more efficiently with his total environment."

The National Advisory Committee on Handicapped Children[27] stated:

> Concurrently, efforts are being made to revise some of the traditional discrete disability categories which have limited service: (1) more direct focus on the educational needs of severely and multiple handicapped children, (2) specific programs to return children, unnecessarily labeled and academically underestimated to the mainstream of education, (3) more rigorous and earlier educational assessment of children with developmental problems and aberrations, and (4) educational intervention to promote effective learning in vulnerable infants and very young children without reference to a specific disability.

There is an urgent need to identify relevant pedagogical variables which maximize the successful adjustment and growth of exceptional individuals in the regular class. There appears to be a need for a description of those variables which appear most relevant to the prediction of successful outcomes and the development of specific intervention programs available to regular classrooms.

Although researchers and clinicians have been expressing discontent with labels for years, little progress has been made toward improving diagnostic procedures. Douglas[28] recommended that it may be worth considering an approach in which the existing diagnostic labels are ignored and individuals are classified according to attention problems and poor impulse control. It was indicated that this approach could be applied to other areas of behavior and/or learning. The author related that sophisticated instruments must be developed and validated before such a procedure is attempted.

Such a system as outlined by Douglas was proposed by Iscoe

---

[27]*Basic Education Rights for the Handicapped*, 1972 Annual Report of the National Advisory Committee on Handicapped Children, p. 2.

[28]Virginia Douglas, "Sustained Attention and Impulse Control: Implications for the Handicapped Child," *Psychology and the Handicapped* (Washington, D. C.: U. S. Office of Education, 1974), pp. 158-161.

and Payne[29] for classifying variables in special education. The authors' system is based upon three educational or behavioral variables with subcategories as follows:

1. Physical Status
   a. Visibility of physical deviation
   b. Locomotion capabilities and limitations
   c. Communication capabilities and problems
2. Adjustment Status
   a. Peer acceptance
   b. Family interaction
   c. Self-esteem
3. Educational Status
   a. Motivation
   b. Academic achievement
   c. Educational potential

The proposed system is not based upon etiological categories, rather it appears to be based upon an educational and sociological system which, in a limited way, appears to be a realistic and workable approach that takes into consideration the functional competencies of exceptional individuals and their developmental needs.

It is apparent to us that the needs of *all* exceptional individuals will not fit into the defined categories as outlined because of the multiplicity of behavioral characteristics. The problem is further compounded when one attempts to define the primary need or status wherein several needs appear to be evident. A case in point might be that of a child with physical problems. Individuals with this condition may also have needs in the adjustment area or in a combination of areas.

The proposed system raises other issues which have numerous implications for educational programming. It would involve a dramatic shift in teacher education. Such a change will require different training approaches and organizational structures.

With additional research, Iscoe's system will offer special education an alternative approach. This approach will delimit the negative consequences of the prevailing system which has often

---

[29]I. Iscoe and S. Payne, "Development of A Revised Scale for the Functional Classification of Exceptional Children," in Trapp and Himelstein (Eds.), *Reading on the Exceptional Child* (New York: Appleton-Century-Crofts, 1972) pp. 7-29.

provided society with prejudiced or stereotyped attitudes toward the exceptional. These attitudes, in turn, have caused many exceptional individuals to develop feelings of apathy or aggressive behavior.

A Developmental Strategy

The developmental approach has been widely used and applied to normal children, but has not been applied extensively to exceptional individuals. The following approach might prove significant for classifying many exceptional individuals; however, as in the classification system proposed by Iscoe and Payne, it must be validated.

1. Sensory Acuity
   a. Visual
   b. Hearing
   c. Tactile
2. Expressive Ability
   a. Verbal
   b. Fine Motor
   c. Gross Motor
3. Perceptual Motor Skills
   a. Coordination
   b. Locomotion
   c. Environmental Influence
4. Ideas and Attitudes
   a. Interpersonal Relationships
   b. Attitudes Toward Learning
   c. Self Concept
5. Conceptual Learning
   a. Individual Learning Patterns
   b. Background of Experience
   c. Classification
   d. Problem Solving
6. Educational Intervention*
   a. Individualized Instruction
      (1). Programmed

*Refer to Chapter VIII. Interventions and/or strategies may be greatly altered based upon research hypotheses or findings, or during the standardization process of any new classification system.

      (2). Programmed
b. Diagnostic Teaching
c. Perceptual Remediation
d. Behavior Modification
e. Peer Teaching
f. Team Teaching
g. Learning Stations
h. Open Education

This model was developed by assessing the ways an individual receives information (input), and the ways he expresses himself (output).

It might be worth considering a developmental classification system in which conventional diagnostic labels are ignored and exceptional individuals are classified on the basis of their developmental needs. As mentioned, an inordinate amount of instrument construction, validation, and experimentation must be conducted to establish objective criteria for classifying children under one or more of the proposed categories. In essence, a battery of well-standardized, valid, and reliable measures must be developed before they can be used as diagnostic and/or assessment instruments.

There is sufficient information, including some techniques already in existence, to begin experimenting with a developmental classification system for classifying, educating, treating, and evaluating exceptional individuals, premised upon the fact that a developmental system has the potential and flexibility to adjust to most areas of functioning. This book's reactions to critical issues that must be addressed before a functional developmental classification system is adapted are similar to those discussed under the Iscoe and Payne "Classification System."

The two proposed systems are more alike than different. The chief difference is that the proposed developmental system indicates specific strategies that may be employed to ameliorate problems, using broad parameters for meeting the educational needs of the exceptional. Both systems outline the value of the physical aspects of learning and allow for basic differences in the learning styles and abilities of exceptional individuals. There are other similar classification systems not addressed in this volume that have been adequately covered elsewhere.[30, 31]

SUMMARY

Special educators in general took great pride and satisfaction in the rapid expansion of special education programs. The most commonly stated goal of special education programs was to meet the needs of exceptional children that were not being adequately met in regular programs.[32] Much controversy exists today because many specialists now generally agree that the special class model or goals, which have been in existence for well over thirty years, have not provided exceptional individuals with a viable education. Thus, the justification of special education programs is questioned, with a plea that special educators stop being pressured into continuing and expanding a special education program that is known to be undesirable for many individuals.[33] Throughout the number of years special education programs have been in operation, research findings have consistently indicated that there are slight, if any, differences in performances between those placed in regular classes and those placed in special classes.

The present special education model has been rejected by several authorities because it focused upon a category of handicaps rather than upon the needs of exceptional individuals. Research findings reported in this chapter have confirmed the negative affects of labeling.

Two classification systems that have numerous implications for mainstreaming most exceptional individuals were reported, as well as issues that constituted major concerns in implementing the proposed systems. A word of caution is in order. For any classification system to be effective, state reimbursement formulas

---

[30]H. C. Quay, "The Facets of Educational Exceptionality: A Conceptual Framework for Assessment, Grouping and Instruction," *Exceptional Children*, 35 (September, 1968), pp. 25-32.

[31]G. D. Stevens, *Taxonomy in Special Education for Children with Body Disorders: The Problem and A Proposal*, University of Pittsburgh, 1962.

[32]H. L. Baker, *Introduction to Exceptional Children* (New York: Macmillan Company, 1959).

[33]L. M. Dunn, "Special Education for the Mildly Retarded — Is Much of It Justifiable?" *Exceptional Children*, 35 (September, 1968), pp. 5-24.

tied to conventional classification systems must be changed. Additionally, federal, state, and local laws should specify exceptional individuals. Brinegar[34] stated:

> Laws should provide the opportunity for any exceptional individual to benefit from appropriate services regardless of exceptionality, thus only a single legal classification should be necessary to cover all exceptional individuals. Exceptional individuals should be defined in educational terms.

We tend to project an optimistic view concerning changes in the present classification systems because of the following:

1. Class actions suits won or pending in several states on behalf of exceptional individuals.

2. Coordination among disciplines and their concerned support for revising the present classification systems.

3. Research and demonstration projects attesting to proven instructional techniques that can be successfully implemented in the regular class for most exceptional individuals.

4. A variety of research activities in learning, technology, and medicine are being investigated which will provide additional insights into the behavioral characteristics of exceptional individuals.

5. A positive change in attitude toward exceptional individuals due to widespread media coverage and support for quality programs launched by concerned groups and political leaders.

---

[34]Leslie Brinegar, "Definitions, Labels, and Classification," in Mann (Ed.), *Mainstream Special Education: Issues and Perspectives in Urban Centers,* Council for Exceptional Children, OEG-0-72-3999 (609), p. 26.

CHAPTER III

INDIVIDUALIZED INSTRUCTION

STANLEY E. JACKSON

THIS chapter is designed to give an overview of the importance of individualizing instruction for the exceptional. It has been stated in Chapter I that the diverse nature of exceptional individuals necessitated the development of instruction based upon their unique abilities and disabilities, not on their handicap category. Individualization purports to accomplish this goal.

Several definitions have been advanced to define individualized instruction. Howes[1] defined the term as meeting, caring for, providing for, or adjusting to individual differences. Scanlon[2] described individualized instruction as an important two-way communication link between the student and the teacher. Smith and Neisworth[3] echoed Scanlon's emphasis. Baker and Goldberg[4] offered a more specific explanation of individualized instruction. They reflected that an individual program should be flexible, in that it provides alternative materials for the student as well as a variety of procedures and techniques. Also, the student should have a substantial voice concerning the content of his educational program, with the counsel of his teacher. Any discussion of the application of individualized instruction to the educational program for exceptional individuals is impossible without an ade-

---

[1]Virgil M. Howes, "Individualized Instruction: Form and Structure," in Virgil M. Howes (Ed.), *Individualization of Instruction — A Teaching Strategy* (New York: The Macmillan Company, 1970), pp. 75-76.

[2]Robert G. Scanlon, "Individually Prescribed Instruction: A System of Individualized Instruction," in James E. Duane (Ed.), *Individualized Instruction — Programs and Materials* (New Jersey: Educational Technology Publications, 1973), pp. 109-110.

[3]Robert M. Smith and John T. Neisworth, "Fundamentals of Informal Educational Assessment," in Robert M. Smith (Ed.), *Teacher Diagnosis of Educational Difficulties* (Columbus, Ohio: Charles E. Merrill Publishing Co., 1969), p. 4.

[4]Gail L. Baker and Isadore Goldberg, "The Individualized Learning System: What It Is and How To Use It," in James E. Duane (Ed.), *Individualized Instruction — Programs and Materials* (New Jersey: Educational Technology Publications, 1973), p. 62.

quate examination of its features. Individualization of instruction strives to acknowledge individual differences and meet individual needs by following a diagnostic-prescriptive model in an effort to implement a flexible, multivaried educational program which is agreed upon by both teacher and student. A generalization may be made that individualized instruction is most notably a student-centered approach to education. Student involvement in the decisions made concerning his educational program imply an inherent goal of individualized instruction which is to promote self-directed learning on the part of the pupil. Accordingly, Burns[5] related that individualized instruction is a system which tailor-makes learning in terms of the learner's needs and characteristics.

COMPONENTS OF INDIVIDUALIZED INSTRUCTION

Individualized instruction is a continual diagnostic and prescriptive process. Scanlon[6] maintained that the prescription should alter congruently with the child's changing needs. Perceptual diagnosis and systematic charting of the student's progress were recommended to facilitate the updating of the prescription. Smith and Neisworth[7] stated just as a particular optical prescription permits each child to have optimal vision, so must an individualized pedagogic program be prescribed for each student's education. Lindvall and Bolvin[8] supported the need for continual diagnostic assessment in the following:

> A basic assumption of IPI is that the desired type of individualized instruction is feasible in a typical school situation only when careful structure and guidance is provided through a carefully defined educational system. The history of our schools indicates that individualization is not achieved by telling

[5]Richard W. Burns, "Methods for Individualizing Instruction," in James E. Duane (Ed.), *Individualized Instruction — Programs and Materials* (New Jersey: Educational Technology Publications, 1973), p. 26.

[6]Scanlon, *op. cit.*

[7]Smith and Neisworth, *op. cit.*

[8]C. M. Lindvall and John Bolvin, "The Role of the Teacher in Individually Prescribed Instruction," in James E. Duane (Ed.), *Individualized Instruction — Programs and Materials* (New Jersey: Educational Technology Publications, 1973), p. 315.

the teacher to "pay attention to individual differences." This has been preached to teachers for decades; little individualization has resulted.

The teacher needs to be assisted by a system which makes individualization feasible. He needs materials that permit a great amount of independent study, diagnostic techniques that provide information as to what a pupil is ready to study, a procedure for monitoring pupil progress, and detailed guidelines that the teacher and pupils can follow to make the total system operate. Only with this type of assistance is it possible for the typical teacher to individualize instruction.

Bolvin's assessment of individualized instruction is similar to the Individually Prescribed Instruction model developed by the National School Public Relations Association.

Individually Prescribed Instruction Program

Various school districts have developed individualized forms of instruction based upon the IPI model.[9] The steps in the program are as follows:

Step 1. Selection of Instructional Objective

The teacher begins planning by stating the instructional objective selected for the student based on student-teacher recognition of student need. The objective may be the acquisition of a mathematical skill, the mastery of a set of scientific facts, the development of a social skill, etc. Whatever the objective may be, it is selected on the basis of what the student needs to learn.

Step 2. Diagnosis of Learning Needs

Before the instruction begins, the teacher pretests the student on the objective to determine what he knows and does not know. In addition, the teacher gathers relevant information about the student's past performance and background. This gives the teacher a set of data upon which to build the student's program. These data are obtained from pencil and paper tests, performance tests,

---

[9]*Individually Prescribed Instruction,* A report prepared by the National School Public Relations Association (Washington, D. C.: 1968).

checklists, informal inventories, standardized tests, cumulative records, etc.

Step 3. Prescription of Student's Program

This is the last phase of preinstructional planning. The teacher reviews all the instructional resources available and prescribes the resources that will help the student master the instructional objective. At the end of this step, the initial design of an individual program of studies for the student is completed.

Step 4. Implementing Prescribed Program

At this point, both teacher and student carry out the program of studies as designed. The student uses the prescribed instructional resources and works toward mastery of the objective while the teacher guides him in following the program. This step is concerned with implementing the program as initially conceived by the teacher.

Step 5. Ongoing Evaluation

As the student is working through his program of studies, his performance provides the teacher with data about the program's effectiveness. The teacher uses the work products and behaviors that the student exhibits as he works in the program as additional diagnostic data. These data tell the teacher whether the student is making progress toward mastery, and suggest reasons for progress or lack of progress. Based on this, the teacher may modify the student's program by repeating some or all of the preinstructional activities (diagnosis and prescription). The cycle of ongoing evaluation, rediagnosis, represcription and implementation is continued until the teacher judges that the student is ready to be tested for mastery of the objective.

Step 6. Mastery Testing

Once the teacher has concrete evidence from the ongoing evaluation that the student has mastered his instructional objective and he can predict a high probability of success on a mastery test, the teacher selects an appropriate mastery test and assigns it to the student. Figure I demonstrates how learning may be individualized for exceptional individuals.

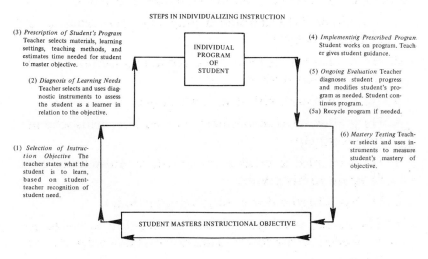

STEPS IN INDIVIDUALIZING INSTRUCTION

(3) *Prescription of Student's Program* Teacher selects materials, learning settings, teaching methods, and estimates time needed for student to master objective.

(2) *Diagnosis of Learning Needs* Teacher selects and uses diagnostic instruments to assess the student as a learner in relation to the objective.

INDIVIDUAL PROGRAM OF STUDENT

(4) *Implementing Prescribed Program* Student works on program. Teacher gives student guidance.

(5) *Ongoing Evaluation* Teacher diagnoses student progress and modifies student's program as needed. Student continues program.
(5a) Recycle program if needed.

(6) *Mastery Testing* Teacher selects and uses instruments to measure student's mastery of objective.

(1) *Selection of Instruction Objective* The teacher states what the student is to learn, based on student-teacher recognition of student need.

STUDENT MASTERS INSTRUCTIONAL OBJECTIVE

Figure III-1.

The IPI is a systematic approach programmed to guide the activities of the learner to the mastery of a stated objective. Bolvin's[10] approach to individualized instruction is similar to the IPI model and is designed to determine the learner's progress toward the: (1) mastery of content at his rate of learning, (2) role in program planning and evaluation, (3) active involvement in learning, and (4) growth in the area of motivation toward learning. In essence, no educational strategy is undertaken without full consideration of its impact upon the student.

In citing the advantages of individualized instruction for both students and teachers, Blake and McPherson[11] also produced evi-

[10]John O. Bolvin, "Implications of the Individualization of Instruction for Curriculum and Instructional Design," in James E. Duane (Ed.), *Individualized Instruction — Programs and Materials* (New Jersey: Educational Technology Publications, 1973), pp. 34-55.
[11]Howard E. Blake and Ann W. McPherson, "Individualized Instruction — Where Are We?" in James E. Duane (Ed.), *Individualized Instruction — Programs and Materials* (New Jersey: Educational Technology Publications, 1973), p. 14.

dence as to the student-centered nature of this educational approach. The advantages listed for the student basically duplicate Bolvin's approach. However, the attributes of the individualized strategy listed as advantageous to the teacher appear to be equally advantageous for the student. The authors outline the following advantages for teachers who individualize instruction:

1. The teacher is freed from teaching many of the routine basic skills of a subject.

2. He is enabled to meet more accurately the instructional needs of each student.

3. He is furnished with diagnostic devices.

4. He is allowed to spend more time with students who need the most help.

5. He is enabled to bring a structured, carefully thought out program to his pupils.

6. He has a higher degree of job satisfaction.

7. The teacher serves not only as a lecturer but also as a guide to the student in his efforts to increase his knowledge of a given subject.

The objective of individualized instruction cannot be fully realized unless time schedules are agreed to and kept. The use of time may be scheduled or unscheduled. An example of unscheduled time is a multiple learning area. The total school is planned for each individual through materials organized around basic learning skills. Each individual selects his own materials and sets his own pace for mastering them.

Efficient use of limited resources must be considered in selecting scheduled or unscheduled time for multiple and single learning areas. Additionally, well-planned procedures must be developed for handling learning activities, scheduled or unscheduled.[12] Some of the procedures that may be instituted to handle learning activities are:

1. Directed activities in multiple learning areas under a regular

---

[12]*Individualization in Schools,* A report prepared by the National School Public Relations Association (Washington, D. C.: 1971), p. 9.

time schedule.

2. Directed activities in multiple learning areas with time unscheduled.

3. Directed activities in single learning areas with time scheduled.

4. Directed activities in single learning areas with time unscheduled.

5. Selected activities in multiple areas with time scheduled.

6. Selected activities in multiple areas with time unscheduled.

7. Selected activities in single areas with time unscheduled.

Where directed activities take place in a multiple learning area with time scheduled, the learning environment tends to be of high quality and the students receive significant guidance from the teacher and the materials.

The elementary school provides the greatest benefits for organizing multiple learning areas and individualized types of instruction. There are many individuals who have similar intellectual, physical, and cultural needs sufficient to build a program with proper balance. It includes opportunities to exercise group inquiry, to offer options that intrigue the interests and motivations of early adolescents, and it gives individuals the opportunity for self-directed and self-sequenced study, along with the opportunity to practice and appreciate the arts.

In summarizing the definitions and advantages of individualized instruction, it should be apparent that emphasis is placed upon the individual. Additionally, most forms of individualized instruction may be categorized under one of the following approaches:[13]

1. In individually diagnosed and prescribed instruction, the school determines what and how the individual will be taught. The school selects material and determines learning objectives and the student is permitted to learn at his own pace.

2. In self-directed instruction, the individual chooses the mate-

---

[13]*Ibid.*, p. 3.

rials and determines how to proceed. The teacher and school administration determine learning objectives and goals.

3. In personalized instruction, the individual sets his own learning goals. The student follows a program established by the teacher and uses specific materials selected by the school to achieve his goals. The student determines his own pace, but as in other individualized learning, the teacher is always available to provide help and guidance.

4. Independent study programs permit the learner to determine his own learning objectives and achievement methods. In most cases only students of high learning capability are permitted to enter these programs.

These approaches to individualized instruction do not eliminate the need for proper diagnosis. Diagnosis is a process by which appropriate data are obtained and analyzed for the purpose of designing individualized programs. It is a time-consuming process but a necessary component of individualized instruction.

INSTRUCTIONAL OPTIONS FOR THE EXCEPTIONAL

Findings reported thus far in this chapter indicate that individualized instruction appears to be a promising technique for assisting children to achieve at their optimum levels of growth. When applied to exceptional individuals, the approach appears to offer additional instructional options because of the wide intra- and interindividual differences that exist among them.

Traditional approaches and methods have not provided most exceptional individuals with a practical education. Trends today indicate a change in school organization for exceptional individuals. Special and regular class structures are rapidly being modified with diagnostic teaching, learning stations, team teaching, and other instructional options that can individualize instruction. Basic to the implementation of any individualized approach will be the need for ample supportive services.

Individualized instruction may be evident in programmed instruction, tutorials, independent study, learning centers, individualized learning kits, and a variety of other approaches. The potentials for individualizing instruction for masses of exceptional individuals are greater today because of advanced media technology that can tirelessly present instruction on demand, maintain records of students' performances, and print out each learner's progress.

The use of technology such as television, videotape recordings, cassette tapes, 8mm film loops, etc. cannot be expected to serve as a panacea for solving educational problems in individualized instruction. It is important that these materials be used as a part of the teaching-learning process and not as the entire teaching media, which may lead to unwarranted expectations about their capabilities. All forms of media are capable of helping learners to comprehend concepts, to acquire skills, and to shape feelings. A variety of automatic and nonautomatic devices and materials should be available to assist exceptional individuals in reaching their optimum levels of achievement. Chapters VI and VII discuss some of these devices and materials.

In individualized instruction, the teacher plays the major role.[14] A climate for learning must be provided that will both stimulate and challenge the learner. Individual learning styles of the learner must be considered. If properly monitored, individualized instruction should help an exceptional individual grow in his own style, at his own speed and in uniqueness.

If individualized instruction is to be of benefit to exceptional individuals, the following are deemed important:

1. Assess the level of skill attainment needed.

2. Select a skill from lists provided in the subject area to be taught.

3. State the skill in behavioral terms.

4. Decide on the best mode for presentation.

5. Decide and select materials that will facilitate the development of the skill.

6. Develop clear and concise directions for individuals to fol-

---

[14]Evelyn Deno, *Instructional Alternatives for Exceptional Children,* Council for Exceptional Children, 1973.

low.

7. Develop an evaluative strategy that will best ascertain whether or not the stated objectives have been achieved.

Thus far individualized instruction has been described as a need-oriented, student-centered, diagnostic-prescriptive educational model which is sensitive to the individual differences of exceptional individuals. This view is still maintained, with the exception that individualized instruction is not synonymous with teaching in an isolated environment on a one-to-one basis. Group activities add to the process and should be introduced as frequently as possible. Isolated educational environments would defeat the numerous attempts to bring many exceptional individuals into the mainstream of education. Exceptional individuals need group activities so that they might interact properly with their environment. Group activities are in agreement with the flexible and varied nature of individually prescribed programs.

To employ isolationism in the classroom as a means of individualizing instruction is ignoring a vital aspect of development for exceptional individuals. This philosophy is congruent with Montagu's, Veatch's and Cardarelli's aspects of development. Montagu[15] remarked that from the symbiotic relation with the mother in the womb to the continuing symbiosis after it, the human organism unequivocally and clearly exhibits a directiveness in its behavioral growth and development, in which growth and development of the self proceed together with increasing growth and development in interdependence, in relation always with others. The directiveness of the organism is toward growth and development in the realization of its need for relatedness. All its needs are so structured as to require stimulations enabling the organism to realize its capacities for relatedness and turn those capacities into acted out abilities. Veatch[16] and Cardarelli[17] con-

---

[15]Ashley Montagu, "Quest for Self," in Virgil Howes (Ed.), *Individualization of Instruction — A Teaching Strategy* (New York: The MacMillan Company, 1970), p. 24.
[16]Jeanette Veatch, "Individualizing," in Virgil Howes (Ed.), *Individualization of Instruction — A Teaching Strategy* (New York: The MacMillan Company, 1970), p. 91.
[17]Sally M. Cardarelli, "The LAP — A Feasible Vehicle of Individualized Instruction," in James Duane (Ed.), *Individualized Instruction — Programs and Materials* (New Jersey: Educational Technology Publications, 1973), p. 151.

curred with Montagu's premise by stating that "no man is an island". Isolation of individuals should not occur in educational settings. Often teachers see a series of one-to-one relationships as the only way to individualize. Educators should be concerned with the growth and development of the whole person. Thus, educational experiences should be designed to develop a well-rounded human being who is able and willing to share with others, and who can participate positively in group activities with his peers.

Research findings concerned with the social development of exceptional individuals support the authors' views. Since the concept of social interaction is amply covered in the professional literature, this book will merely summarize some of its values to exceptional individuals. Social interaction is of prime importance to exceptional individuals. It should be an integral aspect of development where the individual can expand his horizons and seek expression through group involvement and participation. One of the principal qualities of individualized instruction is its humane approach to education. Consequently, isolation of exceptional individuals deprives them of needed group activities that are necessary for them to operate successfully in integrated settings. Views for the successful integration of exceptional individuals into the mainstream of education have been discussed in Chapter II.

Teachers of exceptional individuals must provide individualized forms of instruction with emphasis on group activities to invoke optimal learning and minimize the negative attitudes produced by isolation. Group activities should be an essential part of individualization and principally concerned with the development of behaviors necessary for effective group participation. Effective working groups can be established under the concept of individualization if the teacher is aware of the abilities and limitations of individuals. A teacher can pursue an individually prescribed program by working with individuals who have similar traits, or who have the need to develop similar skills; such an approach can be implemented without regard to labels but based upon the special needs of the individuals. Group approaches designed to remediate some of the individual problems of the exceptional are feasible and advisable when individuals share a particular mutual need. Chapter VIII deals specifically with individualization under a variety of educational structures.

Supportive services and staffing patterns are necessary components of individualized instruction. The teacher, counselor, psychologist, administrator, teacher's aide, and other supportive personnel must work closely as a team to plan, develop, implement, and monitor an individualized program. Teachers of exceptional individuals need expert assistance from consultants who can demonstrate and explain techniques for individualizing instruction, and they need the support of the principal and the school librarian to provide ideas and materials to complement the instructional program.[18] The major goals of individualized instruction are for the teacher to develop independence, to foster greater self-motivation, and to personalize learning to the extent that the exceptional individual can master learning experiences. Further, if the criteria outlined are followed with creativeness and imagination, exceptional individuals will receive maximum benefits from their educational experiences.

SUMMARY

To convert traditional instruction to the individualized format takes much time, for individualized instruction requires an inordinate amount of time for staff planning, and must have a budget which realistically faces the problems of supplying adequate quantities of well-designed and validated materials. It demands an evaluation system which systematically gathers data about successes and failures and which takes a hard look at the validity and reliability of grades. Individualized instruction takes the time-consuming task of the actual production of materials out of the hands of teachers, and allows them to concentrate upon the content and structure of materials. In essence, individualized instruction implies that if exceptional individuals are to be successful in our schools, their individual abilities and disabilities

---

[18]Marcia McBeath, "Teachers Who Individualize," *Today's Education,* 62 (April, 1973), p. 43.

must be programmed with input from parents and from the children themselves as to what and how they will learn.

It is quite evident that the exceptional individual needs a variety of approaches and instructional techniques. As educators become increasingly more aware of the learning needs of exceptional individuals, the range of individual learning differences becomes more and more apparent. Changes in school organization and curricula, development of more advanced teaching technology, provision for more adequate preschools — all are directed toward dealing with individual learning needs. In conclusion, therefore, a synergistic process approach to humanistic teacher education embodies the concepts and educational methodologies needed for the classroom of today and tomorrow.

CHAPTER IV

BEHAVIOR MODIFICATION STRATEGIES

JACK F. GROSMAN, GEORGE R. TAYLOR AND PETER VALLETUTTI

THE last chapter was concerned with the various forms of individualized instruction. It was indicated that individualized instruction could take on many forms and be conducted under a variety of conditions. Thus, behavior modification techniques may be characterized as another form of individualized instruction. These may be adapted to individuals and designed to change unacceptable behaviors in several areas. In this chapter will be discussed strategies which are necessary to implement a successful behavior modification program.

Behavior modification techniques have been applied with great success to a wide range of problems dealing with exceptional individuals. Successful programs have been developed in the areas of social behavior, academic achievement, motor development, and a variety of other behaviors. Bandura[1] indicated that behavior includes a complexity of observable and potentially measurable activities, including motor, cognitive, and physiological classes of responses.

Macmillan and Forness[2] have concluded that behavior modification strategy has tremendous potential for working with exceptional individuals. Special educators who employ behavior modification techniques are using an effective strategy; however, they are seldom provided with sufficient guidance as to when the approach should be used, for whom, by whom, and toward what end.

Kazdin[3] wrote that behavior modification programs can be no

---

[1]Albert Bandura, *Principles of Behavior Modification* (New York: Holt, Rinehart, and Winston, Inc., 1969).
[2]Donald L. MacMillan and Steven R. Forness, "Behavior Modification: Limitations and Liabilities," *Exceptional Children*, 37 (December, 1970), pp. 291-297.
[3]Alan E. Kazdin, "Issues in Behavior Modification with Mentally Retarded Person," *American Journal of Mental Deficiency*, 78 (September, 1973), p. 134.

more successful than the staff who utilize them. He offered four points which should be considered before implementing a program: (1) staff competencies needed to administer the program, (2) strategies required for developing behaviors in clients which are not controlled by the presence of the staff, (3) techniques for augmenting the performance of intractable clients, and (4) methods for the maintenance of client behaviors after the behavior program has terminated. Kazdin's remarks are supported in the findings of Woody[4] who stressed that certain personnel and facilities should be available before a behavior modification program is implemented. Therefore, before special educators attempt to develop a behavior modification strategy for exceptional individuals, they need to know and explore the limitations and liabilities of the strategy.

On the other hand, current literature abounds with studies reporting on the successful application of behavior modification techniques with the exceptional. The basic principles of behavior modification are neither new nor unique, but the systematic application of its fundamentals to specific problems of human behavior has recently been given increased attention by professionals in the field of education. Principles of direct observation, continuous measurement, and systematic manipulation of the environment were preached early in the nineteenth century; and more recently, behavior modification has received increasing attention, especially within special education during the last decade. This increased attention within special education is, in part, because of the emphasis on task analysis and learning theory.[5, 6]

HISTORICAL OVERVIEW

According to Macmillan and Forness,[7] the use of the behavior modification strategy may be traced to 1800 when Itard used rein-

[4]Robert H. Woody, *Behavioral Problem Children in the Schools: Recognition, Diagnosis and Behavioral Modification* (New York: Appleton-Century-Crofts, 1969).

[5]Florence Christoplos and Peter Valletutti, "Defining Behavior Modification," *Educational Technology*, 9 (December, 1969), p. 28.

[6]Thomas Lovitt, "Behavior Modification: The Current Scene," *Exceptional Children*, 38 (October, 1970), pp. 58-91.

[7]Donald L. Macmillan and Steven R. Forness, "The Origins of Behavior Modification with Exceptional Children," *Exceptional Children*, 37 (October, 1970), pp. 93-100.

forcement techniques with the wild boy Victor. The strategy was further refined by Sequin, and during the 1930's and 1940's, psychologists worked to improve the techniques and broaden the application of conditioning principles. During this time span, experiments were mostly confined to the laboratory setting with emphasis on animals and on humans with severe emotional or mental conditions. Skinner's publications concerning animal behavior in the 1950's gave added impetus to the movement. Efforts were then expanded to apply the principles of reinforcement to a wide range of behavior problems.

The 1960's brought an increase in the frequency of use of behavior modification principles. Macmillan and Forness[8] reported that researchers launched investigations into several areas of human behavior: Bijou and Baer (1961) focused attention on the interaction between a child and his learning environment. Lindsley's work (1964) focused on developing special environments for the retarded, the brain-damaged, and the emotionally disturbed. Ayllon and Haughton (1962) employed behavioral techniques to alter the behavior of patients on a psychiatric ward. Bandura (1962) conducted experiments with modeling techniques. Birnbauer and Lawler (1964) made the first attempt to apply a token reinforcement system to a classroom of retarded children. Their work was followed by Hewett (1964) who used operant techniques to teach autistic children to read.

Around the middle of the present decade, behavior modification was becoming increasingly accepted as a strategy which had particular values for educating exceptional individuals. More recently, Goodall[9] remarked that in the past five years behavior modifiers or controllers have increasingly moved away from laboratory like settings of mental hospitals, correctional institutions, and special classrooms and have been applied in public schools, halfway houses, private homes, and community health centers.

Modifying behavior has always been one of the principal goals of educational programs for exceptional individuals. According

---

[8]*Ibid.*
[9]Kenneth Goodall, "Who's Who and Where in Behavior Shaping," *Psychology Today*, 6 (November, 1972), pp. 53-63.

to Christoplos and Valletutti[10] there is nothing radically new about behavior modification. What does appear to be innovative in the field is the emphasis on evaluation or measurement techniques to determine how effectively behavior is actually modified in the direction identified by the educator. These authors outlined and discussed three aspects related to the behavior modification trend: (1) information about the child, (2) information about the task, and (3) information about the management process. It was concluded that only through the integration of the above aspects of behavior modification can curriculum development truly become a functional tool in the service of educators.

DEFINING BEHAVIOR MODIFICATION

Behavior modification is the application of behavioral analysis to correct an individual's maladaptive behavior. According to Krasner and Ullman[11] the term denotes a specific theoretical position in regard to changing behavior. The strategy consists essentially of introducing reinforcement contingencies which encourage the emergence of predetermined response patterns. Both classical and operant conditioning may be employed. The former is achieved by pairing the reinforcer with a stimulus; the latter by making the reinforcer contingent upon a response.[12] Kessler [13] reflected that in classical conditioning, stimuli are associated with an unconditioned response, whereas in operant conditioning, the response operates on the environment to produce certain results. The organism is not a passive participant in the learning process as in conditioning.[14]

Behavior modification techniques include a variety of ap-

[10]Florence Christoplos and Peter Valletutti, *op. cit.*, p. 30.

[11]L. Krasner and L. P. Ullman, *Research in Behavior Modification.* (New York: Holt, Rinehart and Winston, 1965), pp. 1-2.

[12]A. A. Lazarus, G. C. Davidson and D. A. Pollefka, "Classical and Operant Factors in the Treatment of School Phobia," *Journal of Abnormal Psychology*, 70 (June, 1965), pp. 225-229.

[13]Jane W. Kessler, *Psychological of Childhood* (Englewood Cliffs Hew Jersey: Prentice Hall, 1966).

[14]Morris Brigge and Maurice Hunt, *Psychological Foundations of Education*, 2nd Ed., (New York: Harper and Row, 1968), p. 354.

proaches such as operant conditioning, contingency management, behavioral modeling, role playing, and other approaches
designed to alter maladaptive behavior. In operant conditioning,
desired behaviors are reinforced in an attempt to establish new
operant behavior. Shaping is employed to reinforce desired operant behavior. Continuous reinforcement implies reinforcement
after each occurrence of the desired response. Intermittent schedules may be one of several types: (1) fixed interval schedule, (2)
variable interval schedule, (3) fixed ratio schedule, and (4) variable ratio schedule. Since these schedules are amply discussed in
other texts, they will not be elaborated on here.* Contingency
contracting is that behavior modification strategy wherein the
subject knows that a particular reward depends upon the completion of a certain task or tasks. The student is rewarded if he successfully completes his part of the contract. Modeling refers to
copying socially acceptable behaviors. This technique is based
upon the premise that most behavior can be imitated by students
if they are given a correct model to follow.

Castell and Brown[15] have classified behavior strategy as operating on the following techniques: (1) positive reinforcement contingencies, (2) negative reinforcement contingencies, and (3) a
combination of positive and negative reinforcement contingencies. Regardless of the type of reinforcement employed, it is imperative that the reinforcement be scheduled systematically.
Initially, the reinforcement should be given immediately after the
behavioral act; subsequent reinforcement schedules may be
changed depending upon the abilities of the individual. It is of
prime importance that the reinforcement schedule be consistent if
the behavior modification strategy is to be successful in changing
behavior.

DESIGNING A BEHAVIOR MODIFICATION STRATEGY

Krasner and Ullman[16] explained that the behavior modifier

---

*Refer to: *The Analysis of Human Operant Behavior*, by Ellen P. Reese, William C.
Brown Publishers, 1966, pp. 11-19.
[15]Elea Schmidt, D. Castell and P. Brown, "A Retrospective Study of Forty-two Cases of
Behavior Therapy," *Behavior Research and Therapy*, 3 (August, 1965), pp. 9-19.
[16]Krasner and Ullman, *loc. cit.*

must address himself to three points, if he is to successfully implement a behavior modification strategy: (1) define maladaptive behavior, (2) determine the environmental events which support the behavior, and (3) manipulate the environment in order to alter maladaptive behavior. These points are similar to those advanced by Madsen[17] who presented four behaviors for teachers to utilize in the following behavior modification strategy: (1) pinpoint explicitly the behavior that is to be eliminated or established, (2) set up a procedure for recording specific behaviors as they occur over a period of time, (3) establish external environmental contingencies and proceed with the established program, and (4) stay with the program long enough to ascertain its effectiveness. Miron[18] emphasized that a positive atmosphere should be created in implementing a behavior modification strategy. He proposed that the teacher formulate a positive rule, something students can work toward, rather than something to avoid. By this means the student is directed toward a specific desirable behavior rather than merely castigated without an alternative suggested behavior. The importance of involving students in planning a behavior modification strategy was also outlined.

Hewett[19] in his design of the engineered classroom focused upon the teacher establishing a working relationship with each individual. He stated that the teacher's job was to assign tasks that the student needed to learn, was ready to learn, and could be successful in learning. He maintained that this approach permits greater teacher-student interaction. The specific behavior modification strategy, the character of its application, and the nature and quality of the teacher-student interaction must arise out of the teacher's assessment of the individual and his needs and interests. A behavior modification strategy should be flexible in its application while firmly based in scientific method.

It is universally accepted that the identification of potential

[17]Charles Madsen and Clifford Madsen, *Teaching Discipline Behavior Principles Toward a Positive Approach* (Boston: Allyn and Bacon, Inc., 1970), pp. 10, 21, 133.

[18]Charles D. Miron, *Behavior Modification Guide for Teachers*, Behavioral Information and Technology, 1971, p. 20.

[19]Frank Hewett, *The Emotionally Disturbed Child in the Classroom* (Boston: Allyn and Bacon, Inc., 1968).

reinforcers is basic to a behavior modification strategy. Many behavior modifiers, however, use the terms reward and reinforcement interchangeably. According to Ayllon and Azrin[20] there is a distinction between the terms. A reward is typically considered in terms of the subjective reaction that it produces. The distinction between rewards and reinforcers reflects the difference between a humanistic and a behavioral approach to human behavior. A reinforcing stimulus is defined as an event or consummatory behavior that leads to an increased probability of a response. The definition of a reinforcer is always in terms of some measurable stimulus or measurable behavior of the individual. Maehr[21] argued that the Skinnerian conception of motivation was inadequate to explain human behavior. He maintained that in his demand for objectivity, precision, observability, and measurability, Skinner ignored the hard-to-define internal states of men. He felt that in so doing, Skinner severely limited the applicability of his approach. Maehr expressed the view that reinforcement principles are too simple to provide an efficient or easily obtainable solution to the problem of getting the individual to confront the educational task, and then have him persist at it and learn from it.

The Teacher as a Behavior Modifier

Educators attempt to change the behavior of students in ways which they feel will enhance their desire to learn. Using a behavior modification strategy, educators try to determine those reinforcers which will increase the probability of a desired response or behavior. Several difficulties, however, are inherent in the systematic application of a reinforcer. The first lies in the pupil's perception of his current behavior, the target behavior to which he is aspiring, and his relationship to the reinforcer. By providing an individual with arbitrary reinforcers, a teacher

---

[20]T. Ayllon and Nathan Azrin, *The Token Economy* (New York: Meredith Corporation, 1968), p. 57.
[21]Martin Maehr, "Limitations of Applying Reinforcement Theory to Education," in Behrns and Nolen (Eds.), *Behavior Modification in the Classroom* (Belmond: Wadsworth, 1970), p. 83.

focuses the individual's attention, not on the relationship between his behavior and his academic or social success, but rather on the relationship between his behavior and the reinforcement. He sees his behavior as related only to the desired consequence and changes his behavior only to receive the reinforcement, not because the new behavior has meaning for him. The use of natural reinforcers may also be criticized in the same way, although they may more easily be integrated into an individual's frame of reference and thus be more easily related to the desired behavior.

Madsen and Madsen[22] illustrated how aspects of teacher attention and praise may function as a negative reinforcer. They stated that a teacher may utilize an opportune moment to comment favorably or praise another student in front of the class with the intention of sending a negative message to another student. Miron[23] wrote that this type of situation may be called an example of unintended consequences of reinforcement and frequently does not fit the particular life style of the student. In essence, the method might be harmful to the student unless the teacher has considered his individual needs.

Behavior modification is a technique which may be effectively used in conjunction with educational systems and/or content; it is not a program with content of its own.[24] Generally, teachers of special individuals feel that the utilization of a behavior modification strategy is too complex and involves too much preliminary training. These concepts can probably be attributed to the fact that special educators are not often familiar with behavioral principles. Several studies were reviewed which indicate that a behavior modification strategy can be successfully implemented by teachers who have had adequate training.

Jones[25] indicated that behavior modification techniques can be highly effective in the beneficial changes of social and academic behaviors of normal and exceptional individuals. Recent research

---

[22]Madsen and Madsen, *loc. cit.*

[23]Miron, *loc. cit.*

[24]B. R. Gearheart, *Learning Disabilities: Educational Strategies* (St. Louis, Missouri: The C. V. Mosby Company, 1973), p. 117.

[25]Reginald L. Jones (Ed.), *New Directions in Special Education* (Boston: Allyn and Bacon, Inc., 1970), pp. 199-204.

has applied these techniques to preschool children, to school dropouts, to emotionally disturbed children, and to low achieving minority children. The approach that these investigations have taken has been to employ token reinforcers such as colored chips or point cards to improve and maintain improvement of social and/or academic behaviors. Items such as candy, gum, toys, and money have served as back-up reinforcers to these tokens.

ADVANTAGES OF A BEHAVIOR MODIFICATION STRATEGY

Behavior modification techniques have proven extremely successful in eliminating maladaptive behavior in children with behavioral disorders.[26] It was found that after fifty-two days of operant techniques the attending behavior of behaviorally disordered children increased. Many studies concerned with behavior modification have been conducted with retarded children. Although the intellectual deficit of retarded children may add numerous special factors to the conditioning process, and moreover, to the factors underlying the occurrence of problem behaviors, it has been shown that operant conditioning procedures have been effective with the mentally retarded. Numerous forms of behavioral problems have been reported to be successfully modified in children classified as mentally retarded. For example, Hundziak, Maurer, and Watson[27] used an operant conditioning format to toilet train several mentally retarded boys in a residential institution. A reinforcement device issued an object reward of candy for each successful defecation and urination. Elimination and voiding behaviors rapidly improved, and the results transferred to the subject's general behavior outside the experimental conditions.

Brown and Elliot[28] controlled aggressive behavior of boys in

[26]H. C. Quay, "Remediation of the Conduct Problem Child in the Special Class Setting," *Exceptional Children*, 32 (April, 1966), pp. 509-515.

[27]M. Hundziak, Ruth Maurer, and L. S. Watson, "Operant Conditioning in Toilet Training of Severely Mentally Retarded Boys," *American Journal of Mental Deficiency*, 70 (July, 1965), pp. 120-124.

[28]P. Brown and R. Elliot, "Control of Aggression in a Nursery School Class," *Journal of Experimental Child Psychology*, 2 (June, 1965), pp. 103-107.

nursery school by using positive operant techniques. Allen[29] conducted an experiment with a four-year-old subject who displayed nonattending behavior. The subject moved so rapidly from activity to activity until it was nearly impossible to assess his behavior. After the application of behavioral modification strategies, there was a significant reduction in the rate at which he changed activities. At the end of the experiment, the subject was spending fifteen to twenty minutes on each activity. This was then deemed as appropriate for his chronological age. A similar study conducted by Wolf[30] was designed to increase the attention span of children in a third and fourth grade remedial class. Students were given tokens later to be exchanged for candy, clothing, and field trips as a reward for being in their seats at appropriate times. Results indicated that inappropriate out-of-seat behavior was significantly reduced when compared with baseline data.

The sample of research studies was not intended to give the reader a comprehensive view of behavior modification used with the exceptional but rather to indicate that special educators can effectively employ behavior modification strategies in their classrooms. Zimmerman and Zimmerman[31] presented five incidents in which a teacher of emotionally disturbed boys altered unproductive behavior by removing the social consequences of the behavior. Semrau[32] listed the benefits of applying behavior modification for educational purposes:

1. The most significant contribution is that behavior modification helps make education more of a science. It provides a language, including operationally defined terms, which makes precise communication possible. Precise communication helps make possible the replication of studies and the

---

[29]K. Allen, "Control of Hyperactivity by Social Reinforcement of Attending Behavior," *Journal of Educational Psychology*, 58 (August, 1967), pp. 231-237.

[30]M. Wolf, "The Timer Game: A Variable Interval Contingency for the Management of Out-of-Seat Behavior," *Exceptional Children*, 37 (October, 1970), pp. 113-118.

[31]Elaine H. Zimmerman and J. Z. Zimmerman, "The Alteration of Behavior in A Special Situation," *Journal of the Experimental Analysis of Behavior*, 5 (January, 1962), pp. 59-60.

[32]Louise P. Semrau, "An Educator Looks at Behavior Modification," Paper presented at the 45th Annual Convention of the Council for Exceptional Children, St. Louis, Missouri, March, 1967.

validation of results.

2. By utilizing behavior modification techniques, the educator is better prepared to control behavior. Having command of the group or individuals in one way or another guarantees freedom from the disciplinarian role. Consequently, concern can more appropriately focus on educational programming.

3. Any academic subject or problem area can be approached with behavior modification techniques. The contingencies determining the results can be identified whether the task includes reading, writing, arithmetic, or sitting in a seat ready for work. The virtually unlimited potentials for application to a wide range of tasks make it an extremely valuable tool for all educators.

LIMITATIONS OF A BEHAVIOR MODIFICATION STRATEGY

According to Whelan and Haring,[33] behavior modification techniques provide systematic procedures which teachers may implement to change or modify deviant behavior and encourage more acceptable behavior. Skeptical, cautious acceptance and application are certainly indicated. Similarly, Macmillan and Forness[34] indicated that like any tool, behavior modification techniques are themselves morally blind. The authors proposed five limitations to the behavioral approach: (1) the behavioral approach treats only the symptoms and not their causes, (2) it stresses remediation and minimizes prevention, (3) behavioral problems cannot be nullified by a strategy which fails to penetrate environmental or psychological roots, (4) there is no transferable value because out-of-classroom behavior is not affected, and (5) self-discipline is devalued in favor of extrinsic management.

There is ample research to indicate limitations of behavior modification techniques. Redl and Wattenberg[35] stated that

---

[33]Richard Whelan and Norris Haring, "Modification and Maintenance of Behavior through Systematic Application of Consequences," *Exceptional Children*, 32 (January, 1966), pp. 281-289.

[34]MacMillan and Forness, *op. cit.*, pp. 291-297.

[35]F. Redl and W. Wattenberg, *Mental Hygiene in Teaching* (Chicago: Aldine Publishing Company, 1961), pp. 285-286.

teachers are often told to use a positive approach to influence behavior. The danger inherent in this approach is that rewards may impede natural motivation. Better management would help students feel the satisfaction inherent in doing good work for its own sake. Another danger arises when jealousy about the reward sets children apart. When this occurs, those who are given a reward may be treated as the "teacher's pet," thus interfering with their social relationships with peers. In cases such as this, receiving a reward becomes an unpleasant experience. A third danger is when the reward loses most of its value because it can be attained by only a few and is beyond the reach of most. Hewett[36] reviewed a number of studies using behavior modification techniques. He concluded from the research that the use of trinkets, food, and small toys was ineffective for holding children at a task for any considerable length of time because of satiation.

As concern increases with accountability and as the necessity for evaluation increases, another potential source of misuse of a behavior modification strategy is in the area of goal determination. Behaviorally oriented educators such as Madsen and Madsen[37] stressed the setting of specific behavioral objectives to determine the direction for effort, and to provide a precise means for evaluating that effort. A dangerous potential is implicit in this desire for accountability and measurability — the situation whereby that which is measurable becomes the goal. The unfortunate situation thus arises in education, i.e., that it may become more rewarding for centers to teach that which is readily measured. Behaviors which are not easily quantified, particularly those in the affective domain, may thus be excluded from the realm of desirable educational goals.

Mann and Phillips[38] stated that an approach that does not consider the whole child holds some disturbing portents for special education in that it considers the special individual as a collection of indiscrete and unrelated fractions. The basic assumptions underlying the development and utilization of frac-

---

[36]Hewett, *loc. cit.*
[37]Madsen and Madsen, *loc. cit.*
[38]Lester Mann and William Phillips, "Fractional Practices in Special Education: A Critique," *Exceptional Children*, 32 (January, 1967), pp. 311-315.

tional approaches is that human activity may be successfully separated into specific entities, being essentially independent and capable of being individually evaluated and treated. Mann and Phillips defied this approach, and concluded that human behavior is too complex to justify a fractional approach to behavior analysis.

GOAL DETERMINATION IN A BEHAVIOR MODIFICATION STRATEGY

Atkin[39] criticized goal determination on the grounds that the behavioral analyst seems to assume that for an objective to be worthwhile, he must be able to observe progress. Accordingly, goals come first, not the methods for assessing progress toward the goals. Goals, however, are derived primarily from measures. In the determination of adequate behavioral objectives, one of the steps in a behavior modification strategy requires that a teacher work with both short and long range objectives. Without the association between short and long range objectives, the objectives themselves become fractional bits of behavior with little relationship to the process of educational development.

Goal determination in behavior modification research tends to indicate the following: (1) behavior modification cannot be arbitrarily applied because the strategy does not provide teachers with educational goals or philosophy, (2) behavior modification describes learning as a change in observable behavior, disregarding the entire range of covert and unobserved learning, (3) the use of the strategy limits the target behavior to precise, quantifiable, and measurable behaviors, ignoring less easily defined and difficult to measure behaviors, and (4) the strategy concentrates almost entirely on objective measurements, not recognizing the subjective realm of human functioning.

MODIFYING INAPPROPRIATE BEHAVIOR

Behavior modification is a recognized approach for the sys-

---

[39]Myron J. Atkin, "Behavioral Objectives in Curriculum Design: A Cautionary Note," *Science Teacher*, 12 (November, 1972), pp. 22-25.

tematic control of certain behaviors. Its effectiveness in the temporary altering of many overt, observable behaviors is not questioned. The approach eliminates long and possibly fruitless searches for underlying psychological causes that may or may not be susceptible to change or therapy. An accurate description of present behaviors is an indication of how subsequent behaviors can be modified or changed. In the case of some exceptional individuals, the crucial task is to affect a reward system which eliminates undesired behaviors and reinforces those behaviors which are more socially acceptable. While a review of professional literature supports the value of behavior modification, it nevertheless points out some of the limitations and disadvantages of using the strategy with exceptional individuals.

In the field of special education, behavior modification has developed as an acceptable alternative to the psychodynamic method of resolving behavioral problems. It has helped teachers to focus on specific individual behaviors rather than on a general pattern of behavior such as emotional disturbance or learning disability. Additionally, behavior modification has directed teacher effort away from punitive actions for undesirable behavior to reinforcement and encouragement of desirable behaviors.

Finally, behavior modification has focused attention on the environmental contingencies which maintain undesirable behaviors. Educators are provided with an approach which encourages them to analyze and alter classroom environmental situations to bring about desirable change. No longer are they forced to regard classroom behavior as the result of factors outside the classroom and beyond their control.

These views are not supported by all researchers in the field. Opponents of the strategy have attacked the behaviorist position of considering only the overt, observable, and measurable portion of human functioning. They feel that behaviorists are offering a powerful approach to changing human behavior but are neglecting the complex nature of human activity, particularly how individuals learn and how they are motivated. Due to the fact that a behavior modification strategy is based upon specific overt behaviors, it possesses the potential for encouraging teachers to teach those behaviors which fit the system, overlooking affective behaviors.

SUMMARY

The uniqueness of a behavioral strategy lies in its systematic application of a precise technique to bring about behavioral change. Because of its origin in the scientific laboratory, it requires compliance with and acceptance of the demands of scientific rigor. The development of a behavior modification strategy has established a definite structure whereby a teacher can change a student's behavior. It can be employed to increase the occurrence of desired behavior already within a student's behavioral repertoire or to teach new behavior.

Behavior modification is a valuable tool but should not be used as a total approach to classroom learning. This conviction is supported by Hilgard[40] who stated that alternate developmental theories may be more helpful for determining goals. These developmental theories may suggest to the teacher a specific developmental task that the student must master and what specific skills he must acquire in order to achieve subsequent levels of performance.

However, the teacher should be able to recognize the advantages of giving rewards as they relate to a specific goal that is to be obtained. Using this approach, the teacher should be able also to determine when a reward is not working. When the reward becomes the end instead of the means, it becomes a liability. The teacher should become skilled in systematically employing a behavior modification strategy when it will facilitate the acquisition of knowledge and skills designed to make that student a more fully realized individual.

---

[40]Ernest Hilgard, *Introduction to Psychology* (New York: Harcourt, Brace Publishers, 1957), p. 270.

CHAPTER V

PERCEPTUAL REMEDIATION

CATHERINE GROFF

ELSEWHERE in the volume the discussion was focused upon the many deficits found among exceptional individuals. Causes and methods for remediating the deficits were reviewed. This chapter is designed to focus on an important approach in remediating many of the deficits experienced by some exceptional individuals.

As a general principle, the mechanisms of perceptual behavior are dependent on three functions:

1. Awareness of conditions of internal and external environment.

2. Ability to communicate these conditions by the appropriate affector organs.

3. Ability of affectors to cause the organism to effect overt adjustment to the environment.

Physically, the neural aspect of the simple reflex arc is represented by the nervous system which includes the brain. The function of the nervous system is to transmit impulses generated through the sensory structure to the appropriate musculature. This phenomenon, associated with the awareness of the external world through the exterocepter sense, is called perception.[1]

When an individual is thrust into a new environment at birth, he suddenly has the responsibility of caring for his complex systems. He must learn what to do with the radiant energy that enters his eye, with the sound waves that impinge on his ears, with the mechanical energy applied to his skin, as well as the chemical energy exerted on his tongue and nose.[2]

---

[1]P. A. Verdier, *Bio-Psychology* (New York: Exposition Press, 1963), p. 29.
[2]A. A. Strauss and L. Lehtinen, *Psychopathology and Education of the Brain-Injured Child* (New York: Grune and Stratton, 1962), p. 47.

Gestalt psychologists indicated that perception is innate, but Solley and Murphy[3] reflected that one must learn what to do with the stimuli that approach his senses. The infant must learn to interpret sensory stimuli before he can use them to process information in his environment. Development of conceptual configuration is governable by manipulative experiences to which the individual is exposed. If he is to develop proper concepts, he must be motivated by larger perceptual structures commensurate with increase in age. The degree to which each individual's perceptual configuration is organized and its wealth of content depend on one's experiences and native ability to perceive.

Solley and Murphy[4] go further on this subject. They proclaimed that perceptual learning is dependent on the level of maturation achieved by a child. Full achievement of maturation can be facilitated or inhibited by the occurrence or nonoccurrence of specific learning experiences. Neither maturation nor learning can fully unfold independently. To this concept Verdier[5] would add the condition of individual differences. He stated that individuals do not perceive situations with equal realism. As humans vary in physical characteristics, so do they vary in endowment and development of exteroceptive capacity. This bears out Gesell's approach to individual differences through the stages of growth and development.

Strauss and Lehtinen[6] envisioned perception as involving a complex system of integrations between sense fields and between past and present sensory impressions and experiences. Verdier supports the notion that perception is a panoramic screen, storing the past and allowing individuals to utilize long forgotten perceived experiences. Accumulation of old perceptual experiences helps to explain intellectual growth and ability as they combine to make past events meaningful[7] Solley and Murphy would add that changes take place in perception from early child-

---

[3]C. Solley and G. Murphy, *Development of the Perceptual World* (New York: Basic Books, Inc., 1960), p. 145.
[4]Solley and Murphy, *op. cit.*, p. 125.
[5]Verdier, *op. cit.*, p. 78.
[6]Strauss and Lehtinen, *op. cit.*, p. 78.
[7]*Ibid.*, p. 37.

hood to adult life; that perceptions are not fixed from one year to the next.

AUDITORY PERCEPTION

Gesell and Ilg[8] stated that auditory and visual perceptions are learned from infancy. The same holds true for the three other basic senses. The child learns to make associative discriminations of similarities, differences, and combinations in each sensory area.

In auditory perception, characteristic sounds have a quality all their own. Sensory data in audition comes through vibrations transmitted from the outer air to fluid in the inner ear. It is from these impulses that one evaluates pitch (frequency) and intensity. From association and learning one can discriminate similarities, differences, and combinations of sound. As in all perceptions, discriminations are stored so that they may be called upon whenever needed for further learning. The ability to recall auditory sounds is called auditory memory.[9]

In the very young child, audition supports and reinforces motor activities before the skill and dexterity for writing is developed. In the preschool age child, the use of sounds through language allows him to visualize and report on his visualization.

VISUAL PERCEPTION

Sensory information to the eye comes in the form of light. When an image from the light falls on the retina, a series of impulses are set off along the optic nerve to the brain. The output of the sensory stimuli is a patterned response based on past and present experiences with environment. Visual perception is perhaps the most important skill required in our culture. Vision reaches the highest achievement when all developmental processes are incorporated in the guidance and training routines presented as learning situations. The use of motor-integrative-

---

[8]A. Gesell and F. Ilg, *Child Development* (New York: Harper and Brothers, 1949), p. 425.
[9]G. H. Getman, *How to Develop Your Child's Intelligence* (Minnesota: Programs to Accelerate School Success, 1957), pp. 31-32.

perceptual processes enhances every skill in that it prepares the child's entire visual machinery.[10]

Visual perception is the most significant of our perceptual skills in that it is an interpretive skill. It assists us in understanding texture, size, shape, direction, and color. The senses of taste, smell, and touch need more specific contact before they can furnish information on decision and interpretations.[11]

The spiral of development in perceptual skills can progress to where vision alone provides adequate information. For example, one can see an orange and know it is an orange from past perceptual experiences. One does not have to touch, taste, or smell it to know it is an orange. As a distance receptor, vision can help us to understand our world more completely than any other sensory mechanism. Perceptual organizations and conceptual orientations in space start with the child's awareness of his own position in space. A child must learn to know the meaning of up and down, near and far, right and left, vertical and horizontal. In other words, he must learn directionality. This is especially important in learning to read.

The location of objects in space is the result of the integration of a series of visual impressions. Strauss and Kephart outlined that it is necessary to locate objects laterally, with relation to each other and our own bodies. There are clues one may get which enter into the perception of distance under various circumstances.

1. Kinesthetic sensations produced by the convergent and divergent eye movements that estimate the distance away from an object.

2. Kinesthetic sensations of the accommodatory movements of the eye to make accurate judgments of distance.

If one has an idea of the relative size of objects in a field of vision, one can learn to estimate relative distances. One can also learn that brightness, clearness, and color saturation decrease as distance increases.

The differences and similarities which an individual observes

---

[10]Morris Bender, *Disorders In Perception* (Springfield, Illinois: Charles C Thomas, 1952), p. 13.
[11]*Ibid.*, p. 14.

in space are accomplished, not only on the basis of space but time as well. He can learn to change complicated spatial series into a temporal series and back again. Strauss[12] says that if one learns to make such changes, this will lead one to find that differences and similarities go in patterns. This was also stated by Kephart[13] along with the fact that the individual can learn to understand that changes in parts of the pattern change the pattern and present a variation. These authors further stated that a child must build up the whole, which has its own characteristics and which differs from any of its parts.

Distinguishing figure-ground organization is the final process of structuring percepts. According to Solley and Murphy, distinction between figure and ground can be learned. The figure is more easily definable by color connected with meanings and feelings. Knowing these differences is important in reading in that one has to distinguish the symbol (figure) from the page on which it is printed (ground).[14] Hebb[15] supported this concept when he stated that in the course of perceptual learning one goes through the period of paying separate attention to each part of a whole.

DeHirsch[16] concluded that an individual must achieve maturation in the areas of perceptual-motor-conceptual behavior as a reading readiness measure. She felt that movement, like perception, requires patterning. Certain levels of motor skills are indicative of an individual's overall maturity, for one must attain neurological saturation in order to activate specific muscle groups.

It is not within the scope of this chapter to discuss detailed relationships between perception and reading, but to review perceptual training techniques that can be successfully implemented by the teacher in remediating reading disabilities found among many exceptional individuals.

---

[12]A. A. Strauss and L. Lehtinen, *loc. cit.*

[13]N. Kephart, *The Slow Learner in the Classroom* (Ohio: Charles C. Merrill Book, Inc., 1960).

[14]Solley and Murphy, *op. cit.*, p. 263.

[15]D. O. Hebb, *The Organization of Behavior* (New York: John Wiley & Sons, Inc., 1949), p. 303.

[16]K. Katrina DeHirsch, "Test Designed to Discover Reading Difficulties on the Six Year Old Level," *The American Journal of Orthopsychiatry*, 27 (July, 1957), pp. 566-576.

READING

Reading is not one skill, but a number of interrelated skills. For the beginning reader, reading is mainly concerned with learning to recognize printed symbols which represent speech and to respond intellectually and emotionally as if the material were spoken rather than printed. The beginning reader learns to develop skills in the mechanics of reading such as developing a sight vocabulary and identifying unfamiliar words. He also learns to develop skills in comprehension by learning to grasp meanings, to understand main ideas and to understand sequences of events as well as recalling details. He learns to associate printed words with concrete objects and abstract ideas and use them in arranging sentences.

Reading involves the following simultaneously:
1. Sensation of light rays on the retina, reaching the brain.
2. Perception of separate words and phrases.
3. Function of eye muscles with exact controls.
4. Immediate memory for what has been read.
5. Organization of the material so that it can be used.[17, 18]

In order to perceive symbols, there must be good visual mobility in the left to right movements across the reading page as well as visual orientation to the symbols on the printed page. Related to the percepts of form are the percepts of space since forms do involve spatial relationships. Tactile perception gives an indication of size and shape. Visual perception gives one an orientation in space as in left to right, up and down. Visual perception also gives an orientation in space as to size, shape, figure/ground, as well as distance as in near and far. Auditory perception gives one a sense of rhythm, time, and continuity, as he relates to sounds. Space, position, and direction will only have meaning for the child if he has sense of his own body image. Some procedures for determining how well the individual uses his sensory modalities are outlined in Chapter I.

Developmental Readiness

Educators have placed much stress on the concept of readiness

---

[17]Albert Harris, *How to Increase Reading Ability* (New York: David McKay, 1961).
[18]David Russell, *Children Learn to Read* (New York: Ginn and Co., 1961).

as a prerequisite for learning. From the field of child development, the emphasis has been drawn on individual differences in maturational patterns, especially as they relate to children in the earliest school years. Differentiated from intelligence and experimental influences, the factor of biological readiness, which appears to be a reflection of specific integration patterns, plays a major role in the acquiring of speech and the learning of reading and arithmetic. While, for example, aphasia in the adult can generally be traced to known cerebral trauma, in children it is more often maturational in origin and represents a lag in the development of specific language functions. Usually, following the delay, spontaneous compensation occurs, although on later examination a residuum of difficulty may be diagnosed in the form of motor, sensory, conceptual, or mixed aphasia. A similar pattern is followed in older children in relation to reading. Differences in the development of such fundamental techniques as directional orientation and auditory discrimination may be wide in a group of first grade children of comparable intelligence, and the influence of this factor on the learning process is crucial.

A vexing clinical problem for the child psychologist is suggested by these developmental considerations. In some cases early disability can be expected to be overcome spontaneously through growth, and in other cases specific help is needed. Notwithstanding the validity of the developmental lag concept, too often there is a tendency to wait too long for spontaneous compensation to occur, while the individual is neglected, sometimes beyond remediation.

Bryant[19] listed five principles that should be employed if remediation is to be effective with individuals who have special needs:

1. Remediation should initially focus on the simplest, most basic perceptual associational elements in reading: perception of details within the Gestalt of words and association of sounds with the perceived word elements.

2. Perceptual and associational responses should be overlearned until they are automatic.

3. The remedial teacher should plan the learning experience

[19]N. Dale Bryant, "Some Principles of Remedial Instruction for Dyslexia," *The Reading Teacher*, 18 (April, 1965), pp. 567-572.

and modify the presentation of the task and material on the basis on the individual's performance, so that the child is correct in nearly all of his responses.

4. When two discriminations or associations are mutually interfering, the following steps should be taken consecutively:

   a. one of the discriminations or associations should be learned on an automatic level;

   b. the second should then be learned on an automatic level;

   c. the first should be briefly reviewed;

   d. the two should be integrated, starting with tasks where the only difference between the two need be perceived; and finally,

   e. in graduated steps, both should be made automatic when the task requires discriminations and associations in addition to the mutually interfering ones.

5. There should be frequent reviews of basic perceptual, associational, and blending skills, and as rapidly as possible these reviews should involve actual reading.

It appears from the aforementioned principles that successful reading remedial instruction can be influenced by the extent to which the teacher can couple the richness of previous teaching experience with modification in skills and instructional techniques to remediate severe reading problems. Principles advocated by Bryant parallel those advanced by M. Frostig.[20] It was voiced by Frostig that certain perceptual skills need to be practiced until they become fully automated. She further stated that the more automatic the individual's perception and decoding are when he reads, the more fluently he can direct his attention toward the task. Reading readiness should develop percepts of form as they involve the printed letters or symbols a child will need in reading. Vertical, lateral, and oblique lines, plus circles, squares, and angles are the forms singly, or in combination, that make up letter symbols.

---

[20]M. Frostig, "Visual Perception, Integrative Functions and Academic Learning," *Journal of Learning Disabilities* (January, 1972), p. 6.

When discussing perceptual handicaps, reading is one of the most important topics, since nearly all perceptual handicaps affect reading abilities. Haber[21] wrote that reading involves not only language processes, but rests upon incredibly rapid perceptual activity derived from sequentially presented brief exposures of complex information. Further, since reading is so dependent upon constructive processes, anything which disrupts the translation of ongoing perception will have disastrous consequences for reading skills.

Perceptual skills are improved when the individual has opportunities to explore and learn the characteristics of distance and spatial relationships. Often exceptional individuals have not mastered sizes and distances because interpretation and reorganization skills have not been perfected. The individual must learn to perfect this reorganization through repeated perceptual-motor activities of matching experiences with an object to the perception of that object at a distance. The process involves matching eye movement with feeling of the body before the size and distance of an object can be judged.[22]

Reading Retardation

By far the most common area of learning difficulty experienced by children is reading. Estimates of incidence vary widely but probably more than 10 percent of the children who have average intelligence in our schools are reading so inadequately for their grade placement that their total adjustment is impaired. The earliest descriptions traced etiology to a known, specific, focal cerebral lesion. Later numerous other etiologic correlations were described, including chronic illnesses, visual problems, mixed cortical dominance, developmental lag, generalized neurological dysfunctions and emotional problems. In the presence of these and many more etiological possibilities, it is evident that inade-

---

[21]Ralph N. Haber, "Visual Perception," in *Psychology and the Handicapped Child* (U.S. Government Printing Office, 1974), p. 69.

[22]Elsie Blankenship, "A First Primer on Visual Perception," *Journal of Learning Disabilities* (December, 1971), pp. 580-581.

quate reading, like other learning deficiencies, is a symptom rather than a discrete clinical entity in itself. Because of this, the term "reading inadequacy" is suggested to describe all cases of reading difficulties.

The term is used in reference to all individuals whose level of reading achievement is two years or more below the mental age obtained in performance tests. It appears valid to use performance rather than verbal tests as the index of mental age, because functioning on the verbal portions of such psychometric tests as the Wechsler or the Binet is significantly affected by the reading inadequacy itself, whereas the performance subtests are much less so influenced. The two-year discrepancy between mental and reading age is arbitrary, but it has the value of limiting the definitive diagnosis to cases showing significant functional reading inadequacy that inevitably affects school adjustment.

While visual, general health, and other causes occasionally operate alone to produce reading retardation, the large majority of cases fall into three major groups:

1. Capacity to learn to read is intact but is utilized insufficiently for the individual to achieve a reading level appropriate to his intelligence. The causative factor is exogenous, the individual having a normal reading potential that has been impaired by negativism anxiety, depression, emotional blocking, psychosis, limited schooling opportunity, or other external influences.

2. Capacity to learn to read is impaired by brain damage manifested by clear-cut neurologic deficits. History usually reveals the cause of the brain injury — common agents being prenatal toxicity, birth trauma or anoxia, encephalitis and head injury. These cases of brain injury are frequently associated with severe reading retardation.

3. Capacity to learn to read is impaired without definite brain damage suggested in history or on neurological examination. The defect is in the ability to deal with letters and words as symbols, with resultant diminished ability to integrate the meaningfulness of written material.

Neurological Appraisal

Drew[23] has reported on the neurological study of a group of individuals with reading retardation. He describes a characteristic pattern, with much variability from patient to patient. His findings are summarized as follows: "Right-left confusion, various extinction or inattention phenomena, cortical sensory disturbances, mixed hand-eye preferences, nonspecific motor awkwardness, dissociated dysgraphia, and speech and spelling abnormalities are all variously combined with the reading disturbance." Drew concluded that primary reading retardation results from developmental discrepancy rather than an acquired brain injury, and that the dysfunction primarily involves the parietal and parietal-occipital regions. Studies by Critchley, Gerstmann, Rabinovitch and Drew are particularly pertinent in providing directions for much needed further research. It is in keeping with the concepts advanced in Chapter II to reject the term "reading retardation" and substitute "reading inadequacy."

Assuming that the proposition advanced by Drew is accepted, then most reading difficulties can be remediated through perceptual training. This proposition would exclude those children with definite brain damage. Accepting the above proposition, this work accordingly would recommend that perceptual training be employed, after a detailed assessment indicates the absence of an acquired brain injury. The remaining portion of this chapter will be devoted to perceptual training that the classroom teacher can implement without advanced training.

PERCEPTUAL TRAINING

The individual may be deficient in any one or more of his perceptual abilities; furthermore, the impairment may range in degree from mild to severe. The teacher must ascertain the area and the degree of involvement before initiating therapy. (Refer to Chapter I, "Learning Styles.") Some suggested therapies are as follows:

---

[23]A. L. Drew, "Neurological Appraisal of Familial Congenital Word Blindness," *Brain*, 79 (1956), p. 440.

1. Visual Perception
   a. Space
      Develop a left to right sequence (a prereading skill) by the following:
      (1.) Arrange story pictures in a left to right sequence (may use flannel board).
      (2.) Arrange blocks or squares of colored paper of varying sizes, small to large, in a left to right sequence.
      (3.) Use peg and form board placing objects from left to right.
   b. Figure-Ground
      The teacher's goal is to increase the individual's tolerance for distracting backgrounds (gray colors seem to be distracting), thereby increasing his awareness of the foreground. This might be accomplished in two ways: increase the "strength" of the background by first using light lines, dots and small figures, and then heavier lines; secondly, gradually decrease the "strength" of the foreground by decreasing its size and using lighter shades of color.

Perceptual Motor Training

1. Visual Motor
   a. Eye-Hand
      (1.) Show the individual different colored geometric forms, letters, and numbers, and have him trace them in a sandbox, on a chalkboard, on paper, or on sandpaper cutouts. Then have him copy them, and then draw them without copying.
      (2.) Throw rings on a stake and throw beanbags at holes in a board.
   b. Eye-Leg
      Hopping, skipping, jumping, walking a rail.
2. Restricted Perceptual-Motor Abilities
   A number of individuals with impaired perceptual-motor abilities have restricted approaches to activities. They can be

helped by exercises designed to foster different solutions to motor problems, e.g., going across a mat in different ways, i.e., crawling, walking, hopping.

The importance of gross motor training in the development of curriculum for exceptional individuals has been well documented by research findings. Kokaska[24] implied that whereas motor training is important to overall motor development, it is not sufficient in itself. Exceptional individuals need the opportunity to experiment with body movements. Three categories were outlined to assist in the total development of the individual. They were: (1) movement exploration where the individual is presented with a task in which he must seek his own solution, (2) creative expression where the individual is presented with material upon which he improvises movement, and (3) structured activities in which the individual is guided to practice certain skills and games. The importance of setting a definite time for activities were discussed as being essential to the success of movement training.

AUDITORY ACUITY

In order to rule out the possibility of deafness, one must get some idea of the individual's auditory acuity. Auditory tests for individuals may be classified as formal or informal. The formal tests include pure tone audiometry, tuning forks, and speech audiometry, all of which require active cooperation on the part of the individual. Another formal but more objective test is Electrodermal Audiometry (E.D.R.), otherwise known as Psychogalvanometry (P.G.S.R.). Informal tests do not require active cooperation and they include sound instruments, sound toys, and free field noise and voice tests.

Program for Developing Auditory Discrimination

The teacher should begin with the "Awareness Program." In

---

[24]Sharen Metz Kokaska, "Classroom Training for the Mentally Retarded," *Education and Training of the Mentally Retarded,* 8 (April, 1973), pp. 10-14.

this program, the child will develop an awareness of sounds in his environment. These sounds may include sounds in the classroom, at home, at school, in town, at the zoo, and many other places. This is done so that the child can understand what he hears. The teacher should develop with him a vocabulary for these sounds.

The child should be taught to: (1) discriminate between gross sounds, (2) develop an awareness of likenesses and differences between gross sounds, (3) differentiate between loud and soft sounds, fast and slow frequency, high and low pitch, and the location of gross sounds, (4) imitate gross sounds, and (5) use the vocabulary of sounds.

The child then may proceed to the "Auditory Memory" program. Here the child develops the ability to follow directions in sequential order. The child should be aided in developing auditory recognition, retention and recall through stories and questions (increase length of stories and difficulty of questions). This also can be done through rhymes, poems, fingerplays, music, creative dramatics, etc. Creative interpretation can be done without music.

Next, the child learns to discriminate between words and sounds. Before moving to this step, the child must have some of his visual problems corrected. After this has been done, visual clues are developed to discriminate among words using objects as visual clues. Discrimination among words can be made by using pictures and figures. For example:

1. The teacher puts three concrete objects on the table in view of the child. Two are the same (e.g., two boats and one car). In a left to right progression, the teacher points to each object and names it. The teacher asks the pupil to choose which is different or the one that was named only once. The teacher varies the objects in many ways.

2. The teacher puts two different objects in full view. She points to each object naming one of them twice. She asks the child to name the one he has heard only once. She varies the order of the objects named.

If using no visual clues, the discrimination is developed in the sounds of words as the phonetic structure changes. Other auditory exercises are as follows:

1. A game with silly questions answered by "Yes," "No," or "Maybe."

2. Another game in which the child looks for a hidden object and is aided by being told he is "hot," "cold," or "warm," along with other clues. Verbal directions should be given one at a time. Stories can be told after which the child may be asked to retell parts of the story or answer questions about it.

3. The teacher could have the child to classify objects such as naming objects that belong in a house, etc.

4. Have the child state how objects are alike or different.

5. Ask the child many cause and effect questions like, "What would happen if . . .?"

6. Have the child complete sentences generated by the teacher.

7. Sentence structure could be developed with the child. The child should be asked to speak in complete sentences.

8. Have the child repeat sentences word for word.

9. Have the child repeat a short story that has been read to him.

10. Have the child chant groups of words after you chant them.

11. Have the child say sounds separately before attempting to put them into words.

12. Have the child listen to taped lessons and the record player. Here, you could have the child make use of the "Language Master."

13. The teacher should stand near the child when she speaks so that the child can imitate his sounds as well as being able to hear him.

VISUAL DYSFUNCTION

The following is suggested for visual dysfunction:

1. Space Perception
   a. Have the child read a simple passage (if capable of reading).
      (1.) Does he reverse words?
      (2.) Does he read from the wrong coordinate (right to left)?
      (3.) Is he a poor reader?
   b. Have the child write a few simple words, e.g., man, etc. (if capable of writing words).
      (1.) Does he spell the words incorrectly?
      (2.) Does he reverse words (e.g., god instead of dog)?
      (3.) Are letters incorrectly juxtaposed?
      (4.) Does he write from the wrong coordinate?
2. Figure-ground Disturbance
   a. Does the child misread words, numbers, letters, or detect incorrect figures when presented on a checkered or on a different colored background?
   b. Is he unsuccessful in manipulating simple puzzles? (If so, examiner must first rule out perceptual motor or any eye-hand coordination difficulty before deciding on figure-ground as the factor).
3. Distance Perception
   a. Have the child write a sentence.
      (1.) Is his writing close enough to the line?
      (2.) Are his words cramped together?
   b. Have the child color within a circle.
      (1.) Does color extend over the line?
      (2.) Does color come close enough to line?
   c. Have the child throw an object at another object.
      (1.) Does he completely overshoot his mark?
      (2.) Does he completely undershoot his mark?

The following is suggested for tactile dysfunction:

Tests in this area might first include having the child feel certain objects while blindfolded or while his eyes are closed. He is then instructed to open his eyes and identify the object he felt from a group of several objects placed in front of him.

Program for Developing Visual Discrimination

The teacher should help the child develop an awareness of shapes before the awareness of the configuration of letters and words. The child should also be helped to develop the ability to use the words for shapes (square, circle, etc.).

The child should learn top to bottom, left to right progression. He should be aided in developing the concept of order in the placement of objects, and should develop the use of words such as first, last, second, next.

The child should be taught to develop an awareness of self in relation to his environment (body image) and be helped to identify right and left in regard to the self. He should develop memory for position in space (location of articles in the room, route to school or the library).

The child should be taught to discriminate among details (shades of colors, concepts of soft and hard, rough and smooth).

Also, the child should learn to comprehend shapes through tactile sense. He can be aided in developing the ability to identify objects by feeling and in developing a suitable vocabulary of shapes using the tactile sense.

The following are a few exercises that will help the child improve in the visual areas:

1. Visual Memory

   a. Show the child slides of movies that tell a story; have the child talk about it or retell it after it is over.

   b. Have the child look at a page of pictures and after the pictures have been removed, have him try to pick out the pictures like those he has seen.

   c. Place objects in a certain order, mix them up, and have the child put them back in the original order.

    d. An idea for sequencing numbers is to help the child learn his telephone number and the telephone numbers of friends and relations. If there is a toy telephone, he should be allowed to dial the numbers at appropriate times.

    e. Provide sequential exercises progressing from the very gross discriminations to the very fine ones.

    f. Place three pictures in front of child. Have the child hide his eyes. Remove one picture. Ask: "Which one is missing?" Show the child three letters. Take them all away. Have the child write the letters he saw.

2. Visual Reception

    a. Have the child identify objects in picture dictionaries, catalogs, or magazines.

    b. Have the child identify colors, letters, numbers, and geometric forms.

    c. Have the child identify the meaningful content of an action picture.

    d. Have the child tell stories of pictures.

3. Visual Association

    a. Have the child group pictures by class (birds, animals, etc.).

    b. Have the child find the picture that is not like the others in a group, and have him tell how the other pictures have something in common (i.e., truck, car, bike, house).

    c. Give the child pictures, each of which tells a part of a story, and have him place them in sequential order.

4. Visual Closure

    a. Have the child name shapes of shadows, ink blots, or cloud formations.

    b. Have the child find partially hidden objects in a picture.

    c. Have the child complete a picture by looking at a finished model.

    d. Have the child connect dots or numbers to make some

shape or picture and name it before it is finished.

5. Verbal Expression

    a. Have the child describe an object and tell a story about it.

    b. Show the child pictures of home life, children playing in the street, etc., and have him talk about it.

    c. Have the child explain how to do some task or play some game.

SUMMARY

Before anyone can professionally treat an individual's needs, he must be aware of what his needs are. This can only be accomplished after a correct diagnosis has been obtained. Even then, however, an individual cannot be helped to achieve his potential until stumbling blocks which might impede his progress are removed. Behavior problems must first be obviated if learning is to take place. The individual cannot retain stimuli if he cannot attend to the stimuli for a sufficient length of time. Similarly, the hard of hearing individual must be provided with improved channels (and/or new channels should be developed) through which he can learn.

No rigid habilitation program can be devised for any group of exceptional individuals; rather, each individual must have an individual program that is geared to his individual needs, as outlined in Chapter IV. Not every individual will need all of the perceptual training discussed in this chapter. However, many exceptional individuals exhibit different kinds of minimal problems which often go undiagnosed or untreated. The teacher and the principal should know the individual's abilities and his limitations before a program of treatment is started.

The individual needs several hours each week of specialized remedial instructions in very small groups with teachers who are competent in both diagnosing and presenting alternate instructional techniques. Alternate instructional strategies are covered in Chapter VIII.

CHAPTER VI

PROGRAMMED INSTRUCTIONAL DEVICES AND MATERIALS

STEPHANIE LAFOREST BROWN AND GEORGE R. TAYLOR

PRINCIPLES that operate in modifying behavior, as reported in Chapter IV, are evidently needed for programmed instruction. Both strategies demand overt responses, immediate reinforcement, a gradual move from the simple to the complex, and continual evaluation and revision. Additionally, both strategies are premised upon the principle of reinforcement. For many exceptional individuals, reinforcement must be applied immediately and consistently if they are to master expected skills.

Programmed instruction is broken down into small sequential steps, thus making it a viable strategy for instructing the exceptional; it can aid immeasurably in individualizing instruction. This chapter will address itself to some of the current trends and components of programmed instruction.

During the last decade there has been a surge of interest in automated and programmed instruction for education. Educators are closely examining the feasibility of incorporating educational technology into educational programs. By and large, these techniques are experimental in nature; however, research has indicated that automated and programmed instruction may prove to be an effective and efficient method for the instruction of exceptional individuals.

Programmed devices and instruction have not been employed in the schools as rapidly as programmers had envisioned. There are several reasons that have possibly attributed to this trend. Branson[1] wrote that teachers were reported to oppose automated and programmed devices on the ground of being replaced by

---

[1]Robert K. Branson, "The Criterion Problem in Programmed Instruction," *Educational Technology*, 10 (July, 1970), p. 36.

them. Administrators frequently lack the courage to try new methods. Finally, the expense involved in many automated and programmed instructional materials prohibited their use in the schools. Although some of the above may be true, presently where automated and programmed modes of instruction are being employed, they are used to supplement the regular instructional process. Examples might include the use of computer-assisted instruction for individualized instruction, audiotapes to reinforce a previously learned skill, and a variety of teaching machines for self-instruction and analysis. Automated and programmed instruction are used to support the teacher in giving the exceptional individual specialized instruction that he normally could not provide alone. Programmed materials may be used with various types of individualized approaches, such as programmed modules or learning stations, diagnostic and prescriptive teaching, behavior modifications, and open education.

Programmed and automated instruction have been an impetus for several other important developments in instructional technology. Computer-assisted instruction, programmed films, tapes, programmed texts and booklets are but a few specific by-products.[2,3,4] The most important contribution that programmed and automated instruction has made to education is the concept that instruction should be designed and presented in a systematic way in order to lead to expected outcomes, and that instruction is revised on the basis of the learner's feedback until expected outcomes are achieved.

Diversity is the general rule to be applied when the exceptional individual is discussed. The differences in learning patterns constitute unique problems for special educators. The early identification, assessment, and management of a pupil's learning differences or difficulties can prevent more serious and often irreparable learning problems from occurring. By careful observa-

---

[2]Geary A. Rummler, "PI Where the Action Is," *Educational Technology*, 10 (July, 1970). p. 31.

[3]J. H. Harless, "A Technology of Performance Problem Solving," *Educational Technology*, 10 (July, 1970), p. 34.

[4]Robert Morgan, "A Decade of Programmed Instruction," *Educational Technology*, 10 (July, 1970), p. 30.

tion, identification, and assessment of the pupil's educational needs, appropriate programming can be undertaken.[5] Step by step instruction can be carried out on an individual basis by adapting various programmed and automated techniques for each individual, permitting the evaluation of the total process of learning and instruction in terms of highly specific goals and objectives. In programmed approaches, tasks are sequenced into small manageable steps, allowing the exceptional individual to proceed at his own rate. Properly sequenced, these tasks can lead to reinforced learning situations.

Programmed and automated instruction offer an effective approach for meeting many of the unique needs of the exceptional. Special educators have the responsibility and opportunity to experiment, modify, and adopt highly reliable and sophisticated automated and programmed instructional devices and techniques to improve educational opportunities for exceptional individuals.

PROGRAMMED STRATEGIES

Special education is presently being pressured to justify its programs. Much of the controversy is due to the fact that exceptional individuals often fail to learn effectively when conventional teaching strategies are employed. Programmed devices and materials appear to have meaningful application to the problem of improving the present status of special education. Research indicates that they have the capability of programming practically every subject area. For purposes of this chapter, automated devices will be referred to as teaching machines or hardware. Included in programmed instruction will be software materials such as films, textbooks, booklets, filmstrips, etc. In essence, automated instruction involves the use of machines and materials, whereas in its generic sense, programmed instruction includes various forms of materials and media without the support of machines.

---

[5]Maryland State Department of Education, Teacher Manual, "Teaching Children with Special Needs," (Owings Mills, Maryland: Division of Instructional Television, 1973).

AUTOMATED INSTRUCTION

As indicated, automated instruction involves the use of technology designed to employ the use of both machines and materials. An automated device or teaching machine is only as good as its software. Examples may include an instructional television without videotapes, a motion picture machine without film, or a cassette player without tapes. Not all automated devices are programmed, but with the present technology, practically all automated devices can be programmed providing that acceptable materials are designed for their particular use. Automated devices include various forms of computer instruction: computer-assisted instruction, computerized talking typewriter, various types of dictating machines, and a variety of teaching machines, to name but a few. Those devices that appear to have the most significance for exceptional individuals will be discussed.

Computer-Assisted Instruction

In computer-assisted instruction multisensory presentation allows for a variety of individual responses. The computer can maintain a detailed response record for each individual, and may interact with the record to give a unique sequence of immediate diagnosis and instructional feedback. This is particularly important when dealing with exceptional individuals, who might be in need of strong support, attention, and encouragement through each step of instruction. Computer-assisted instruction appears to offer a systematic approach in this regard.

For the purposes of this section, CAI will be employed to denote computer-assisted instruction. Salisbury[6] enumerated that twenty-one terms can be found in the literature which describes all or part of the process belonging to computer-assisted instruction. Consequently, such terms as computer-administered instruction (CAI), computer-assisted testing (CAT), computer-managed instruction (CMI), and computer-based instruction (CBI) are frequently used synonymously.

---

[6]A. R. Salisbury, "Computers and Education — Toward Agreement on Terminology," *Educational Technology*, 11 (September, 1971), pp. 35-40.

Utilizing computer technology to assist with instruction appears to be one of the most promising developments in education. The concept is equally important when applied to instructing exceptional individuals. Pedrini[7] wrote that students who fall under the auspices of special education are those who, for one reason or another, have not been able to learn adequately or effectively in the regular classroom setting. These students have special problems and require special techniques and programs if they are to profit sufficiently from their educational experiences. Computerized instruction is programmed to move from one phase to another and makes a reappraisal of skills at each level. This permits the establishment of lower skills that can be associated with more advanced skills at a later stage. The acquisition and retention of lower skills are essential to mastery of the subject content.[8, 9, 10]

In addition to being adaptable, computers do not get tired or frustrated. They can be utilized to serve many individuals at once, so that highly individualized attention can be provided.

Computer-Assisted Instruction Versus Standard Programmed Instruction

CAI involves the interaction of students with computers. The computer's memory capacity enables storage of test items and instructional materials sufficient to diagnose and instruct a wide variety of students in several content areas. A typical terminal will consist of a typewriter, an image projector, and an audio unit. These components, all under program control, enable flexible, multisensory presentation of materials and a variety of student responses. This specification creates a unique sequence of diagnosis and instruction for each student. Thus, CAI provides an

---

[7]Bonnie Pedrini and D. T. Pedrini, "Operant Conditioning for Special Educators," *ERIC No. ED. 064815* (Nebraska: University of Nebraska, 1972).

[8]"Guidelines for Program Development," *Special Education*, Vol. 1, Bulletin 673 (Austin, Texas: Texas Education Agency, 1965).

[9]R. Mackie, *Teachers of Children Who Are Mentally Retarded* (Washington, D. C.: Government Printing Office, November, 1967).

[10]*Programs for the Handicapped*, U. S. Department of Health, Education and Welfare (Washington, D. C.: Government Printing Office, November, 1967).

exciting new approach for individualizing diagnosis, instruction, and evaluation.[11]

The flexibility inherent in CAI offers many advantages over standard programmed instruction. For example, many exceptional individuals are handicapped by poor reading abilities. While the effectiveness of most standard programmed instruction is dependent upon the student's ability to read, CAI can partially overcome this difficulty through a multisensory presentation of instructional materials.

Most programmed instruction is linear in design, i.e., all students proceed through the same sequence of instructional material. Certain programs, however, are designed to provide extra practice for students experiencing difficulty. The decision as to whether or not a given student has extra practice is usually dependent upon his response to one or two test items. In contrast, CAI can be programmed so that each student's cumulative response record will determine not only whether or not he needs more practice, but also which one of several skills he should learn next and which type of presentation of instructional material will be most effective for him.[12]

All programmed instruction, including CAI, provides some sort of immediate feedback for each student response. However, in standard programmed instruction the feedback usually consists of no more than telling the student the correct answer. CAI feedback can be highly diversified and appropriate to the individual student response. With CAI, if the student's response is incorrect, he is usually given additional information or help so that he will eventually be able to come up with the correct answer himself.

Modification of CAI and Automated Instruction To Meet the Needs of the Exceptional

In many instances, little modification is needed in CAI for the

---

[11]Eugene Kerr, "An Instructional System for Computer Assisted Instruction on a General Purpose Computer," *Educational Technology*, 10 (March, 1970), pp. 28-30.
[12]Dean Jamison, "Cost and Performance of Computer Assisted Instruction for Education of Disadvantaged Children," *ED 054978* (California: Stanford University, July, 1971).

exceptional since program content can be sequenced to meet their needs. Tondow [13] outlined the positive effects of using computers in special education. It was related that where the quality of the student is low, CAI appears to be a teacher with infinite patience, readily adaptable to the student's special problems. Similarly, Suppes[14] indicated that the use of the computer in the classroom finds its way into many areas of the curriculum where it meets the needs of the deaf, blind, and other exceptional individuals. The computer regularly informs the special teacher of each pupil's progress and frees him to work with individual problems.

Knutson and Prochnow[15] analyzed a computer-assisted instructional module to teach educable mentally retarded students the survival skill of making change. Behavioral objectives were determined through consultation with various interested personnel, including the staff of the Vocational Training Annex at the Austin State School and the staff of the Mary Lee School of Special Education. After determining subskills by task analysis it was determined that the ability to identify the denominations of coins and to know the proper value of each was a necessary minimal entering behavior.

The IBM 1500-1800 computer system was chosen for its reliability and sophisticated terminals. A mental overlay keyboard was designed containing ten oversized keys; this allowed actual coins to be placed on the keys. Thirty-eight subjects were involved in the program, ranging in ages from twelve to thirty, and having IQ ranges from 45 to 80. Twenty-one students completed all parts of the course. Every student who completed the course improved his score from pre- to posttest, and retention appeared substantial. Student responses were studied as the basis for future revisions. William's and Gilmore's[16] findings were essentially the same.

[13]M. Tondow, "Computers in Special Education — An Introduction," *Exceptional Children*, 31 (November, 1964), pp. 113-116.

[14]P. Suppes, "Computer in the Classroom: Handling Student Differences," *Education Digest*, 33 (October, 1967), pp. 8-20.

[15]Jack Knutson and Robert Prochnow, "Computer-Assisted Instruction for Vocational Rehabilitation of the Mentally Retarded," *ERIC No. 044039* (Texas: Texas University, 1970).

[16]Charles William, "Programmed Instruction for Culturally Deprived Slow Learning Children," *Journal of Special Education*, 11 (Summer-Fall, 1968). pp. 421-438.

They reported that teaching machines were found to stimulate attention and interest in learning materials, and contributed to higher performance in work acquisition, arithmetic, and reading skills when used with the retarded.

A computerized talking typewriter was used with two severely emotionally disturbed boys whose psychological disorganization was manifested most directly in the motor area. Subjects were thirteen years old and were taught simple typing skills on the programmed machine by pressing keys in response to a computer voice. They learned to observe short time delays, developed simple keyboard maps, and attained a specific motor patterning as a result of the response system.[17]

Van Duyn[18] discussed a program conducted at Stanford University using the computer as a catalyst in the treatment of nonspeaking autistic children. The program is based upon the following facts: (1) all children like to play games that are lively and noisy, (2) according to clinical observations, autistic children favor playing with machines, and (3) computers do not have nerves; they are persistent and ask the same question over and over until the child gives a response.

In one group of seventeen nonspeaking autistic children there were four who did not respond to the program. When the children realized they could not wear down the machine, they soon began to respond. The computer treatment program consisted of short games. A word or sentence first appeared on a screen. At the same time, a voice repeated the word or sentence, and gave directions for the child to repeat the word or sentence. This child was exposed to the word or sentence in a three-dimensional way — audio, visual, and interpretive. The computer has a lot more patience than people, and this patience and persistence are getting nontalkers to talk. It was recognized that although the program is an advance for many autistic children, additional experimentation and research are needed.

---

[17]Leonard Colbrinik, "Programmed Learning in the Treatment of Severely Disturbed Children: The Role of Motor Patterning," *Paedopsychiatrica*, 39 (November, 1972), pp. 11-21.

[18]J. Van Duyn, "Magic Machines for Autistic Children," *Early Years*, 2 (March, 1972), pp. 56-58.

Fletcher and Stauffer[19] described a CAI system for instructing the hearing impaired. The system operated in fifteen residential and day schools located in four states and the District of Columbia. Over 3,000 students were registered in the program. Curriculum content included reading, mathematics, language arts, computer programming, foreign languages, and logic. Instruction was programmed from the kindergarten through the university level.

The language difficulties of the hearing impaired were analyzed and individualized language instruction was tailored and programmed for each student. As in many programmed approaches, CAI waits for the student to respond. If the student responds with the correct answer, the program types CORRECT and moves to the next exercise. The order of lessons can be changed by typing a special command to the computer. This allows for remediation and review. Each lesson contains one or more checkpoints. Results determine whether students continue with the practice or are branched for reinforcement and remediation.

Several experimental procedures were developed to assess the effectiveness of the program. Preliminary data indicated that the experimental groups (those in the CAI program) showed significantly favorable posttest performance when compared with the control groups.

Garner[20] described an experimental program conducted by Project Life, a subdivision of NEA, concerning the values of using a teaching machine with the hearing impaired. The machine was equipped with a four-button response mode for discriminating frames. The program provided for immediate reinforcement for each correct response. The program is presently being field-tested at various centers to validate its contents. A similar experiment was conducted by Karlsen.[21] He used a teaching machine

---

[19]J. D. Fletcher and C. M. Stauffer, "Learning Language by Computer," *The Volta Review*, 75 (May, 1973), pp. 305-309.

[20]Waunita L. Garner, *The Life Programming Process*. (Washington, D. C.: National Education Association, 1972).

[21]Bjorn Karlsen, *A Research Basis for Reading Instruction of Deaf Children*. (Minneapolis: University of Minneapolis, Department of Special Education, 1965).

called the Honeywell-University of Minnesota Instructional Device. The machine has a three choice response system and is fully automatic with no auditory stimulus used. Phonetic color coding was used with fading techniques to diminish clues. Concept development stressed employing a variety of methods. Progress was measured by the child's performance. Initial findings indicated favorable results with five and six-year-old hearing-impaired children.

Driscall and Abelson[22] formulated a hypothesis to determine whether programmed instructional materials were more effective than using therapeutic instruction with a group of learning-disabled boys. Dictating machines were employed to improve the eye-hand coordination skills of the subjects in the experimental group. The control group was exposed to therapeutic instruction. Findings showed that after six months the experimental group (those using programmed instruction in the dictating machines) made significantly greater gains in improving eye-hand coordination skills than the control group which was instructed by therapists.

Atkinson[23] noted results from a recent experiment using the computer to teach reading. The children were first grade students classified as culturally deprived. By the end of the year, they not only had learned to read better than the control group taught by teachers, but also had demonstrated how, and with what effect, computer technology and learning theory can be combined and put into practice.

The experiment by Atkinson alluded to is called the Stanford Project. It was begun in 1964 under a grant from the U. S. Office of Education. Initial years of the project were devoted to experimentally testing computer-assisted instruction in initial reading and mathematics. It was related that evaluations from the project have indicated a number of experiments and analyses that might be profitable for laying the groundwork for a theory of instruction

---

[22]Mary Driscall and Carol Abelson, "Programmed Instruction Versus Therapist Instruction: For Children with Learning Disabilities," *American Journal of Occupational Therapy*, 26 (March, 1972), pp. 78-80.
[23]Richard C. Atkinson, "The Computer As A Tutor," in *Readings in Psychology Today*, 2nd Ed. (Del Mar, California: Communication Research Machines, Inc., 1972), pp. 81-87.

useful to special education.

Literature abounds with descriptive studies outlining automated programmed instruction for the exceptional. The cited research is by no means comprehensive enough to represent the preponderance of studies. Rather, its intentions were to indicate that automated programmed instruction has proven to be a valuable asset in teaching exceptional individuals. Additional empirical studies are needed to objectively validate the practicability of using automated programmed instructional devices with the exceptional; however, automated programmed instruction offers a great promise for the future.

These convictions are supported by Uttal.[24] He stated that some day a machine may be produced that will respond to the students with as much imagination and flexibility as a flesh-and-blood tutor. Uttal's position does not imply that automated programmed instruction will replace the classroom teacher. Perhaps the number of teachers needed in the future will be reduced, and advanced technology will enable programmers to develop programs with a higher degree of accuracy. These machines would reduce the amount of individualized work required by today's teachers, but because of intrinsic values, namely motivation, classroom teachers will be needed.

NONAUTOMATED PROGRAMMED INSTRUCTION

Earlier in the chapter was delineated the difference between automated devices and programmed instruction. In essence, both are forms of programmed instruction. Accordingly, automated devices are classified as hardware and programmed instructional materials as software. Automated devices (teaching machines) are no better than the software constructed for them. The proceeding chapter will deal with nonautomated programmed instruction.

As other strategies outlined in the volume, programmed instruction can be developed to fit the interests and needs of exceptional individuals if a careful analysis of their abilities and disabilities is made. Materials can then be programmed into

---

[24]William R. Uttal, "Teaching and Machines," in *Readings in Psychology Today*, 2nd Ed. (Del Mar, California: Communications Research Machines, Inc., 1972), pp. 88-91.

sequential steps for the exceptional individual to master. As indicated, both programmed and automated programmed instruction are premised upon the principle of reinforcement. Programmed instruction comes in many forms. Books are available which are linear or branching in design. Filmstrips and tapes can be programmed very effectively to meet the needs of exceptional individuals.

Various studies have shown that programmed instruction can be used very effectively in special education because of the sequence of steps in learning. Positive reinforcement is given most effectively for right responses after each step in the learning process. Learning is usually ineffective if each successive step is not mastered in turn as the material may become confusing and aversive. Small steps lead the student from the simple toward the complex, and require him to lean more and more on what he has learned.

Active participation is more effective than passive reception and hence an individual, who is personally responding in the step-by-step process and receiving positive reinforcement for right responses, will learn faster and remember longer.

Individuals learn faster when they make fewer mistakes, as mistakes are time-consuming and often frustrating. Many errors may make the learning situation aversive, which may result in a decline of natural motivation to learn. When many mistakes are made it means that one step does not lead logically to the next step and/or the steps in the process are too large. For many exceptional individuals, massive frustration is experienced when success is not immediate, or when they experience prolonged failure. Learning is achieved best when individuals are reinforced based upon their rate of understanding. A well-constructed program takes into consideration the individual learning styles of exceptional individuals, and proceeds to the next lesson after students have succeeded with the previous steps. Strategies outlined throughout this volume are premised upon the aforementioned principles.

MODIFICATION OF PROGRAMMED INSTRUCTION

Individualized instruction for exceptional individuals in past decades frequently meant repetitive drills to reduce deficiencies. Today, because of advancements in programmed instruction, it is now possible to individualize whole units of instruction through programmed materials that are designed to reinforce skills in practically every area of the curriculum. The trend in education is gradually moving toward the use of programmed materials for many exceptional individuals who have been unable to profit from traditional methods or techniques. Research findings indicate that exceptional individuals who have been exposed to programmed instruction have shown significant growth in various areas of the curriculum.

Rainey[25] has attested to the value of using programmed instruction with retarded children. He included eighty-two educable mentally retarded subjects in his experiment. A commercially programmed textbook and two teacher-made programs were used. The teacher-made programs were constructed on the basis of observed needs of the individuals. Findings indicated that subjects showed growth in both programs; neither was superior to the other. Implications from the study seem to indicate that educable mentally retarded children can profit from the use of commercially constructed materials in conjunction with teacher-made programmed materials. The latter is more likely to be based upon the unique needs of the children. Teacher-programmed materials can serve a useful purpose, providing that teachers are properly instructed in developing packets. Johnson's[26] findings gave support to the value of using programmed instruction with the retarded. He concluded that programmed instruction was more efficient for teaching arithmetic skills to educable retardates than conventional methods. Pinegar[27] stated that because of the success factor, programmed instruction

---

[25]Don Rainey, "An Evaluation of a Programmed Technique As Applied to Teaching Addition and Subtraction Combinations to Normal and Educable Mentally Retarded Boys," Unpublished Doctoral Dissertation, University of California, 1964.

[26]Gordon F. Johnson, "An Investigation of Programmed Procedures in Teaching Addition and Subtraction to Educable Mentally Retarded Subjects," Unpublished Doctoral Dissertation, University of Oregon, 1966.

[27]Rex Pinegar, "A Comparison of Conventional Teaching Techniques with Programmed Instruction Techniques As Applied to Teaching Addition and Subtraction Combinations to Normal and Educable Mentally Retarded Boys," Unpublished Doctoral Dissertation, The University of California, 1967.

appeared to have an intrinsic motivational value superior to other approaches. Meanwhile, Knaus[28] concluded that retarded children taught with programmed materials demonstrated significant performance when compared with the integrative or sequence control approach. Findings also revealed the retarded individuals preferred to be taught by the teacher in conjunction with the use of programmed materials.

There are a group of studies dealing with developing programmed instruction for the retarded in the areas of motor skills and recreational activities, self-care skills, and language instruction. Guidelines and methods include terminal behaviors, prerequisite skills, necessary instructional materials, errorless learning, and programming for the classroom teacher.

The lesson plans in each session of the self-care program are programmed to maximize the child's success at each level of learning. Detailed guidelines instruct the parent or child care worker in what he should say and do at each step of instruction.[29] Activities for motor skills and recreational activities follow the same format as outlined under self-care. Children must demonstrate that they have mastered the terminal behaviors when the final task is completed. The justification for each skill selected, prerequisite skills, necessary instructional materials, and advanced skills are explained.[30] In the area of language instruction, controlled statements are programmed to limit the stimuli to which the child responds. Provisions are made for the child's response at each level. Tutorial instruction is built in at each level for remediation and reinforcement.[31]

[28]William J. Knaus, "Three Methods of Presenting Programmed Instruction to Mentally Retarded Adolescents," Unpublished Doctoral Dissertation, The University of Tennessee, 1967.

[29]Maxine Linford, et al., *Systematic Instruction for Retarded Children: The Illinois Program, Part III. Self-Help Instruction* (Illinois: Illinois University, Institute for Research on Exceptional Children, August, 1960).

[30]Anthony Linford and Claudine JeanreNaud, *Systematic Instruction for Retarded Children: The Illinois Program, Part IV. Motor Performance and Recreation Instruction* (Illinois: Illinois University, Institute for Research on Exceptional Children, August, 1970).

[31]James Tawny and Lee Hipsher, *Systematic Instruction for Retarded Children: The Illinois Program, Part II. Systematic Language Instruction* (Illinois: Illinois University, Institute for Research on Exceptional Children, August, 1970).

Morin[32] listed several values for using programmed instruction with the visually handicapped: (1) programmed instruction can meet individual needs at an accelerated pace, (2) it provides for more accurate measurement and evaluation, and (3) the student becomes directly involved in the learning process with immediate feedback on errors. He cautioned that the unique needs, abilities, and interests of the visually handicapped must be carefully planned into the programmed sequence.

Commercially prepared instructional films are being employed in several institutional settings to instruct the deaf. Special educators are now realizing the values of using films in their instructional strategies. Moreover, the materials provided supply some much needed earlier stimulation to reading readiness as well as auditory training.[33] Grigonis and associates developed and field-tested a program of instruction for young deaf children. The program contained two major areas of instruction: verb vocabulary and sentence structure. Subjects ranged from five to ten years of age. From the total population of seventy-nine children, 77 percent achieved mastery in verb vocabulary, and 83 percent in sentences. It was concluded that the program represented a very effective, as well as efficient, method of teaching written language to young deaf children.[34]

A review of the literature pinpointed the lack of specific studies dealing with certain groups of exceptional individuals. Most of the programmed instructional studies addressed themselves to the education of the deaf, retarded children, children with normal intelligence, and other types of perceptual disorders. Some of the research problems included difficulties in deaf children acquiring language, abnormalities in visual perception and behavioral problems of the retarded and emotionally disturbed. As of the completion of this text, available evidence does not justify or support the widespread acceptance of programmed instruction in

[32]Edward A. Morin, "Programmed Instruction: Today's Challenge in Educating The Visually Handicapped," *Education of the Visually Handicapped,* 2 (March, 1970), p. 40.
[33]James J. Kundert, "Media Services and Captioned Films," *Educational Technology,* 10 (August, 1970), p. 40.
[34]Dorothea Grigonis, et al., *Development and Evaluation of Programmed Instruction in the Teaching of Verbs to Deaf Children in the Primary Grades,* Final Report (Georgia: Atlanta Speech School, Inc., March, 1970).

all areas of exceptionality. It does appear that there have been sufficient studies to support its usage with the retarded and the hearing impaired. The potential uses of programmed instruction with other exceptional individuals need to be further explored employing scientific methods of validation.

Programmed instruction may be linear or branching in design. Research studies have reported the use of each design with exceptional individuals. In the linear program each student follows the same program. The program is designed by levels and steps, thus permitting some individualization. While in the branching program, students follow a design which is determined by their response. Branching also considers the individual needs of students by providing remediation or additional reinforcement depending upon their responses.

Programmed instruction, as well as automated devices, customarily embrace the following characteristics if instruction is to be properly classified as programmed:[35]

1. The intents (proximate criteria) must be stated in behavioral terms such that the learner's outcomes can be independently verified.

2. There must be a provision for interim feedback to the learner on his own progress.

3. The utility of the materials or processes must be established through use with the target population, and the materials must be evaluated on the basis of data generated in the tryout.

Presumably, all forms of instruction could be modified to fit the programmed model. Generally, highly efficient instruction cannot be obtained unless the materials and procedures are designed for use by individual students rather than groups.

SUMMARY

Programmed and automated instruction have created controversy and concern for special educators. Some of the confusion is due to a lack of understanding of principles underlying the

---

[35]Robert K. Branson, *op. cit.*, p. 37.

concept. Some teachers fear that they will be replaced and still others have not been informed adequately about the potential value that automated and nonautomated programmed instruction have for improving the quality of instruction offered to exceptional individuals. With advancements in technology, additional research, and the move to make the schools accountable for the learning experiences of exceptional individuals, it is hoped that much of the confusion will dissipate. Exceptional individuals need all of the assistance available to maximize their learning. Programmed and automated programmed instruction appear to offer some feasible and practical solutions to assure that exceptional individuals receive the best education possible.

Helvey[36] proposed that teachers of the future will be relieved from those chores which a machine can do better than man. The education in future decades will be based on results obtained by advanced teaching machines, which will automatically determine a student's aptitude, maturity, background information, dexterity in handling experiments, and personality traits. No grades or examinations will be necessary because the machine will evaluate the student's degree of achievement through its manifold feedback system.

Education is an information-processing activity which involves both the learner and the teacher. The process includes the teacher communicating with the learner, interpreting the learner's response, and generating new specific materials relevant to instruction in facilitating understanding. Although much research is needed to perfect programmed and automated programmed instruction, the ability of programmed instruction and teaching machines to perform those three tasks performed by a teacher appears to be achievable with advanced research and technology into the various ways an individual processes information. The achievement of these tasks by programmed instruction and teaching machines will ally them with the human tutor and distinguish them both from other types of traditional teaching techniques now in use for the exceptional.

---

[36]T. C. Helvey, "Cybernetic Pedagogy," *Educational Technology*, 9 (September, 1969), p. 22.

It is not within present knowledge to predict that automated and nonautomated programmed instruction will replace teachers in the future. Helvey's view is that an effective teacher can never be replaced by a machine or programmed instruction. Instructional technology appears to be a tool that can aid the teacher by reducing the demands made upon his time.

CHAPTER VII

NONPROGRAMMED DEVICES AND MATERIALS

STANLEY E. JACKSON, LAFAYETTE MERCHANT, AND LING SONG

THE preceding chapter projected that the schools of tomorrow will be automated with various forms of programmed devices to assist special education teachers. So that today's teachers may profit from these devices in the future, they need suggestions immediately for the selection and purchase of instructional materials. To this end, this chapter was designed.

A variety of nonprogrammed devices and materials have been used to improve teaching methods for the exceptional since the inception of special education. Because of wide deviation in learning characteristics, social and physical behaviors of exceptional individuals, many teachers must develop instructional materials or devices for their own uses. Hall[1] remarked that it is very important when purchasing materials and programs, to ensure that they are suited to the exceptional individuals for whom they are intended. Even more important are the objectives or expected outcomes to be achieved by individuals.

To assist special education teachers with the selection and purchase of materials, Boland[2] has outlined the following steps: (1) find out how much money has been allocated, (2) find out which materials and equipment are available on short or long term loan from libraries, school districts, or local or regional instructional media centers, including state and federal, (3) inventory all the instructional materials on hand, (4) assess the needs of the children, (5) seek other opinions relative to materials, (6) consider any special needs one has as a teacher, (7) review materials from the

---

[2]Irma Hall, "Educational Uses of Physical Activities," *Journal of Learning Disabilities*, 5 (November, 1972), p. 64.
[2]Sandra K. Boland, "Managing Your Instructional Material Dollar," *Teaching Exceptional Children*, 6 (Spring, 1974), pp. 134-139.

IMC, instructional materials, displays, advertisements in professional magazines and commercial catalogs, and (8) consider all of the listed factors and order. By employing the aforementioned steps, materials will be more readily accepted by individuals and will aid in the attainment of stated objectives.

Armstrong[3] related that often materials which are developed and sold by commercial producers are distributed without any formal evaluation of their effectiveness. A model was developed to field-test selected materials based upon the relationship between materials and learners' characteristics. The model specified twelve major steps in the material development, research, and evaluation process. They were: (1) research rationale, (2) program rationale, (3) planning of experiment, (4) program writing, (5) test writing, (6) package production, (7) field contacts, (8) field testing, (9) program evaluation, (10) experiment evaluation, (11) revision, and (12) dissemination. The author concluded by stating that this model will pinpoint weakness in materials before being implemented by the classroom teacher. Any difficulties encountered can be solicited and revisions made based upon criticisms or appraisals of the materials during the execution of the model to determine readiness for mass distribution.

RESOURCE-AID MATERIALS FOR EXCEPTIONAL INDIVIDUALS

The federal and state governments, as well as some local school districts, have developed instructional materials based on the steps outlined by Armstrong. These materials are presently being tested and validated for a wide range of uses with exceptional individuals. Such a program was conducted by the Baltimore County public school system. Part of Chapter X and Appendix A deal with the development of prototype materials.

The New England Materials Instruction Center* developed a

---

[3]Jenney R. Armstrong, "A Model for Materials Development and Evaluation," *Exceptional Children*, 38 (December, 1972), pp. 327-333.
*Additional information may be obtained by writing to: New England Instruction Center, Boston University, School of Education, 704 Commonwealth Avenue, Boston, Massachusetts, 02215.

Speech and Language Resource Packet of materials to develop oral communicative skills. The center was developed to meet expressed needs of the region for specific materials for the remediation of speech and language disorders, as well as for the stimulation of language in children. This comprehensive resource covers procedures involved in phonation through remediation for the expressive speech problem. Specific instruction and materials have been developed and divided into seventeen response type categories.

The federal government has aided special education in providing instructional materials for exceptional individuals through its Regional Media Centers and Special Education Instructional Materials Centers. The centers are located in regions throughout the country. (See Appendix B.) Materials are collected and categorized for exceptional individuals. All centers will loan materials to special education teachers within their region for a short time. This affords the teacher an opportunity to experiment with various materials and to make decisions relevant to the selection of materials suited to his class.

The regional centers provide professional assistance to special education teachers who wish to develop instructional materials for specific purposes. The demands for assistance in developing instructional materials, compounded with the increased requests for borrowing materials, resulted in the establishment of associate centers. These associate centers work in direct conjunction with the regional centers. Many of these associate centers are now operating their own mobile units. Services have expanded to in-service training for many special education teachers. Field teachers from mobile units frequently make direct presentations of the usage of instructional materials to classes.[4]

Special Education Materials, Inc. has developed a variety of instructional materials that may be used with the exceptional. Materials have been constructed for the following areas: (1) testing and evaluation, (2) visual perception, (3) cognitive development, and (4) various subject content areas. Audiovisual

---

[4]LeRoy Aserlind, "The Special Education IMC/RMC Network," *Educational Technology*, 10 (August, 1970), p. 35.

equipment and materials are also available; much of the materials produced by the company are programmed.* State, federal, and private agencies have developed a host of instructional materials applicable for exceptional individuals. See Appendices C and D for free and inexpensive sources.

The states of Illinois and New York have developed materials and instructional centers supported by state funds to serve their exceptional individuals. The state of New York has opened two centers: one center will coordinate the activities of a city university system, and one will coordinate the activities of a large public school system within the State. Research and experimentation can be developed at the university center, and practical application can be conducted within the public schools. These centers could become a part of the regional centers, operating as associate centers as outlined by Aserlind.[5]

The Library of Congress, Division for the Blind and Physically Handicapped, operates regional libraries throughout the country. Instructional materials include braille books, recordings, and large prints. Service is free to registered users of the library and includes borrowing materials and free postage. These services are free for blind or physically handicapped individuals from age six on. A special education teacher may write to any of the regional offices, explaining the handicapping condition of the individual. This will permit the individual to borrow materials. Additional information concerning this service may be obtained by writing the Library of Congress.†

ADAPTATION OF INSTRUCTIONAL
MATERIAL AND EQUIPMENT

According to Jackson[6], teachers of the deaf have long used books, study guides, pictures, charts, and other visual aids for

*For additional information or a catalog, write Special Education Materials, Inc., 484 South Broadway, Yonkers, New York, 10705.
[5]Aserlind, *op. cit.*
†The Library of Congress, Division for the Blind and Physically Handicapped, Washington, D. C., 20025.
[6]William D. Jackson, "The Regional Media Centers for the Deaf," *Educational Technology*, 10 (August, 1970), pp. 45-48.

instruction. Only in recent years have comprehensive audiovisual centers been expanded to meet the needs of deaf children in the nation's schools. To meet the demand for additional materials, the Captioned Film Program was developed. This led to the establishment of Regional Media Centers for the Deaf. These centers support various agencies in the country by producing materials and models for improving the education of hearing impaired individuals.

In spite of the recent impetus to develop materials for deaf children, Pfau[7] indicated that most materials developed are adult-conceptualized and uninteresting to students. He recommended building intrinsic motivation into materials. This will ensure acceptance by students. He also recommended that field testing of materials should be completed on various development levels before being introduced into the classroom. Applying this procedure will enable teachers to determine the effectiveness of materials for their classroom. More importantly, the materials are likely to appeal to the interest of children. Pfau's remarks concerning instructional materials are similar to those advanced by Boland and Armstrong, who recommended stringent field testing.

Aserlind[8] reported the results of a survey conducted in 1964 concerned with the availability of audiovisual materials for the retarded. The survey revealed that very few audiovisual materials existed for the mentally retarded. He further stated that many of the films used in special classes were too abstract and too long for the attention span of the retarded learner, and that repetition of basic concepts, so badly needed for retention, was lacking. Although this survey was conducted approximately ten years ago, it is suspected that the availability of suitable audiovisual materials for the retarded has not materially changed.

Two years later, McCarthy[9] wrote that the need for adequate supply of effective and appropriate educational materials for use with the mentally retarded remains a critical and unsolved prob-

---

[7]Glenn S. Pfau, "Built-In Motivation," *Hearing and Speech News*, 40 (March-April, 1972).

[8]Aserlind, *op. cit.*, p. 33.

[9]James J. McCarthy, "Education Materials for the Mentally Retarded: A Quandry," *Education and Training of the Mentally Retarded*, (February, 1966), pp. 24-30.

lem. The material shortage is so widespread and so chronic that it has been accepted as the *status quo,* partly due to the fact that no one has been specifically charged with the material supply task, but everyone generally charged with it. He proposed that the development of material centers with specific objectives in mind would be one solution to the shortage. McCarthy's proposed guidelines for the development of material centers was partly solved with the development of Instructional Material Centers throughout the country. Although these centers serve a much needed avenue for instructional materials, there is still a shortage of materials needed to instruct the retarded, especially the trainable and the profoundly retarded.

The multiple handicapped, visually impaired child has disabilities in several areas. The development of instructional materials to meet the unique needs of this population constitutes an area of concern. Materials must be developed to suit the individual learning modes of each individual child. Special education must attempt a number of approaches and methods, and a great deal of creativity must be employed to communicate with a child who uses neither braille, print, or listening modes. Instructional materials need to be designed to encourage independent functioning as much as possible. Many materials will not interest the child; therefore, it is extremely important that materials be carefully selected based upon assessed needs of the child. Due to the diverse nature of multiple handicapped, visually impaired children, teachers must frequently construct their own materials to maximize learning.[10]

Due to the heterogeneity of emotionally disturbed children, there is a tendency to focus on the adaptation of existing special or regular instructional materials. This lack of specificity in the creation of materials for different groups of disturbed children has perhaps inhibited the growth of knowledge concerning ways of handling information, and the impact of this information, on certain kinds of children. If materials and instructions are not designed specifically to reduce the individual problems of

[10]Fay Leach, "Multiple Handicapped Visually Impaired Children: Instructional Material Needs," *Exceptional Children,* 38 (October, 1971), pp. 153-156.

emotionally disturbed children, they serve little value in amelio-
rating basic problems. Consequently, materials should be designed to reduce or neutralize anxiety or other arousing
tendencies.[11]

Other researchers have developed materials designed to lead to
interpretation of behaviors, and the promotion of mental health
within educational settings. The research indicated that carefully
designed instructional materials based upon adequate assessment
have considerable potentials for strengthening ego processes
needed for successful school experiences. Because of the many
problems inherent with emotional disturbance, the development
of instructional materials will take many forms. The psychological or physical problems present will largely determine the nature
of the types of materials that are to be developed.[12, 13]

The intent of this section was not to report a comphehensive
view of instructional materials being used with exceptional individuals, but to indicate that there is a critical need to develop
materials attuned with the abilities and disabilities of the exceptional. The market is proliferated with a variety of materials;
however, these materials are frequently not suited for exceptional
individuals, or modifications must be made if they are to be effectively used. This does not rule out the possibility of using available materials. Often these materials serve a useful need. Special
education teachers should have a variety of materials to employ as
the need arises.

NONPROGRAMMED DEVICES

Chapter VI covered some current programmed devices in use
with exceptional individuals. There it was indicated that a programmed device is no better than the software constructed for it.
The same rule of thumb applies to nonprogrammed devices. The
major differences between the two sets of equipment is that the

[11]Don C. McNeil, "Developing Instructional Materials for Emotionally Disturbed
Children," *Focus on Exceptional Children,* 6 (November, 1969), pp. 2-5.
[12]R. H. Ojemann, "Investigations on the Effects of Teaching and Understanding an
Appreciation of Behavior Dynamics," in Kaplan (Ed.), *Prevention of Mental Disorders in
Children* (New York: Basic Books, 1961).
[13]H. C. Quay, "Some Basic Consideration in the Education of Emotionally Disturbed
Children," *Exceptional Children,* 30 (September, 1963), pp. 27-41.

latter does not have step-by-step sequence, does not require the learner to reply to previous questions before proceeding to the next segment, and does not supply the correct answer in which a learner can compare with his own response (immediate feedback and reinforcement).

A variety of nonprogrammed devices are being used to instruct exceptional individuals. A few such devices are television, tape recorders, phonographs, motion picture projectors, the radio, and various technological device combinations. The instructional use of these devices can be adapted to serve a variety of purposes for exceptional individuals. Examples include the filmstrip and carrousel projectors with specially selected software to reinforce a previously learned skill, audio recordings for diagnostic purposes, instructional TV and the radio for self-instruction and analysis. Presently, there are trends that indicate that many nonprogrammed devices and materials will be programmed in the near future. The technology is present; all that is needed is an acceptable market.

Instructional Television

Chapter I was addressed to the various learning styles that exceptional individuals display. A list of activities was outlined to assist special educators in determining which sense modality the exceptional use best.

The Maryland State Department of Education[14] has constructed a telecourse to give teachers introductory information in the observation, identification, and management of exceptional individuals. The telecourse consists of sixteen half-hour instructional telelessons* in the areas of teacher attitudes, observation of behavior, behavior problems, learning styles, oral receptive language, informal assessment of reading, analytic approach to reading, synthesis approach to reading, mathematical problems, and referral process. The teacher's manual assists the teacher in developing

---

[14]Maryland State Department of Education, Teacher Manual, "Teaching Children With Special Needs," (Owings Mills, Maryland: Division of Instructional Television, 1973).
*For additional information on the telelessons write to Maryland State Department of Education, Division of Instructional Television, Garrison Forest Plaza, 10317 Reisterstown Road, Owings Mills, Maryland, 21117.

follow-up activities after each telelesson. The objective for each lesson is expressed in clear operational terms.

Goldstein[15] voices that retarded children do not readily learn through reading, but that audiovisual presentations seem to provide a suitable alternative. Allen's[16] remarks were directly related to the use of television as an instructional tool. He stated that with television one can program a variety of activities for increased learning. Striefel[17] stated that in spite of the large amount of time retardates view television, and the success that other children have received from its instructional utility, it has received little exploration as a medium for training retarded children in language or general functions.

Striefel[18] further stated that instructional TV programs could be designed specifically to maintain institutional children's attention while at the same time providing appropriate language models and functional content. The author indicated that ITV programs could be very economically developed and could reach a larger number of individuals than a traditional training model. During the ITV program, behavior of retarded children could be recorded and reinforced. These recordings could show a continuum of behavior in speech development providing that tapes are constructed for retardates to imitate.

Striefel's[19] preliminary study indicated that imitation of TV models occurs regardless of whether the subject is familiar with the TV model or not. The initial results of his study pointed out the instructional value of using the TV for language development of the nonverbal severely retarded by conditioning them to make verbal imitations.

Baran[20] supported the instructional use of TV in teaching

---

[15]Edward Goldstein, *Selective Audio-Visual Instructions for Mentally Retarded Pupils* (Springfield, Illinois: Charles C Thomas, 1964).

[16]W. H. Allen, "Research Verifies the Value of Audio-Visual Materials," *Today's Psychology*, 41 (January, 1952), p. 49.

[17]Sebastian Striefel, "Television as a Language Training Medium with Retarded Children," *Mental Retardation*, 10 (April, 1972), p. 27.

[18]*Ibid.*

[19]Sebastian Striefel, Television Viewing Behavior of Severely and Profoundly Retarded Children, Parsons working papers, Parsons, Kansas, 1971.

[20]Stanley J. Baran, "TV and Social Learning in the Institutionalized MR," *Mental Retardation*, 11 (May, 1973), pp. 36-37.

retarded children, but cautioned that other programs that are essentially noninstructional must be considered. He discussed the importance of using the TV as a medium of social learning. His review of the research indicated that aggressive behavior can be learned by children who view such behaviors in a video presentation. Conversely, a child who is rewarded for imitating will learn to imitate.

Genensky[21] and his associates have been experimenting with a closed circuit TV system as a medium to instruct the partially sighted. Subjects involved in the experiment were all classified as legally blind.* The age range was from ten to eighteen; a variety of eye conditions were reported among the groups.

The construction of the TV permitted a wide range of magnified images, designed to fit the degree of magnification needed by the individual to complete a learning task. By using a remote controller, the teacher could control the image size at the students' monitors, as well as focus on many activities in the classroom, thus permitting many partially sighted children to engage in a variety of academic pursuits. Results from the experiment have shown that closed circuit TV is significantly more useful to many legally blind people than any purely optical aid in use.

Advantages and Disadvantages of Using Instructional Television

Research outlined earlier in this section has emphasized the importance of using instructional TV with some exceptional individuals. Hall[22] proclaimed that with time provided to study and prepare, a teacher's television lesson may be more dramatically effective than his normal classroom presentation. Using special

---

[21]Samuel M. Genensky, "Closed Circuit Television and the Education of the Partially Sighted," *Educational Technology*, 10 (August, 1970), pp. 27-31.

*The author referred the term partially sighted to legally blind people who are able, with or without the aid of corrective lenses or devices, to read material and to write with a pen without tactile aids, and also to people who are not legally blind but whose corrected vision in their better eye is no better than 20/100.

[22]James E. Hall, "The Potential of Closed Circuit Television as an Effective Instructional Medium," Teacher and Technology (March, 1970, in *Educational Technology*, 10 (March, 1970), in *Educational Technology*, 10 (March, 1970), pp. 519-520.

effects, visuals and a well-paced format, a teacher can bring a new dimension into his students' learning processes. Programs produced by teachers and students can deal with a variety of subjects and are limited only by their imaginations.

One of the roadblocks in using instructional TV is posed by educators themselves. As indicated in Chapter VI, many feel that it will replace them in the instructional process. Generally, educators have not been adequately apprised of the instructional value of using TV. Much of this is due to a lack of adequate research attesting to the values derived from using this medium, as well as school personnel competent in the areas of television programming.

The Radio

The radio has proven to be an effective audio-learning tool. It is a way of bringing learning experiences into the classroom, where related visual experiences may often be coordinated with the radio instruction, in which the combined effect of voice, environmental sound, and music, can capture the pupil's attention and arouse his imagination. Whereas instructional television often provides whole courses, the radio is seldom thought of as offering complete instruction, but rather as supplementing day-to-day activities and instruction.[23]

Taylor[24] claimed that the radio, as a means of communication, is but approximately forty-eight years old; as an instructional tool, it is even younger. Radio programs for schools are generally three types: direct instruction, appreciation, and enrichment. In most cases, the content is directed toward a specific classroom use. A few of the school systems that have had success with experimental programs using the radio are: St. Louis, Newark, New York, Wisconsin, and Washington, D. C.

A study was designed to determine the motivational capability

[23]Walter A. Wittich and Charles F. Schuller, *Audio-Visual Materials: Their Nature and Use* (New York: Harper and Row, 1967), p. 323.
[24]George R. Taylor, "The Radio: An Experiment in Communication Skills," *AV Guide — The Learning Media Magazine*, 51 (May, 1972).

of the radio when used as a reinforcement stimulus in the classroom for improving communication skills. Two hundred and seventy-four public school children constituted the sample. Subjects were classified as culturally deprived by the school system index. They were in grades three through senior high school. The program consisted of broadcasting four different sound programs in relation to the grade levels in ten schools. The complexity of the sounds were commensurate with the developmental stages of the subjects. Teachers' guides were distributed before the broadcasts with suggestions for stimulating class discussions, essays, dramatizations, art, and various language activities.

Findings showed that the broadcasts generated an enormous amount of interest among students. Teachers also voiced favorable comments toward the broadcasts. Students were stimulated to voluntarily participate in discussions which not only enabled the teachers to give them immediate help in self-expression, but also gave the teachers a chance to ascertain the nature and degree of basic language deficiencies. The radio was viewed as a powerful motivational force in improving the communication skills of deprived students.

The study supported the concept that the radio can reinforce instruction in several areas of the curriculum. As indicated, it provided enrichment both for the pupils and teachers. In addition to specialized information, the radio can provide teachers with effective models which often demonstrate new ideas and approaches for instruction. It is also concluded that radio programs can be constructed or modified to facilitate the instructional process of exceptional individuals.

Audio Recordings: Cassette and Audiotapes

Cassette tapes can be developed for a variety of academic programs. Developing materials for use with cassettes is essentially no different than preparing other AV media for instructional use. The basic equipment needed is a cassette recorder, a microphone, earphones and some blank cassette tapes. Teacher-prepared cassette lessons come in a variety of formats. Three of the most widely used are: listening only, listening and visuals, and listening and responding.

Children can be instructed by the tapes to perform a variety of activities associated with a learning experience. Frequently, teachers and students can develop tapes for their own use. The major advantage of teacher-made tapes over commercially made ones is that activities can be taped that are tailor made for a class. Giorgio[25] has outlined several tips for successful taping: (1) try not to exceed the normal attention span of your children, (2) always introduce a lesson by incorporating some motivating techniques; (3) maintain a normal speaking voice during the teaching portion of the recording; (4) introduce another voice if the lesson is lengthy; (5) keep the instruction clear and simple whenever the lesson requires the use of response sheets or other media forms; (6) be sure clear and adequate directions are given for all following activities; and (7) always end the taped lesson with a brief summary of what the child has learned, and with a few words of encouragement.

Connor's[26] study appeared to have conformed to the steps outlined by Giorgio. Programs were planned separately for approximately forty-seven severely retardates, and designed to meet their needs. Rehearsal and practice were provided to motivate and to introduce activities in the tapes. Several staff members participated in the recordings, thus providing a variety of different voices in the activities. Activities were taped and played on a cassette player. The tapes provided activities to improve self-help skills, motivation, motor skills, attention span, and language development.

At the end of the year, findings showed that children were engaging in more cooperative play activities as opposed to fighting among themselves as they did before the advent of the program. Self-abuse has been reduced to a point where many of the helmets, bandages, and other restraints were removed, or used sparingly. Occupants who would formerly run away from attendants demonstrated no such behavior at the conclusion of the program. Parents voiced that skills learned were transferred to the

---

[25]Joseph F. Giorgio, "The Cassette for Learning," *Early Years*, 4 (January, 1974), pp. 51-53.
[26]George N. Connor, et al., "Intensive Programming for the Severely Profoundly Retarded Using Pre-Recorded Audio Tapes," *Mental Retardation*, 10 (August, 1972), pp. 40-42.

home when children visited.

Research by Allen[27] and Fargo[28] has proven the value of using videotapes in recording a variety of classroom experiences for effective use in discussion and analysis of teaching techniques. Videotapes can provide a reliable, objective, and immediate picture of the actual teaching situation. Properly employed, the tapes can facilitate an understanding of the teaching-learning process through the use of immediate and repetitive play.

This technique permits teachers and their associates to review and evaluate the effectiveness of their teaching strategies. Because of the extensive and intricate behavior problems of exceptional individuals, teachers need as much information as possible to improve the teaching-learning process. Videotapes will reveal how the behavior of the teacher might influence the total teaching-learning process and could indicate possible avenues for improving interaction among teacher, pupil, and the instructional process.

Instruction utilizing audiovisual presentation does not necessarily need expert assistance. In many instances, a familiar voice will communicate to exceptional individuals more effectively than a trained voice recording. There are times when teachers' voice recordings are best for communicating at a level which makes students feel more comfortable. This is especially true when instructing exceptional individuals.

The Motion Picture

There appears to be a scarcity of research studies involving the use of the motion picture as an instructional tool with the exceptional. According to Kundert[29] the motion picture has failed in bridging the communication gap between the screen and the deaf population. The process of adapting films for the deaf includes inserting captions at the bottom of the picture. Captions are

---

[27]D. E. Allen and D. B. Young, *Television Recordings: A New Dimension in Teacher Education,* (Palo Alto, California: Stanford University, School of Education, 1966).

[28]George A. Fargo, et al., "Using Videotapes in Training Teachers of the Mentally Retarded," *Education and Training of the Mentally Retarded,* 4 (December, 1968), pp. 202-203.

[29]Kundert, *op. cit.*

correlated with the audio in the film. Films are currently being used with the deaf for training in lipreading, as well as classroom instructional filmstrips, transparencies, and slides. The Regional Media Centers can provide the special education teacher of the deaf with these rich sources of instructional materials.

Regional Media Centers and private companies are also experimenting with developing film services for the emotionally disturbed. The films will be designed to initiate self-care skills needed for the emotionally disturbed to improve his academic and social skills. These films will have instructional values for other exceptional individuals since the motion picture appeals to the two basic senses of seeing and hearing. These two senses can be stimulated simultaneously or singularly. As with instructional television, the motion picture can reinforce an already new concept or provide insight into new problems. Films can affect the whole climate of instruction for the exceptional. When selected carefully, their use can result in positive changes in students' interests, learning, and retention of skills. All instructional materials, including the motion picture, must be selected based upon the teacher's objectives as well as the assessed and demonstrated needs of the pupils.

SUMMARY

The development of instructional materials and equipment was once closely related to technological advances in our society, rather than to meet the expressed needs of exceptional individuals. In past decades, teachers of the exceptional had to construct their own materials or modify existing materials. Today, much progress has been made in instructional materials. Currently, instructional materials are being designed to expressly meet the needs of the exceptional. The federal government has been chiefly responsible for much of this growth through its Instructional and Regional Media Centers.* These centers can provide the special education teachers with a wide variety of instructional materials to be examined and experimented with before being adapted for

---

*See Chapter X for description of The Council for Exceptional Children's Information Center: An Educational Resources Information Center (ERIC) Clearinghouse on Handicapped and Gifted Children.

their class. Various local, state, and private agencies have also contributed to the wide reservoir of materials currently in use.

One might readily conclude from the contributions of federal, state, and private agencies that the crisis in instructional materials for the exceptional has finally been overcome. Where it is recognized that the aforementioned agencies have substantially contributed to the development and construction of materials, there is still an urgent need to develop more materials suited for individual deviations among exceptional individuals. Equally important is the need to scientifically test materials. Several authors have recommended that all instructional materials be field tested before being adapted for widespread classroom use. Without question, this procedure will reduce the material lag in special education. However, no matter how individually designed materials and equipment may be, without the skills of the teacher making decisions regarding their use, little can be accomplished. Active student involvement with instructional materials should facilitate the student's learning, if employed appropriately with his instructional program.

The learning tasks to which several combinations of instructional materials can be used are, in essence, left to the imagination and ingenuity of the teacher. Teacher-made materials combined with commercially prepared materials can often be individually designed to meet the unique needs of exceptional individuals. Learning experiences that involve a combination of media must be carefully planned and prepared, and provisions for evaluation and follow-up activities should be included.

CHAPTER VIII

ORGANIZATIONAL AND INSTRUCTIONAL STRATEGIES

Stanley E. Jackson, Inez Lattimore, Colonel Hawkins, and Rae Jones

A RECENT U. S. Office of Education publication[1] stated that approximately 40 percent of the identified handicapped children today receive special education of some type. It was estimated that there are a large number of exceptional children who are unidentified in terms of their impairments and special services needed. In 1969, a nationwide survey revealed that a variety of programs were conducted for exceptional children in this country. The following programs were found to be representative:

Full-time special education in a residential school.

Full-time special education in a day school that serves one type of handicapped child.

Full-time special education in separate classes with a regular public school.

Part-time special education for children who receive part of their instruction in regular classes.

Resource room programs in which children spend much of the school day in regular classes but go out for some special instruction.

Itinerant programs in which part-time special education is offered by traveling instructors who visit schools, homes, and hospitals.

Consultant programs which combine full-time regular education with consultative services through which special education materials may be provided for handicapped children;

---

[1]U. S. Department of Health, Education and Welfare, *The Education Professions 1971-72*, Washington, D. C., U. S. Government Printing Office, 1973, p. 1.

assistance may be offered to the regular teacher and directly to the children.

The survey found two programmatic trends were evident across the country; (1) that an increased number of exceptional children are being placed in regular schools, and (2) that there is increasing emphasis on the early diagnosis of handicaps and placement in special programs as soon as possible, preferably at the preschool level.

The exclusion of a significant number of exceptional children from the mainstream of public education is observable in the aforementioned report which reflects the historical models of special schools and other educational institutions. Research findings[2,3,4,5,6] indicate that categorical programs in special education, in many instances, have compounded the problems of racial segregation and have been responsible for serious self-concept impairment for a significant number of exceptional children.

Many handicapping conditions can be dealt with successfully without special equipment, educational settings and methods, or specially-trained teachers. Many exceptional individuals, who are educated in self-contained classrooms and by special teachers, have needs which can be met with equal effectiveness by teachers of regular classes. Of course, there are some exceptional children who must have specialized assistance and instruction outside the realm of regular education.

Innovative techniques and strategies for educating exceptional individuals may be implemented in several organizational structures. Many of the organizational structures that will be discussed in this chapter may be individualized to meet the needs of exceptional individuals, as noted in Chapter III. Flexible organizational structures permit large and small groups, one-to-one relationships, independent learning activities, peer teaching,

[2]Keith Beery, *Models for Mainstreaming* (California: Dimensions Publishing Company, 1972).

[3]Philip H. Mann (Ed.), *Mainstream Special Education: Issues and Perspectives in Urban Centers,* The Council for Exceptional Children, OEG-0-72-3999 (609), pp. 24-43.

[4]Christoplos and Renz, *op. cit.*

[5]Dunn, *op. cit.*

[6]W. Baldwin, "The Social Position of the Educable Retarded Child in the Regular Grades in the Public School," *Exceptional Children,* 25 (November, 1958), pp. 106-112.

learning centers and team teaching. An organizational structure permits various resource personnel to plan independently for the exceptional in the regular classroom on a full or part-time basis, in a resource room, or a special facility on a full or part-time basis, depending upon their handicapping conditions.[7] The analytical or learning problem approach to meeting the needs of exceptional individuals lends itself to implementation in many different educational settings. Traditional as well as open schools can readily adapt teaching techniques as long as the philosophy of the school incorporates principles of individualization.[8]

Educational programs for exceptional individuals, for the good of all, should be located as much as possible within the regular school facility with ample opportunities provided for personal interaction among all who use the facility.[9] Whereas total segregation of exceptional children in the schools should be criticized, severe handicapping conditions will not permit many exceptional children to profit sufficiently from full-time regular classroom participation. However, it is believed that many exceptional individuals can participate to some degree in part-time regular classroom instruction and activities.

The aspirations of this work for mainstreaming exceptional individuals are in concert with those advanced by Davis.[10] He enumerated ten guidelines that should be supported by the federal government in improving education. All of the statements have relevancy for educating exceptional individuals. The statements are as follows:

1. To move from a mass approach to teaching and learning, toward more individualized diagnosis and teaching.

2. To move from the traditional emphasis on reciting and listening, toward more participation and creative activity on the part of students.

3. To move the school from its ivory tower aloffness, toward

---

[7]Beery, *op. cit.*
[8]Mann, *op. cit.*, pp. 114-115.
[9]Robert Smith and John Neisworth, *The Exceptional Child: A Functional Approach* (New York: McGraw-Hill Company, 1975), p. 268.
[10]Don Davis, Associate Commissioner of Education, U. S. Office of Education, in an unpublished memorandum, April, 1969.

existence in and involvement in the total community and its problems.

4. To move from negative attitudes toward youth who are different, toward a positive attitude of valuing and developing every pupil for his own unique potential.

5. To move from a white middle-class orientation in curriculum and activities, toward a multicultural point of view that will build strength from diversity.

6. To move from a fear of instructional technology, toward effective utilization of appropriate new media.

7. To move from academic snobbism and prestige complexes, toward a recognition of many kinds of excellence.

8. To move from the crystallization of meeting requirements and passing courses, toward evaluation that measures meaningful performance in life situations.

9. To move from an educational system that seems to be run for the convenience and comfort of the administrator, toward a philosophy and practice that stimulates and encourages teacher creativity in solving educational problems.

10. To move from the pattern of self-contained teachers presenting a self-contained curriculum in a self-contained classroom, toward flexible and differentiated approaches that utilize diversified talents of a teaching team in the most effective fashion.

A SYNERGISTIC PROCESS APPROACH

These statements suggest a synergistic process approach to educating all children. This approach is essential in instructing exceptional individuals and embodies a combination of creative innovative teaching skills, techniques, strategies, and services integrated to provide a humanistic approach to education. The synergistic process approach to humanistic teacher education incorporates the recommendations of Davis, Coleman[11], and

---

[11]J. Coleman, "The Children Have Outgrown the Schools," *Psychology Today*, 5 (February, 1972), pp. 72-75, 82.

Bruner[12], who suggested that the purpose of schooling should shift from acquiring knowledge solely for knowledge's sake to an emphasis on schooling-in-action content that will teach learners how to put information to work in personal and social constructive programs.

To support a synergistic process approach, education must be humanized and personalized to such a degree that exceptional individuals will receive maximum benefits from their educational experiences. The remaining part of this chapter will be devoted to organizational structures and strategies that will humanize and personalize instruction for exceptional individuals.

REGULAR CLASSROOM APPROACH

In keeping with the concept of mainstreaming exceptional individuals, experienced regular classroom teachers are rapidly being trained to instruct children who demonstrate a variety of learning problems. The child with a learning problem may be one who, for a variety of reasons, has not had experiences or opportunities similar to most children, or his pattern of growth and development may be impeded. The actual cause of the problem may be difficult to define since the problem may be a complicated combination of behavior and physical problems. Individualization affords the teacher the opportunity to program to reduce or minimize behaviors associated with the child's secondary characteristics.

Individual evaluation is the key to effective planning. The teacher must be able to evaluate the child's behavior and performance and convert his own findings and those of others into practical day-to-day activities. An adequate program of pupil appraisal and evaluation should include the following: (a) observations, (b) listening and recording, (c) special ability scales and profiles, (d) autobiographies and diaries, (e) sociograms, (f) the child's cumulative record, (g) intelligence, aptitude, achievement and teacher-made tests, and (h) assessment charts.

---

[12]J. Bruner, "Nature and Uses of Immaturity," *American Psychologist*, 27 (August, 1972), pp. 687-708.

Part of a comprehensive evaluation design includes procedures which provide for pupil personnel specialists to administer a series of specific diagnostic instruments and tests which are used to assess the causes of special problems and to recommend corrective procedures and treatments.

Most importantly, Lysaught[13] states that schools do have the knowledge and the capacity to reform. If they are to stand the test of relevance, however, they must develop instructional systems that are parallel in effectiveness to systems already in use, such as programmed and automated devices and materials.

Walker[14] described an experimental program testing the efficacy of the resource room for educable mentally retarded children. When results were compared between children in the special class and children in the resource room program, children in the resource room program were significantly better academically and socially. The experimental group of children (the resource program) obtained significantly better residual gains in word reading and vocabulary when compared with children in the special class program (the control group). Results indicated that the academic, social, and emotional needs of the educable mentally retarded can be met as well, if not better, in the resource rooms.

Many programs have been initiated to maintain exceptional individuals in regular classes through resource teacher support.[15] Resource teachers are not a new phenomenon in educational practice. Curriculum specialists who provide help to regular teachers in basic skill or content areas, such as reading, math, art, music, or physical education are often called "resource teachers," "consultants," or "helping teachers."

In the Baltimore County public schools, the resource room has an academic focus.[16] This program is suitable for any child who can profit from a highly individualized program without being

---

[13]Jerome Lysaught (Ed.), *Individualized Instruction in Medical Education* (New York: The University of Rochester, 1968).
[14]Valaida Smith Walker, "The Efficacy of the Resource Room for Educating Retarded Children," *Exceptional Children*, 40 (January, 1974), pp. 288-289.
[15]Deno, *op. cit.*
[16]Baltimore County Public Schools, Curriculum Information, Towson, Maryland, 1970.

removed completely from the regular school program. Teachers work with children individually or in small groups and prepare instructional materials to be used in the regular classroom. The resource room teacher provides both direct and indirect services to children and their teachers.

The program provides for remediation activities and places more emphasis on prescriptive teaching than traditional approaches. An additional attribute of the program is that children receive most of their instruction in the regular classroom. The resource room is designed for children to use specialized equipment and to receive specialized instruction either individually or in small groups. Children participating have the same or similar needs for special instruction.

The resource room serves the needs of a number of exceptional individuals with abilities ranging from above average to below average in several areas of learning. The children may be scheduled for one to three periods a day on a regular basis until their particular problems have been minimized or resolved. Diagnostic techniques are utilized and an educational prescription supplements the curriculum of the regular classroom for those periods that children are absent from regular instruction. Children are reassigned full-time to the regular class as soon as their problems have been corrected.

Consultant services are provided to the regular classroom teacher through periodic formal or informal discussions followed by visitations. The major purpose of the program is to provide temporary services for pupils who exhibit a functional disorder in one or more behavioral areas.

The traditional practice of placing children in special classes by handicapping conditions or by standardized tests results is not practical. The selection for placement in this program is governed within the limits of mental and physical maturation, need for the acquisition of various skills, and by chronological age levels of each individual. Other factors include severe physical, sensory, or emotional problems that would necessitate specialized treatment. Endorsing the approach outlined by the Baltimore County public schools, this work strongly recommends that other school districts develop similar approaches as alternatives in teaching children with special needs.

Role of the Resource Teacher

The resource room teacher, in cooperation with the regular classroom teacher and principal, schedules the appropriate amount of time for children who have been assigned to the resource room. They are divided into small groups of one to six by the screening committee for one, two, or three periods a day.

Since the resource room teacher has been trained as an educational diagnostician, he frequently may identify a child's problem through teaching.

It is the responsibility of the resource room teacher to:

1. Group one to six children each period according to learning needs as indicated on learning profiles.

2. Spend approximately 20 percent of his time in consultation with the regular classroom teacher to apprise him of special needs of children assigned to his classroom.

3. Confer with others on the screening committee.

4. Assign his aide to assume classroom responsibility, either in the regular class or the resource room, so that the resource room and regular classroom teachers may confer.

5. Work with his aide to prepare materials for the resource room or for distribution to regular classroom.

6. Confer with parents in regard to:
   a. The nature of the child's learning problem.
   b. What is being done in the school for the child.
   c. What the parent may do in the home to assist the prescribed school program.

7. Provide intensive tutorial services to children.

8. Cooperate with the regular classroom teacher in supplementing the regular curriculum.

9. Work with classroom teachers to help them implement the prescribed program (demonstrate, describe, and prepare materials).

10. Prepare anecdotal records on each child (in duplicate) so that the regular classroom teacher may have an up-to-date record.

Time and resources are necessary to implement strategies in the schools for educating exceptional individuals. Unfortunately, many school systems have not seen the need for change or have not reemployed their resources to personalize or humanize their instructional procedures. Somehow special resources must be made available for the support of special educators who undertake the difficult task of redesigning special education programs. The United States Congress is addressing itself to the critical issue of providing additional resources to school districts in order that they might improve services for exceptional individuals; hopefully, legislation will be enacted that will enable school districts to implement quality programs for exceptional individuals.

TEAM TEACHING APPROACH

Measures of students' and teachers' attitudes toward team teaching have generally favored the approach. Schools that have incorporated team teaching have often found it necessary to move toward flexible modular scheduling. It has been shown that by bringing students into contact with a variety of teachers and instructional materials, the goals of flexible modular scheduling have been facilitated.[17]

Trow[18] suggested that team teaching is an effective method for enhancing learning in the various domains as well as improving communication among school personnel. He outlined some suggested guidelines that should be considered in implementing a team teaching approach. They are as follows:

1. A teaching team consists of three to seven, or more, teachers jointly responsible for the instruction of 75 to 225, or more,

---

[17]Harris Taylor and Katherine Olsen, "Team Teaching with Trainable Mentally Retarded Children," *Exceptional Children*, 30 (March, 1964), pp. 304-309.
[18]William C. Trow, *The Learning Process* (Washington, D. C.: The National Education Association, 1971).

pupils in one or more grades or age levels.

2. Teams may have teachers assigned different levels of responsibility depending on their ability and experience, with higher salaries and higher status given to the senior teachers and the team leader.

3. Team teaching programs emphasize the team, rather than the individual teacher, in the planning, teaching, and evaluating cycle. The stress is on the team as a unit, not the individual teacher.

4. In the classroom situation, however, teaching teams protect the professional autonomy of each teacher and stress the use of his unique abilities in the instruction of children.

5. In many team teaching programs, each member of the team specializes in a different curriculum area and helps all other members of the team plan, teach, and evaluate in his area of speciality.

6. All team teaching programs emphasize the effective utilization of the strengths of each staff member.

7. As team teaching promotes nongradedness within the school, so does nongradedness promote team teaching. The theory of continuous pupil progress is basic to most team teaching programs.

8. Team teaching programs emphasize varying class sizes and class lengths based upon instructional objectives, contexts, techniques, and pupil needs.

9. Class size and length of period are closely related to the flexible scheduling practices for pupils and teachers.

10. Most team teachers make more effective use of mechanical and electronic equipment than in traditional programs.

Trow has outlined some general guidelines to follow in developing a team teaching program. However, while these guidelines are invaluable in implementing the team approach, specific duties and responsibilities of the team leaders should be clearly defined. The team leaders play a crucial role in determining the success of a team approach. An example of the team leader's responsibilities is reported by the District of Columbia public schools.[19] According to them, the team leader should:

1. Be responsible for the success of his team — this is a key position and the teacher assuming this role should be released from one-half of his teaching load.

2. Arrange for team input during the week to be discussed at weekly scheduled team meetings.

3. Plan with the team in adjusting schedules for individual children.

4. See that team members are objective toward one another, emphasizing that all members should be interested in the overall success of the program, and advancing the point that criticism should never be personal but aimed at improving the program.

5. Report to parents and schedule conferences to review students' progress.

6. See that new students are oriented to the program and assigned student buddies until they are adjusted to procedures.

7. Keep the administration in tune with the feelings of the team.

8. See that instructional packages are properly prepared and validated.

9. Report students' progress to homeroom teacher on a weekly basis in writing.

10. Assist in assigning teachers to the team based upon their expertise in subject content.

In reviewing the listed duties of team leaders in the District of Columbia public schools, it appears that team teaching and leadership require an inordinate amount of planning in order to meet the individual needs of children. It is also evident that large groups of children can be instructed utilizing this approach if they have similar needs or interests. One of the salient points of

---

[19]District of Columbia Public Schools, In-service Training Team Teaching Program, Washington, D. C., 1972.

this approach is that teachers with expertise in various areas must plan cooperatively to meet the individual needs of pupils.

Cooperative planning, based upon the unique needs of exceptional individuals, is a necessary ingredient in mainstreaming. Of course, as reflected throughout this volume, all exceptional individuals will not be able to participate in many of the strategies discussed on a full-time basis. The same principle is true for team teaching. However, opportunities should be provided for them to participate in activities that are not restricted by their handicapping conditions.

PEER TEACHING

In order for exceptional individuals to receive quality educational experiences, some of their experiences must be related to real life situations. In peer teaching, children and teachers as partners build and extend the needs and interests that arise out of their ongoing experiences in the school. Goals for learning are defined and experiences selected that are relevant to real life. Within these experiences plans should be made for children to work on their own and in small groups. Peer teaching permits the development of positive relationships within the group.

A peer teaching approach is thought of as child-centered rather than task-centered, although the amount of work accomplished may go far beyond what is envisioned by most preplanned programs. Because the approach is child-centered, there are planned opportunities for children to explore problems that are of interest to them.

Essential to a successful program will be the need for human resources such as aides, volunteers, and tutors from the community to supplement and support the teacher's efforts.

Balmer[20] described a peer teaching program using students from the fourth through sixth grades as tutors for the EMR. Findings revealed that the tutors discovered that EMR students possessed abilities that teachers had not discovered or recognized. The tutors implemented methods that were more effective with

[20]Joan Balmer, "Project Tutor: Look I Can Do Something Good," *Teaching Exceptional Children*, 4 (Summer, 1972), pp. 166-175.

some of the more limited children than any approach that had been previously attempted. Finally, the tutors acquired positive feelings toward the EMR which were not evident at the inception of the project.

Csapo[21] reported the results of using peer models with emotionally disturbed children. The role of the peer models was to perform behaviors noted by the teacher as appropriate in the presence of the emotionally disturbed peers. Results showed that the number of inappropriate behaviors displayed by the emotionally disturbed after a fifteen-day intervention phase decreased significantly. Modeling behavior was not confined to the classroom. One disturbed boy continued to imitate his buddy in line, on the playground, and in the gymnasium. The study supported the proposition that peer reaction does have a positive influence on most children's behaviors. Peer modeling appears to be a viable technique for controlling inappropriate behaviors of emotionally disturbed children. It might be one of the approaches employed in mainstreaming disturbed as well as other handicapped children.

Other studies have demonstrated that peers can be enlisted as effective behavior modifiers.[22, 23, 24, 25, 26] Peers can be taught to observe and record behavior and to directly reinforce one another to effect positive growth in terms of cooperation and self-control. Children have also proven to be effective tutors, a fact that has significant implications for implementing individualized instructional programs.

[21]Mary Csapo, "Peer Models Reverse: The One Bad Apple Spoils the Barrel," *Teaching Exceptional Children* (Fall, 1972), pp. 20-24.

[22]Alan Gartner, *Children Teach Children* (New York: Harper and Row, 1971).

[23]J. H. Meyerowitz, "Peer Groups and Special Classes," *Mental Retardation*, 5 (October, 1967), pp. 23-26.

[24]R. L. Hamblin and Woodarski, "Group Contingencies, Peer Tutoring and Accelerating Academic Achievement," in Ramp and Hopkins (Eds), *A New Direction for Educators: Behavior Analysis* (Kansas: University of Kansas, 1971), pp. 41-53.

[25]V. W. Harris, "Effects of Peer Tutoring on the Spelling Performance of Elementary Classroom Students, in Semb (Ed.), *Behavior Analysis and Education* (Kansas: University of Kansas, 1972), pp. 222-231.

[26]G. R. Patterson, "Teachers, Peers, and Parents as Agents of Change in the Classroom," in Benson (Ed.), *Modifying Deviant Social Behavior in Various Classroom Settings* (Oregon: University of Oregon, 1969), pp. 13-48.

As indicated by the aforementioned research, peer teaching is often successful in changing inappropriate behaviors of exceptional individuals wherein teacher intervention has not been successful. Nelson[27] indicated that in many instances peer-related reinforcement develops more appropriate standards of behavior than those developed by teachers. This is especially true for older exceptional individuals who have been exposed to repeated failure in the schools.

THE OPEN CLASSROOM

Open education was derived from the concept of the British Infant School. This informal approach permits students to choose between educational alternatives, which are usually highly individualized, until they have achieved prescribed objectives. Rosenberg[28] wrote that open space per se does not indicate open education. Open education, as in other organizational strategies, may operate within the walls of a traditional classroom providing that the student is given freedom to choose alternatives and that help and guidance are provided by the teacher.

The application of open education techniques to instructing exceptional individuals is an emerging trend. Implied in the technique is the development of strategies to enable the exceptional to function independently to the extent that their abilities will permit. Team work is essential in operating an open education program. Coordination of activities are too complex for the individual teacher to implement successfully. As indicated earlier in the chapter, diversity among exceptional individuals requires supportive services from several areas to meet their unique needs. Some of the functions of the team will include: (1) assessment, including mental, physical, and social factors, (2) programming, designing functional and relevant curricula, (3) constant evaluation and monitoring of progress, (4) interaction of team

[27]Michael Nelson and Judith Worrell, *Managing Instructional Problems* (New York: McGraw-Hill Book Company, 1974).
[28]Elihu Rosenberg, "Open Education for Trainable Mentally Retarded," *The Journal for Special Educators of the Mentally Retarded*, 9 (Winter, 1973), pp. 98-99.

members, including cooperation and communication.

Open education appears to be one approach that attempts to match teaching styles, learning styles, and the expectations and needs of parents and children. Optional learning environments are based on individual choices by teachers, students, and parents. It is designed to enhance the teacher learning process. Planning for use of space and organizational structures for various aspects of open education is under constant modification, to adjust to the individual's growth and the achievement of exceptional individuals. (See Appendix E.)

One very important feature of the open space, individualized learning concept is that it usually results in the abandonment of the traditional letter grade system. Individualized instruction connotes continuous growth, and continuous growth cannot be evaluated in the traditional way. Children are not asked to compete against one another. Their growth is not thwarted or stunted by artificial and frustrating barriers to learning. Their progress, therefore, is evaluated in terms of individual growth and development, measured in terms of self-capability.[29]

Another basic difference between the traditional and open classroom is one of structure. In the traditional classroom, desks are usually placed in rows with the students facing the teacher. Frequently the entire class is taught as a group. The degree of freedom to pursue independent activities is limited by the teacher. In the open classroom, there is no front of the room in the traditional sense. Upon entering the classroom, one often has to look around for a while to find the teacher who may be sitting with a small group of students on the floor, playing a game or conducting a minilesson.

Some educators insist that the open classroom, in contrast to the traditional one, has no structure and is utterly chaotic. In fact, they can get messy at times, with too much noise and not enough learning, but these conditions are true of some traditional classrooms as well. At any rate, it is more important and accurate to say that open classrooms have structure, although it is dramatically different from the structure of the traditional classroom.

---

[29]Herbert R. Kohl, *The Open Classroom* (New York: Random House, Inc., 1969), p. 64.

The room is invariably divided into separate areas, often called interest centers, each representing different aspects of the curriculum, such as science, art, and language arts. In a good open classroom these areas are filled with thought-provoking learning materials. A language center might have word games, learning stations for a variety of reading and language skills (new and review), and books for a variety of reading levels. Other interest centers may include animals, balancing and measuring equipment for math, games, blocks, and even sandboxes. The classroom is like a miniature carnival with a wide variety of multisensory materials available.

Each bay or learning center is set up in such a way that materials are readily available for selection by the children. Small racks or book shelves are combined with cardboard cartons, shoe boxes, plastic containers, and a variety of other storage devices so that children can have what they need in the very place where they are learning. The storage facilities help children to develop a sense of order. Adequate storage also helps them learn to arrange and classify materials, and to care for them so that the next child can also find what he needs.

It is important to reduce the number of visually stimulating objects in any classroom, but it is absolutely imperative that they be reduced for many exceptional individuals. Individual cubicles for each exceptional individual are recommended. A sound-deafened cubicle is large enough to permit the child and the teacher to sit side by side. The cubicle prevents the child from being visually distracted by activities in the room as well as by other children.

The philosophy of the open classroom is as radically different from that of the traditional one as its physical appearance. A basic tenet of this philosophy is that children learn even such basic skills as reading in an almost random way and at their own pace, and that, therefore, they cannot be programmed to learn what teachers think they ought to learn according to a predetermined sequence. One child might be reading on a second grade level in kindergarten, while another might only be ready to start reading at the end of the first grade.

Paramount to the open classroom philosophy is the idea that

the child's self-motivation is a crucial factor in the retention of what he learns. So, teachers who follow this method tend to encourage play, spontaneity, and individual creativity much more than is found in traditional classrooms.[30] Often the degree of freedom and openness that a teacher allows will depend upon the success of an open classroom. Some teachers cannot tolerate a high noise level and constant movement in their rooms. Needless to say, that this type of teacher will encounter serious problems in an open classroom structure for exceptional as well as normal children.

DIAGNOSTIC PRESCRIPTIVE APPROACH

Diagnostic teaching has come into focus as a direct result of a growing recognition among educators and psychologists of the irrelevancy and serious negative consequences of traditional psychomedical diagnostic labels. Since its inception, diagnostic teaching has been implemented in various educational settings throughout the country.[31] For educational purposes, the term would be defined as a careful and meticulous analysis of behaviors for the purpose of understanding present behaviors and relationships which serve to develop clearly specified behaviors and skills.

Teaching activities should be designed to modify or remediate a specific academic skill. According to Sabatino,[32] the above can be accomplished through a concentrated multidisciplinary diagnostic assessment and a behavioral profile covering many areas of functioning. The profile would be employed for initiating diagnostic/prescriptive teaching. This approach will permit objective evaluation to be made on the abilities and disabilities of exceptional individuals, and will answer the question as to whether or not the stated objectives established through diag-

---

[30]*The Campus Learning Center Experience* (New York: State University College, 1973), pp. 6-15.

[31]R. Prouty and D. Prillaman, "Diagnostic Teaching: A Modest Proposal," *Elementary School Journal*, 70 (February, 1970), pp. 265-270.

[32]David Sabatino, "A Scientific Approach Toward A Discipline of Special Education," *The Journal of Special Education*, 5 (Winter-Spring, 1971), p. 20.

nostic assessment have been achieved. Diagnostic assessment should be made in several areas of functioning.

While medical examination and psychological testing have other useful purposes, the result of using them to determine educational needs has been that of stigmatizing individuals with clinical labels. This often leads to inappropriate placement of individuals and rarely provides any meaningful guidance to the teachers who have the responsibility of working with children so categorized. Often exceptional individuals who have been placed in special classes only need modification in their instructional programs which could have been met in the regular class.

Some diagnostic principles that special educators should be aware of are as follows:

1. Diagnosis should be directed toward formulating methods of remediation based upon each students's unique needs.

2. Diagnosis and remediation are no longer the special privileges of the slow learner — they are extended to the gifted and the average as well.

3. Diagnosis may be concerned merely with the symptomatology, but genuine diagnosis looks toward the cause of the symptoms.

4. The causes of pupil inadequacy are usually multiple rather than single.

5. The teacher needs more than simple skill in diagnosing the causes of the child's difficulty. He needs ability to modify instruction to meet the needs identified by diagnosis. (See Appendix F.)

6. Decisions based on diagnosis should flow from a pattern of formal and informal test results.

7. Instructional materials should be viewed as teaching tools which can be modified or adopted to meet any given needs. The flexibility of a tool lies in the many ways that the same tool can be applied. This also depends on the perceptiveness and creativeness of the user.

8. The user of any instructional material must bear three

things in mind when selecting materials:

a. Does it suit the learner's interests and ability so that some element of success is inherent?

b. Can it directly or indirectly help accomplish the desired goal?

c. Is it presented in the mode that best suits the learner's style of learning, e.g., visual, auditory, tactile, or multi-sensory?

The purpose of diagnosis should be to determine the educational relevance of handicaps. Prescriptive teaching is based upon diagnostic findings arrived at through the use of standard evaluation techniques. Data are integrated and focused on the educational relevance of the disability. Diagnostic, predictive, and therapeutic teaching are bound together in a dynamic interrelationship. Evaluation of the therapeutic relationship is an aspect of diagnosis as well as the follow-up study.

When the assessment has been completed and remedial procedures have been explored, the diagnostic/prescriptive teacher should then make the appropriate recommendations for a prescription. Possible assignments for the child are: the resource room or regular classroom with recommended teaching techniques and/or prescriptions. Other than children with severe handicapping conditions, assignment to any class other than the regular class should be temporary and some indication should be given as to when the child will be reassigned to the regular class.

As an integral part of the educational assessment, the diagnostic/prescriptive teacher should schedule conferences with the regular classroom teacher who referred the child. This is to gather additional information which is pertinent to the diagnosis and the recommended prescription. The diagnostic/prescriptive process is a complex assessment of the child's abilities and disabilities. In order to accomplish this task, the teacher should have expertise in the areas of educational diagnosis and curriculum development for exceptional children.[33]

In evaluation and remediation, the diagnostic teacher need not

---

[33]Beery, *op. cit.*

be overly concerned that every technique must be supported by a reason for its use. He should be free to experiment with a variety of techniques and materials, discarding those which do not fit the needs of a particular individual. The diagnostic classroom is not necessarily curriculum bound with an academic purpose dictating the teacher's every procedure.

The function of the program, as its title states, is to diagnose through teaching. The diagnostic/prescriptive teacher may work with one to three children at a time to identify the areas in which they are having difficulties. Once the problems have been identified, the teacher should develop remedial educational programs.

As a first step, diagnostic teachers should not administer standardized tests to determine the strengths or weaknesses of children, but should diagnose through teaching. If, after a diagnostic/prescriptive teacher works with the children, he suspects certain areas of weakness, he may administer a formal or informal test to confirm his suspicions. Emphasis is placed on informal techniques rather than standardized testing instruments. Thus, the diagnostic/prescriptive teacher should be concerned with: (1) present behavior, not etiology, (2) the best instructional process to use, not exposing the child to techniques that have produced failure, (3) individualized form of instruction, not group instruction, (4) whether the child can be motivated to read, not with whether he can read a selection from a book.

Diagnostic techniques can assist exceptional individuals in achieving their optimum level of growth, if executed properly. Diagnostic teachers should perform the following:

1. Provide educational evaluation for children referred by the principal or screening committee.

2. Provide consultative services to regular classroom teachers. (Approximately 50 percent of the diagnostic/prescriptive teacher's time should be allocated for this purpose.)

3. Diagnose through teaching to determine the academic strengths and weaknesses of the children.

4. Administer tests to substantiate beliefs or hunches, corroborating present behavior.

5. Develop a prescription for teaching each child (whether regular classroom, resource room, etc.).

6. Recommend placement for the child in regular classroom or resource room, with recommended teaching techniques, methods, and materials in advance of team approval.

7. Prepare materials to be utilized by the regular classroom teacher.

8. Demonstrate the use of suggested materials to the regular classroom teacher.

9. Assign aides to take the regular classroom teachers' classes for a designated period of time so that the regular classroom teachers can observe the diagnostic/prescriptive teacher working with the children.

10. Participate in screening committee conferences.

11. Maintain anecdotal records of all diagnostic information, prescriptions, and other pertinent information for each child referred.

12. Communicate with parents in regard to:
    a. The nature of the child's learning problems.
    b. What is being done in the school for the child.
    c.) What the parents may do in the home to assist the prescribed school program.

Diagnostic techniques, as well as other strategies, should be designed with one purpose in mind and answer this question: What are the best techniques to employ in aiding the exceptional individual's return to the regular class as soon as possible? In order to answer the question systematic procedures must be applied, as outlined in this volume.

LEARNING STATIONS

A learning station is one segment of a learning center which stresses one skill, concept, or interest. Learning stations may be designed to individualize teaching. The learning station approach can be the medium through which each child can learn how to learn, to think independently, to make choices, to plan, and to evaluate. Children may go or be directed to listening, speaking, reading, or writing stations, where learning tasks are performed. This program can be implemented in any situation, as discussed in this chapter, by a simple rearrangement of classroom furniture, and a teacher's commitment to individualized teaching.

In this connection, an adaptation from the Lida Lee Tall Learning Resource Center[34] will be discussed. The following tasks have been outlined by the center for teachers and pupils:

Teachers' Tasks

1. Take an inventory of class interests and abilities through questionnaires, teacher observation, and general classroom performances.

2. Determine the curriculum area around which the experiences can be planned.

3. Collect audiovisual aids, reference materials, art materials, etc.

4. Set up stations according to pupil needs and interests.

   a. Designate areas in the room for speaking, writing, reading, and listening stations by bold captions, displays, etc.

   b. Rearrange furniture making sure that each station has access to boards, charts and/or cabinets.

   c. Design various tasks for accomplishing a specific purpose that will provide for the differences of children in thinking, performing, and expressing.

   d. Decide whether or not the stations will operate full-time or part-time.

   e. Equip each station with teaching aids.

5. Provide a specific area for the pupil-teacher conferences.

   a. Evaluate pupil progress and suggest the next step.

   b. Plan individual projects.

---

[37]Lida Lee Tall Learning Resource Center, Baltimore, Maryland: Towson State College, 1972.

    c. Determine weaknesses and/or problems.

    d. Plan corrective activities.

    e. Summarize.

6. Provide a multilevel variety of individual assignments.

    a. Based upon outcomes of skill developments.

    b. Direct pupils to keep notebook records of purpose for doing assignment.

    c. Provide folders for completed work.

    d. Use devices that ensure privacy to collect work of individuals when suggestions or reinforcements are needed.

7. Orient pupils as to how the stations will function through demonstrations and graphics.

    a. Establish routines.

        (1.) Designate a number of pupils to work at each station.

        (2.) Determine the amount of time to be spent at each station.

        (3.) Establish procedures for orderly movement.

    b. Provide a master schedule.

        (1.) Include time blocks for work/group work, independent work, conferences, and sharing periods.

        (2.) Provide for economic use of class time.

    c. Post a "Learning Stations Directory."

        (1.) Include skills being reinforced.

        (2.) Provide space for children to sign up according to their choices.

        (3.) List names of children being directed to specific learning tasks by the teacher.

        (4.) Allow space for pupils to check off tasks completed.

    d. Provide for self-evaluation.

        (1.) Use individual checklists and diagnostic sheets.

        (2.) Use teacher-pupil conferences.

(3.) Use work folders and informal tests.

8. Evaluate the Learning Stations Program in terms of:

   a. The success the pupils have in accepting responsibility for their own learning.

   b. The degree and maintenance of interest.

   c. The acquisition of skills and concepts by pupils.

Pupils' Tasks

1. Pursue the solution of a problem.
2. Think and react to what has been read or done.
3. Share procedures, ideas, and solutions in reaching an objective.
4. Use and apply knowledge to understand, to discover, and to effect change.
5. Make choices as to how to solve a problem, and assume the responsibility for following through on tasks.
6. Complete self-evaluation.
7. Plan the next step in the pursuit of knowledge.
8. Request assistance with problems that cannot be solved individually.

Children using learning stations must be introduced to this concept gradually and in a planned manner so that they have time to develop independence and responsibility. The teacher's chief responsibility is to serve as a guide and/or helper. If the child is instructed properly in how to use learning stations, he should rarely have problems requiring teacher assistance. Three examples of learning stations are illustrated in Appendix G. The concepts illustrated can be generated to more advanced forms of learning.

Arranging a physical environment that is responsive to the changing requirements of children, teachers, and instruction is a frequently expressed desire of special educators. This goal was one of the primary objectives in a recent renovation proposal for a Special Education Center in Ithaca, New York.[35]

---

[35]Virginia Rapport, *Learning Centers: Children On Their Own* (Washington, D. C.: Association for Children's Education International, 1970).

The redesigned space and equipment provided a minimum of fixed or permanent locations such as "wet" areas for art and science use. Logically, the sink became a focal point for these activities with a secondary science area created along the window providing a plant-growing area. The other fixed area was the bathroom. All the other spaces remained versatile, providing the opportunity for environmental change and creating learning areas or centers as required. It is recognized that an environment that is altered too frequently can lose some of the familiar and visual cues for the children. However, choices in the use of surface materials helped alleviate this problem.

By using flexible partitions, caster-mounted storage units, movable coat storage units and fold-up work surfaces, considerable accommodation to structured or unanticipated change became possible.

The original carpeted surfaces remained except for the wet areas where a vinyl asbestos tile surface was recommended. Retaining carpeting on the floor helped control scraping and impact noise, as well as making a more pleasant surface to sit on. Carpeting could be applied to the rear of storage cabinets, to partitions, and walls to act as a very suitable sound absorber, back area, and tactile surface. Folding and movable partitions were suggested to provide space formation, sound control, privacy, and circulation area definition.

A very useful and flexible multiple use unit was proposed to provide support for a variety of activities. The proposed units consisted of three fold-up study carrels, a pull-down table, built-in lighting and electrical outlets, plus chalkboard area in the study carrel. It could be combined with the movable storage units to create learning centers. One of the important functions of the program was the close working relationship between teachers, administrators, maintenance staff, and the students.

With changing curricula, personnel, and the accountability movement in the field of special education, innovative strategies and options must be evident. New approaches and alternatives must be explored and experimented with if special education is to challenge these societal trends. Learning stations appear to be one of many strategies that may be instituted to provide maximum learning opportunities for exceptional individuals. Concepts advanced in this section were intended to assist special educators in achieving a user-oriented environment for educating the exceptional.

SUMMARY

The need for dynamic programs in the schools was brought about by the demands of a continually changing society. The very technology that created this need is the same that will provide the solution to creating a dynamic school program.

Since the standard approach to classroom instruction for exceptional individuals has produced only neutral or negative response, new approaches or strategies are proposed. Etiological categories are of little use for educating exceptional individuals; therefore, deliberate efforts must be employed to change the present classification systems which have had adverse affects on the total adjustment of exceptional individuals.

It appears that the regular classroom offers the best approach for changing the self-concept of most exceptional individuals. Most regular school facilities for normal children can be the same for the exceptional, although facilities and strategies must be altered to meet severely handicapping conditions of some exceptional individuals. In this book some of the strategies that will make mainstreaming feasible and practical have been outlined.

As Kemp[36] indicated, successful innovation in education requires at least three major elements: (1) teachers who are deeply concerned about their teaching effectiveness and are motivated by a desire for improvement, (2) administrators who willingly encourage and support these teachers, and (3) carefully designed plans for developing improved instructional practices.

Implementing the major elements advanced by Kemp should be based upon our knowledge of human behavior and learning. These insights should be used to establish relevant educational environments, materials, and instructional strategies. The educa-

---

[36]Jerrold E. Kemp, *Instructional Design* (California: Fearon Company, 1971), pp. 5.

tional environment for exceptional individuals must become a change agent for genuine self-realization to develop what Maslow refers to as the "self-actualizing personality."[37]

---

[37]A. H. Maslow, *Motivation and Personality* (New York: Harper and Row, 1954), pp. 90-91.

CHAPTER IX

COLLEGE AND UNIVERSITY PROGRAMS

Peter Valletutti and Jack F. Grosman

STRATEGIES and services presented in this volume cannot be effectively implemented unless institutions of higher learning develop and provide nontraditional approaches for training teachers of exceptional individuals. The institutions of higher learning are currently developing models of teacher preparation in special education which set aside diagnostic categories and emphasize transdisciplinary approaches. Teacher preparation programs based solely on a traditional educational model appear to be too narrow in scope to produce effective educators for the varied situations and roles special educators are expected to fill. Training models must not only be responsive to changing patterns of community and educational services and programs for the exceptional, but also must provide the leadership needed to promote new and innovative programs for this population. Training models must keep pace with changing attitudes, recent legislation, and legal decisions which will profoundly change the direction of educational programming for the exceptional. As society strives to normalize the lives of all of the exceptional, and as schools attempt to mainstream the mildly handicapped individual and provide comprehensive programming for the severely and profoundly handicapped, teacher preparation programs must change.

In order to accomplish the goal of a free, quality public education for all the exceptional, regardless of the degree of the handicapping condition, age of the individual, or the educational setting, the college and university must prepare enough teachers with sufficient knowledge and performance-based competencies required to educate exceptional individuals.

College curricula must, therefore, provide: (1) course work designed to acquaint its students with the theoretical foundations of general and special education including developmental psychology, learning theories, and the philosophical, historical, biological, psychological, and sociological perspectives of special education, (2) experiences which develop skills in educational diagnosis and evaluation, (3) activities which foster competencies in establishing curriculum objectives, writing educational programs, and selecting appropriate methods and materials, (4) learning experiences which provide skills in classroom organization and management, and (5) course work designed to facilitate the acquisition of competencies in communicating with other professionals involved in the total habilitation/education of the exceptional.

PRACTICUM AND INTERNSHIP

Existing educational settings in the community, such as public schools, day care centers, private schools, community agencies, and institutions usually provide enough facilities for college and university field and practicum instruction for training relative to all exceptional individuals. Properly coordinated, these settings can serve as a laboratory for preservice and inservice teachers.

Lecture and discussion experiences can be invaluable in imparting theoretical knowledge to students preparing to teach. Performance competencies, however, can only be developed by blending lectures, discussions and teacher demonstrations with practica experiences involving exceptional individuals. Practica experiences, therefore, must be an integral part of the teacher preparation program from its inception. The college instructor should demonstrate the specific skills in actual classroom settings. After the students have been given the opportunity to witness skillful instructional and/or classroom organization and management practices, they should then be given the opportunity to practice these skills with exceptional individuals. Teacher preparation must increasingly take place in the schools rather than within the artificial college setting.

A further value in providing practica experiences early in a student's academic career is that this early exposure will help him to confirm or reject his vocational aspirations and commitment to working with exceptional individuals on the basis of the hard data of experience. The teacher preparation program must not only provide frequent practica experiences but must ensure that they are quality experiences. This emphasis on learning through demonstrations and modeling requires that college instructors be skilled practitioners themselves.

A NONCATEGORICAL
COMPETENCY-BASED APPROACH

Increased attention is being given to redefining the role of the special educator. The traditional model in which a special educator is assigned to a self-contained classroom, a resource room, or an itinerant position has frequently placed the special educator in an isolated position.[1] According to Reynolds[2] there is a rising revulsion against simplistic categorizations of human beings. The field of special education has been especially vulnerable to attack because, in defining itself, it has tended not only to categorize or stereotype individuals but to use negatively loaded terminology. Societal trends indicate that labels are not a justified means of categorizing handicapped students. Teacher preparation programs must also provide educators with those skills which will enable them to systematically program for exceptional learners. Effective teachers of the exceptional must be assisted in ignoring nonrelevant categorical clues and in programming for the exceptional learner on an individual basis. This program should be based upon the learner's idiosyncratic constellation of abilities and disabilities, not on a hypothetical trait assigned to his diagnostic subgroup.

The goal of individualizing or personalizing instruction can perhaps best be met by teachers prepared under a noncategorical competency-based model of teacher education. A noncategorical approach in teacher education is concerned with grouping exceptional individuals by common goals rather than by symptoms of

---

[1]Wietse deHoop, "Multi-Level Preparation of Special Education Personnel," *Education and Training of the Mentally Retarded*, 8 (April, 1973), p. 37.
[2]Maynard C. Reynolds and Bruce Balow, "Categories and Variables in Special Education," *Exceptional Children*, 38 (January, 1972), p. 257.

disability.[3] A competency-based program in special education identifies specific goals planned in detail in advance of instruction. It is characterized by vigorous reliance on objectives which are directly related to the instructional process. Emphasis is placed on the student's ability to demonstrate specific competencies in the field. Opportunities for learning, an environment which facilitates the student's progress toward achieving the competencies, and appropriate evaluative procedures and instruments must all be directly related to the stated competencies. A teacher preparation program which identifies expected behavioral outcomes by specifying competencies must also provide objective criterion measures and select instructional techniques designed to achieve these stated behaviors.

The identification of teaching competencies requires a conception of the goals of education in relation to the roles of teachers. Lindsey[4] wrote that a conception of teacher roles may be developed from available bodies of knowledge and drawn heavily from reported empirical evidence about practice. Using the same knowledge, it is possible to make substantial translations from educational goals to ideal teacher roles, to competencies essential in performing these roles, and to develop a set of theoretically derived competencies.

Once these competencies have been identified through precise validation, the instructional strategies and their relationship to the competencies must be clearly delineated. Some prior knowledge of the student's ability, conditions necessary for facilitating student progress, techniques to be employed by the teacher, and ways of assessing and evaluating competencies must all be considered and programmed in order to determine whether or not the stated competencies have been acquired.

Houston's[5] assumptions concerning the designing of competency-based instruction are similar to those advanced by

---

[3]Florence Christoplos and Peter Valletutti, "A Non-Categorical and Field Competency Model for Teacher Preparation in Special Education," *Journal of Special Education*, (Spring, 1972), pp. 115-120.

[4]Margaret Lindsey, "Performance-Based Teacher Education: Examination of a Slogan," *Journal of Teacher Education*, 24 (Fall, 1973), pp. 184-185.

[5]W. Robert Houston, "Designing Competency-Based Instruction Systems," *Journal of Teacher Education*, 24 (Fall, 1973), pp. 201-202.

Lindsey. He listed six procedures that have been employed in specifying competencies: (1) Goals are rewritten as behavioral objectives, some attempt is made to individualize the instructional delivery system, and instructional units are referred to as modules; (2) Professional roles are listed and from this list a set of competencies is drawn. The professionally competent may be observed and/or the professional staff may speculate upon the relevant tasks to be performed in attempts to formulate this list; (3) The needs of learners must also be considered. This approach utilizes the ambitions, values, and perceptions of students in identifying competencies; (4) Needs assessment of numbers and types of handicapped students and school or community programs and services help determine the type of teacher education programs required; (5) Theoretical positions imply that teacher education programs are developed around a theoretical construct. From this proposition, elements of the teacher training program may be designed to educate teachers as applied behavioral scientists who can demonstrate selected skills and concepts which support the theoretical position; and, (6) The cluster approach deals with several general program areas. Each area is deductively analyzed to identify related competencies.

STRATEGIES FOR ACHIEVING COMPETENCY-BASED EDUCATION

The fundamental process for competency-based teacher education curriculum development research is the systems analysis approach. Systems analysis is a general term for the process of applying scientific thinking to large scale problems.[6,7] Systematic specification permits the reduction of competencies to a series of interrelated behavioral objectives that can be empirically evaluated.

Shores, Cegelka, and Nelson[8] conducted a recent survey by

[6]Dean Dickson, "Reform in Teacher Education Through Developing Performance-(Competency) Based Teacher Education Programs," Paper delivered at the 1972 ICET World Assembly, pp. 51-52.

[7]Ruben Altman and Edward L. Meyen, "Some Observations on Competency-Based Instruction," *Exceptional Children*, 40 (January, 1974), p. 8.

[8]Richard E. Shores, Patrician T. Cegelka and C. M. Nelson, "Competency-Based Special Education Teacher Training," *Exceptional Children*, 40 (November, 1973), pp. 192-197.

reviewing over fifty books and articles on competency-based instruction. Part of the survey was designed to ask a sample of personnel from prominent special education institutions to share information concerning their activities and products. Findings revealed that many teacher-training institutions had not stated competencies in behavioral terms. Competencies were either generally stated or were specific to categorical areas of special education. Many could not, however, be generalized to other programs. There was little evidence that competencies had been empirically validated.

In order to implement the strategies outlined by Dickson and Shores, institutions responsible for preparing special educators should derive competencies from experimental procedures rather than from expert opinions. Experimental procedures should involve direct observation of teaching behavior, isolation of the relationships through observation and scientific investigation.[9]

Well-designed modules can facilitate the learner's demonstration of competencies. These units are sets of related specific teacher skills that can be observed in the individual's actual professional performance. This approach permits a concrete baseline from which to judge whether or not the materials presented transfer to actual teaching performances. The knowledge and skills of one competence module should be a part of the next. Traditional college programs often lack this continuity. Modules allow a number of interrelated skills to be developed as a unit and allow for the acquisition of substantive skills as opposed to atomized tasks.[10, 11]

Modules may be of several types. Typically they include five major parts: (1) a prospectus or outline of major activities plus a presentation of prerequisites that are related to later modules and the relationship of the module to the total program, (2) a set of behavioral objectives stated in explicit terms, (3) preassessment, including a diagnostic assessment of subobjectives in the module,

[9]Christopolos and Valletutti, *loc. cit.*
[10]Timothy Rochford and Richard Brennan, "A Performance Criteria Approach To Teacher Education," *Exceptional Children*, 38 (April, 1972), pp. 636-637.
[11]Meyen, *op. cit.*, pp. 261, 263.

(4) enabling activities, which specify instructional alternatives for achieving module competence, and (5) postassessment, which measures successful completion of the module.[12] In addition to the five parts of a module listed above, Klingstedt[13] would add a sixth one, the resource section. He stated that the resource section is the place where all needed materials, media, and readings are listed. Also included may be such things as flow charts, time requirements, and evaluation forms. Learning modules provide a way for the learner to progress at his own rate through self-pacing. They also allow flexibility in terms of instruction and learning styles. Properly developed modules can integrate isolated curriculum into unified instructional strategies.

Meyen[14] indicated at a conference held at the University of Missouri in 1971 that the noncategorical approach to educating exceptional children has become a clear mandate. Current trends in special education are in the direction of increasingly integrating children with learning and behavioral problems into regular classes. This trend is based on evidence that segregated classes do not serve the cognitive and affective needs of exceptional individuals. Nor is there any evidence to the effect that normal children are adversely affected by the presence of exceptional students in their classes. Indeed, experience with wide variations in human behavior and other differences is likely to have beneficial effects on the social tolerance and social competencies of all children, normal as well as the exceptional.

IN-SERVICE EDUCATION

The present century has produced many advances in educational research and educational technology. The wide range of materials and equipment and the growth of knowledge have made it difficult for teachers to keep abreast of innovations in the field of

---

[12]Houston, *op. cit.*, p. 203.
[13]Joe Lars Klingstedt, "Learning Modules for Competency-Based Education," *Educational Technology* (November, 1972), pp. 21, 30.
[14]E. L. Meyen, "Proceeding of the Missouri Conference on the Categorical/Non-Categorical Issue in Special Education," University of Missouri, 1971.

special education. The day-to-day planning, coupled with the diversity of pupils' needs, does not leave the teacher much time to attend professional meetings, peruse journals in the field, or seek additional college credits. Because of the acceleration in technology and research, in-service education becomes extremely important.

In-service programs should be designed to upgrade the skills of all school personnel working with the exceptional. Appropriate facilities, sufficient funding, and skilled personnel, however, are frequently not provided. There often has been a lack of coordination and a disenchantment with the outcomes of in-service training. Some believe that local school districts should be responsible for coordinating in-service efforts while others believe that the coordination of in-service training should be the responsibility of institutions of higher education. It appears reasonable to conclude that many colleges and universities have excellent facilities and resources to implement training programs. Similarly, local school districts have personnel with expertise and resources to improve teacher education. The local school district has a distinct advantage in that it has the students needed to provide the enrichment of practica experiences. In-service training could be greatly improved if school districts and institutions of higher education developed closer interrelationships. Joint participation should be evident. Institutions of higher education and school districts could develop and implement in-service and preservice programs, each drawing on the experiences, resources, facilities, and competencies of the other.

Interinstitutional cooperation might also resolve some of the problems which relate to the development of teacher competency-based preparation programs. Clear philosophical guidelines, arrived at by interinstitutional concensus (colleges, public school systems, and state agencies), must be formulated.

MacIntyre[15] stated that pre-and in-service training and professional skill improvement of various sorts have become crucial to the maintenance of adequate education for the handicapped. The issue of mainstreaming the special student has created an urgent

---

[15]Robert B. MacIntyre, "In-Service Training Through Short Term Conferences," *Exceptional Children*, 38 (January, 1972), pp. 412-415.

need to develop in-service models for regular classroom teachers. To meet the manpower need, he recommended a wide range of short-term conferences and in-service activities. To assure the success of training programs the following elements should be evident: (1) clearly stated objectives, (2) carefully selected procedures and techniques, (3) built-in feedback and evaluation for the conference staff, and (4) demonstrated concern for the individual.

Many school districts have recognized the importance of in-service training for school personnel. In some instances, consortia have been formed for pooling resources to improve the effectiveness of services for exceptional individuals. Tenorio and Raimist[16] described a program operated in Northern Virginia. The George Washington University Diagnostic/Prescriptive Teacher Model was used in selected target schools. The program clearly demonstrated that many problem children can be maintained in the regular classroom provided that consultative and supportive services were made available to the classroom teacher by a school-based educational specialist. (See Chapters IV, V and VIII for diagnostic and other approaches that regular teachers may employ.)

Yates'[17] rationale for training regular classroom teachers was similar to the concept advanced by Tenorio and Raimist. He evaluated a regular teacher preparation model which used a laboratory/experiential approach. Forty regular classroom teachers were involved in the study. Of this number, thirty served as the experimental group, ten served as the control group. The experimental group was exposed to 100 hours of instruction. Findings revealed that a laboratory/experiential teacher preparation model does increase the amount of special education information for regular classroom teachers. The experimental group of teachers did significantly better than the control group of teachers.

The Baltimore City Schools,[18] Division of Exceptional Chil-

[16]Sue C. Tenorio and Lewis I. Maimist, "A Non-Categorical Consortium Program," *Exceptional Children*, 38 (December, 1971), pp. 325-326.

[17]James R. Yates, "Model for Preparing Regular Classroom Teachers for Mainstreaming," *Exceptional Children*, 39 (March, 1973), p. 471.

[18]Baltimore City Public Schools, Division of Exceptional Children. Special Learning Conference, 1974.

dren, developed an in-service program during the summer of 1974. The program was formulated around a special learning conference. Surrounding institutions of higher learning were invited to participate in the organization, planning, and instructional aspects of the program. In order to assure that the conference was based upon needs of the participants, school personnel surveyed what teachers in the system perceived as important in developing teaching competencies. Topics were categorized and grouped around teacher input. This procedure assured a high degree of motivation and participation, especially since graduate credits were given by participating institutions.

The conference was divided into eight basic parts, thus providing the participants with a choice of topics from which to select. Participants were instructed to keep in mind the objectives they had selected in choosing topics.

The workshop consisted of the following topics and/or activities:

1. Large group presentations where nationally known speakers in the field of special education addressed the group.

2. Extensive study sessions were designed to follow up theoretical information with practical application in the classroom. Various media were used such as videotapes and films. Topics covered were: individualized instruction, reading techniques, language development, diagnostic teaching, resource room teaching, techniques of supervision, and continuum services.

3. Clinical study sessions were concerned with applied experiences with children, mostly based upon theoretical constructs. Techniques of behavior modification, diagnostic and prescriptive teaching, and reading difficulties were covered under this category.

4. Intensive study sessions offered intensive instruction in specialized areas such as resource teaching, techniques of counseling with emphasis on parental involvement, behavior management, specialized reading and math techniques, classroom management, administration and supervision, and techniques of adapting instructional materials for

exceptional individuals.

5. Ministudy sessions included a variety of topics developed to provide an introduction to subjects that participants wanted to know more about.

6. Master teacher demonstrations were planned to provide a teaching model on a teacher-to-teacher basis. Master teachers were selected to share their skills and expertise on selected topics, including specialized reading, math, and writing techniques. In addition, proper use of audiovisual equipment, learning centers, and demonstrations in speech therapy were discussed and explored.

7. Special interest symposia were created to encourage a free flow of information and discussion. These symposia were conducted by school and college personnel. Some of the topics discussed, as indicated by participants, were: teacher evaluation, certification requirements in various areas, in-service training for administrators, mainstreaming, parental involvement, and adapting materials to the needs of children.

8. Material displays were provided by several publishers for examination by participants. Demonstrations were given concerning their instructional use.

The National Education Association is presently spearheading a drive to make in-service education a regular, ongoing part of a school district's program for the professional development of its staff. In-service education must be substantially more than extension courses offered by institutions of higher learning. One of the most valuable and least used resources exists in the teachers themselves. Effective in-service education affords teachers an opportunity to get together within a college setting to discuss common problems and to pool their resources in developing new approaches to teaching.[19]

Preparation of personnel for meeting the needs of exceptional individuals will become increasingly complex as school systems

---

[19]William J. O'Keefe, "Some Teacher-Centered In-Service Programs," *Today's Education,* 63 (March-April, 1974), p. 39.

identify and program for exceptional individuals who are more severely and profoundly handicapped. State and local school boards will demand more qualified personnel to meet the complex and multidimensional needs of these students and their families. New types of personnel will be needed to provide a wide range of educational and therapeutic services to this handicapped population. The demands of mainstreaming will require, in the years ahead, personnel resources in each and every school to a degree unanticipated by educators until recently. To meet the challenge of future decades, both innovated pre- and in-service models must be developed to educate school personnel.

TEACHER COMPETENCIES AND TEACHER PERSONALITY

Due to the diverse learning patterns of exceptional individuals, it is desirable that teachers exhibit certain personality traits. Many exceptional individuals learn at a slow pace. The teacher must be satisfied with minimal changes made by the children and must not be distressed because they must teach skills automatically acquired by most children. This should not, however, preclude the teacher from programming learning experiences based upon the abilities of the students. All should not be expected to achieve at the same rate. Individual and intraindividual differences must be taken into consideration. Exceptional individuals are likely to show growth and changes in behavior if instruction is geared to their needs, built upon relevant student competencies, and sequenced into small steps that they can understand, provided that there is no medical or physiological reason which would contraindicate it.

Teachers of exceptional individuals should be flexible. When a student is not mastering concepts, other approaches and procedures should be introduced. It might be necessary to return to a lower level of instruction and sequence the task into smaller steps. The teacher should also consider the appropriateness of the materials, the interest of the student, the quality of his interaction, and the environmental and medical factors which might be operating to impede student progress. Very often it is necessary to temporarily ignore a teaching objective, rearrange teaching priorities, and to return to a task at a later date.

A review of the literature indicated that the most extensive study on teacher competencies were conducted by Mackie, Dunn, and Cain.[20] Respondents represented a cross section of special educators throughout the country, in several institutions and/or agencies responsible for education programs, serving exceptional children. Findings showed that: (1) in evaluating technical knowledge in specialized areas, teachers placed the highest value on social and psychological understandings; (2) curriculum development and specialized teaching techniques were not rated as high as personal characteristics needed by teachers. Teachers who rated this item as very important indicated their concern for individualizing the curriculum and using appropriate teaching methods, (3) counseling and guidance were rated by successful teachers as "very important." This item was considered especially important for teachers of the physically handicapped child, (4) use and interpretation of records and reports were rated as "important" but not of the highest value to aid teachers in working with handicapped children, and (5) generally, teachers evaluated knowledge of specialized teaching methods in other areas of exceptionality as low. Teachers did not place a high value on specialized teaching methods for instructing children with multiple handicaps.

The authors concluded from the results of the study that most of the respondents evaluated personal characteristics as very important in working with exceptional children. Flexibility, resourcefulness, a great deal of patience and understanding were among the teacher personality traits viewed as important in working with exceptional individuals.

Evidence presented by Getzels and Jackson,[21] Meisgeier,[22]

---

[20]Romaine Mackie, L. Dunn, and L. Cain, *Professional Preparation for Teachers of Exceptional Children: An Overview*, Washington, D. C., Government Printing Office, 1960, pp. 100-101.

[21]J. W. Getzels and P. W. Jackson, "The Teacher's Personality and Characteristics," in N. L. Gage (Ed.), *Handbook on Teaching* (Chicago: Rand-McNally, 1963).

[22]C. Meisgeier, "The Identification of Successful Teachers of Mentally or Physically Handicapped Children," *Exceptional Children*, 32 (December, 1965), pp. 229-235.

Scheuer,[23] and Nunnally,[24] indicated that teacher personality is an important factor in the classroom. Although Shores[25] supported much of the research on teacher personality as an important factor, he outlined that the relationship between teacher personality and attitudes was not sufficiently addressed in the above studies as they relate to classroom teachers — in essence, no cause-effect relationship was established. It was indicated that operational definitions of personality and attitudinal variables reflected in observable behavior would increase the cause-effect relationship between teacher-pupil interaction. If more were known about the personality characteristics of potential teachers of exceptional students, understanding of variables related to special class teaching would be greatly facilitated.

Jones and Gottfried[26] summed up some of the problems of teacher competencies and their validation by stating that little is known about what makes the special education teacher effective and competent. Nearly a decade has passed since their statement, and research still has not found a solution to this complex problem.

With the recent move toward competency-based education it is hoped that special educators will be able to scientifically validate competencies needed by teachers of exceptional children. The Office of Education (BEH) and the American Council on Teacher Education have spearheaded the movement toward competency-based education on a national level. Institutions of higher education are addressing themselves to the development of selective competencies for potential and in-service teachers. Competencies identified by institutions should be developed in concert with school systems and available community resources. Without this approach, competencies developed by institutions of higher education may not be relevent to the communities that they serve. Equally important, competencies developed by institutions should meet the rigid requirements of scientific inquiry.

---

[23]Arnold Scheuer, "The Relationship Between Personal Attributes and Effectiveness in Teachers of the Emotionally Disturbed," *Exceptional Children*, 37 (1971), pp. 723-731.
[24]J. C. Nunnally, *Psychometric Theory* (St. Louis: McGraw-Hill, 1967).
[25]Shores, *op. cit.*
[26]Reginald Jones and Nathan Gottfried, "Psychological Needs and Preferences for Teaching Exceptional Children," *Exceptional Children*, 32 (January, 1966), p. 314.

SUMMARY

There is a national movement to make schools more accountable for the learning experiences of students. Special education has been severely criticized for not providing a viable education for exceptional individuals.

As the programs at the local education level start to integrate the mildly handicapped into the mainstream of educational life, and as more and more severely and profoundly handicapped are provided free public education, special and regular class teachers will be expected to be highly skilled professionals. As special educators evolve in their philosophy and advance to the point where they view the exceptional as an individual with a unique constellation of abilities and weaknesses, they will realize that educating them is no different from educating the normal. The materials, equipment, and the level of curriculum objectives may be different but the teaching strategies are the same. Teaching competency is the essential factor, not erudition on the medical, psychological, or sociological aspects of disability.

CHAPTER X

NEW DIRECTIONS IN SPECIAL EDUCATION: FEDERAL, STATE, AND LOCAL ROLES IN MAINSTREAMING

PAUL AREND

PRECEDING chapters in this volume were concerned with trends that have proven to be of significance in the education of exceptional individuals. As stated in previous chapters, federal, state, local, and other agencies must continue to explore innovative avenues for adequate fiscal support, individualization of instruction and improvement in the present classification systems. Successful integration of exceptional individuals into the mainstream of education cannot be successfully accomplished without the full cooperation and endorsement of these agencies.

This chapter is intended to discuss the roles of federal, state, local, and other agencies in their efforts to mainstream exceptional individuals. Outlined are suggestions for improvement to aid these agencies in their endeavors to provide quality educational experiences for children with special needs.

The growth of special education programs and services for the exceptional was unprecedented during the first half of the twentieth century. Indeed, by the year 1973, it was considered a "major event" and commanded national attention in publications not usually connected with the education of the exceptional. The April, 1974 *Phi Delta Kappan* magazine was a special issue on Special Education. Other publications such as *Today's Education* published by the National Education Association (NEA) and *Educational Leadership* published by the Association for Supervision and Curriculum Development (ASCD) devoted space to specific Special Education articles and followed through at their national conference with programs concerned with exceptional individuals.

The focus on special education in 1973 prompted Ben Brodinsky, a special consultant for the Educational Press Association of America, to include special education in his annual list of "ten major education events." Mr. Brodinsky is quoted by the *Kappan*[1] as saying: "Educators and government officials showed new and historic concern for the handicapped, mentally retarded, and other children with special educational needs."

Special education forged to the foreground with many states passing comprehensive laws to ensure the education of all exceptional individuals. School districts were required to provide special education programs and were mandated to devise plans for their state departments of education. All states in the Union, with the exception of two, demanded that school districts provide special education programs for the major categories of exceptional individuals. In 1973, judicial rulings in various states supported the 1971 order by the U. S. District Court requiring Pennsylvania to educate all children. The "right to education" concept was extended to include the physically, mentally, and emotionally handicapped.[2]

PHILOSOPHICAL CONCEPTS

The roles of the local, state, and federal agencies during the present decade have not only improved, but are promoting an extensive broad philosophy of special education. Special education is viewed as a legitimate area of education and is clearly reflected in the educational system of the public. It is not to be conceived as a separate entity for those exceptional individuals who could not achieve in the regular classroom or school. Special education is viewed as part of a continuum of services geared to meet the needs of the total school population.

The *Phi Delta Kappan's* extensive and systematized educational goal search of 1973 indicated eighteen goals of education which clearly reflected the same objectives special educators desired for exceptional individuals. These goals are listed below in

[1]"Special Education — A Major Event in 1973," *Phi Delta Kappan*, 5 (April, 1974), p. 513.
[2]*Ibid.*

the order of importance as rated by Kappans (not necessarily the order of all special educators).[3]

The Goals of Education

1. Develop skills in reading, writing, speaking, and listening.
2. Develop pride in work and a feeling of self-worth.
3. Develop good character and self-respect.
4. Develop a desire for learning now and in the future.
5. Learn to respect and get along with people in daily life.
6. Learn how to examine and use information.
7. Gain a general education.
8. Learn how to be a good citizen.
9. Learn about and try to understand the changes that take place in the world.
10. Understand and practice democratic ideas and ideals.
11. Learn how to respect and get along with people who think, dress, and act differently.
12. Understand and practice the skills of family living.
13. Gain information needed to make job selections.
14. Learn how to be a good manager of money, property, and resources.
15. Practice and understand the ideas of health and safety.
16. Develop skills to enter a specific field of work.
17. Learn how to use leisure time.
18. Appreciate culture and beauty in the world.

The White House Conference on Children in December of 1970 was attended by 3,700 delegates. They developed a list of overriding concerns for education. Within the eight concerns listed were

---

[3]Harold Spears, "Kappans Ponder the Goals of Education," *Phi Delta Kappan,* 55 (September, 1973), pp. 29-32.

specific references to special education. The concerns were as follows: (1) a recording of national priorities beginning with a guaranteed basic family income adequate for the needs of the children, (2) programs to eliminate racism, (3) comprehensive family-oriented child development programs to include health services, day-care, and early childhood education, (4) health, welfare, educational, and bilingual-bicultural programs, (5) a federally financed national child health care program, (6) a system of early identification of children with special needs, (7) immediate, massive funding for the development of alternative, optional forms of public education, and (8) the creation of a national cabinet post concerned with children and youth.[4] These concerns engendered basic concepts related to the broad philosophy held by educators of the exceptional.

The NEA in their 1973 program objectives for the federal government considered two major components of federal responsibility for public education. These were general financial assistance to education in an amount to raise the federal government's share of cost to not less than one-third the total educational expenditures and full funding of existing categorical aid programs. In both of these components, aid to the exceptional was a specific target for support by the NEA.[5]

FEDERAL ROLE IN SPECIAL EDUCATION

Special education is administered on three levels: federal, state, and local. While state and local agencies provide the prime efforts for direct services to exceptional individuals, the federal government provides funds for training personnel, research, and exemplary services which give supplementary support.

There were no provisions in the Constitution of the United States for public education. It was through the interpretation of the "general welfare clause," found in the Preamble and Article 1, Section 8 of the Constitution, that Congress assumed certain positive powers affecting education. This power took the form of

---

4"White House Conference Produces 'Concerns' and Unofficial Actions," *Today's Education*, 60 (February, 1971), p. 3.
5"Work with the Federal Government," *Today's Education*, 62 (January, 1973), p. 49.

levying taxes to promote educational endeavors via the federal government. These endeavors were basically geared to supplement state and local efforts and were never intended as primary regulatory measures.

The traditional role of the federal government in education was to promote, stimulate, and improve education. This was accomplished through providing funds and resources to aid state educational programs; establishing limited educational programs for various groups such as Indians and military personnel; providing scholarships and fellowships; establishing advisory, consultative, and research services; and disseminating information on education. In the mid-seventies, federal activities in the education of the exceptional prompted legislative makers to see a need to reexamine this federal role. Federal legislation was not only being formed to supplement state and local special education programs, but also, in some cases appeared to be the basic element of provision for such programs.

Recognition of Needs of Exceptional Children: Handicapped Defined

A tremendous stride was made with the enactment of Title VI, Elementary and Secondary Education Act Amendments of 1969 (PL 91-230). It was in Part A, Section 602 of this Act that the term "handicapped children" (for the context of this federal law) was defined. The definition included the following handicapping conditions:

> ...mentally retarded, hard of hearing, deaf, speech impaired, visually handicapped, seriously emotionally disturbed, crippled, or other health impaired children who by reason thereof require special education and related services.

In addition, children with learning disabilities were defined as:

> ...those children who have a disorder in one or more of the basic psychological processes involved in understanding or in using language, spoken or written, which disorder may manifest itself in imperfect ability to listen, think, speak, read,

write, spell, or do mathematical calculations. Such disorders include such conditions as perceptual handicaps, brain injury, minimal brain dysfunction, dyslexia and developmental aphasia. These terms do not include children who have learning problems which are primarily the result of visual, hearing, motor handicaps, mental retardation, emotional disturbance, or environmental disadvantage. (Sec. 602)

Bureau of Education for the Handicapped

The Act (Part A) also established a bureau for the education and training of the handicapped in the United States Office of Education (USOE) within the United States Department of Health, Education and Welfare (HEW). The bureau was designated as the principal agency in the USOE for administering and carrying out programs and projects related to the education and training of the handicapped.[6]

The initial years of the Bureau of Education for the Handicapped (BEH) was spent on consolidation of programs and reor-

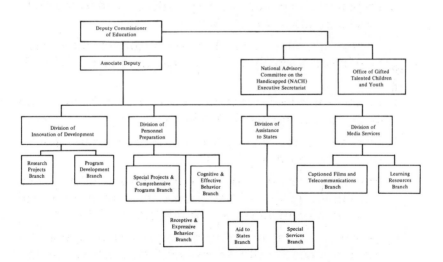

Figure X-1.

---

[6]George Neill, "Washington Report," *Phi Delta Kappan*, 55 (April, 1974), p. 580.

ganization of the bureau. In April of 1974, the following organizational chart for the Bureau within the USOE was approved.

During the fiscal year 1973, fifteen different programs were identified by BEH as under their administration or their monitoring responsibility. These programs had the following purposes:

1. Strengthen educational programs for handicapped children in state-operated or state-supported schools (PL 89-313).

2. Initiate, expand, and improve educational and related services to handicapped preschool, elementary, and secondary children (PL 91-230).

3. Develop model preschool and early childhood programs for handicapped children (PL 91-230).

4. Develop centers for educational diagnosis and remediation of handicapped children (PL 91-230).

5. Develop centers and services for deaf-blind children and their parents (PL 91-230).

6. Prepare teachers and other specialists to educate handicapped children (PL 91-230).

7. Improve recruitment of education personnel and disseminate information about educational opportunities (PL 91-230).

8. Promote and demonstrate new knowledge in the education of the handicapped (PL 91-230).

9. Promote research on physical education and recreation for the handicapped (PL 91-230).

10. Advance the handicapped through film and other media, including a captioned film loan service for cultural and educational enrichment of the deaf (PL 91-230).

11. Provide an instructional media and materials support system for handicapped learners and their teachers and parents (PL 91-230).

12. Provide research and training of personnel and operate

model centers for children with learning disabilities (PL 91-230).

13. Strengthen neighborhood resources for facilitating development of children presenting behavioral or developmental problems (jointly funded and monitored by BEH, National Institute of Mental Health, Rehabilitation Services Administration, and administered by BEH).

14. Provide grants for innovative and exemplary programs and projects which are designed to demonstrate ways of making a substantial contribution to the solution of critical problems in the field of special education (Title III, ESEA).

15. Provide vocational and career educational services to handicapped children and youth (PL 90-576).

Other Federal legislation

As early as 1879, the United States Government recognized the need to promote education for the blind with an act creating the American Printing House for the Blind. This nonprofit institute, located in Lexington, Kentucky, supplied educational materials and tangible apparatus to the blind and multihandicapped children as well as adults. There was a perpetual fund established by Congress for the implementation of this act.

For more than 100 years, Gallaudet College, Washington, D.C., carried out its program with funds voted upon by the U. S. Congress. This private, nonprofit educational institution provided undergraduate and graduate programs for the deaf, a preparatory school for deaf students, a graduate school program in the field of deafness and an adult education program for deaf persons. Through Public Law 89-694, the Secretary of HEW was further authorized in concert with Gallaudet College to establish a Model Secondary School for the Deaf. This secondary school primarily served the residents of Washington, D. C. and nearby states, thereby providing a model for similar programs across the nation. In 1965, Public Law 89-38 authorized the construction and operation of a residential facility for postsecondary technical training and education of persons who were deaf. The purpose was to prepare the deaf for successful employment. The National Technical Institute for the Deaf was founded and located at the Rochester Institute of Technology in Rochester, New York. This Institute provided a sound psychological setting, educating deaf students among the hearing.

Other U. S. laws also recognized the need for special education programs. The Vocational Education Amendments of 1968 (PL 90-576), Title I, provided provisions to ensure that 10 percent of the funds would be spent for the handicapped (Sec. 122). In addition, the National Council on Vocational Education, created within the Act, had to contain one member who was experienced in the education and training of handicapped persons. The Act further required State Advisory Councils to also contain such a member. Grants were made available to the states to assist them in rehabilitating handicapped individuals as part of the amended Vocational Rehabilitation Act (PL 66-236). The Act also called for the federal government to fund the operation of a National Center for Deaf-Blind Youths and Adults. The center, designed to provide intensive services (Sec. 16), is the Industrial Home for the Blind located in Brooklyn, New York.

The physically handicapped who had exceptional academic potential and were from low income families were financially supported to continue or resume their postsecondary education through the Higher Education Amendments of 1972 (PL 92-328). In this Act, loans were provided to college and university students with the promise that they would teach handicapped children in the private or public sector. Once the teaching commitment was fulfilled, the actual loan was then satisfied. One part of the Act, Title V — Education Professions Development, provided fellowships leading to advanced degrees for teachers and related educational personnel in special education for the handicapped children (Sec. 521). This also included projects for preparing such personnel to meet the needs of exceptionally gifted students.

The handicapped were also recognized in other federal legislation. In the Headstart Program, Economic Opportunities Amendments of 1972 (PL 92-424), policies and procedures were established to ensure that at least 10 percent of the enrollments throughout the nation consisted of handicapped children. Title

V, Social Security Act of 1935 as amended, authorized a program to help reduce the incidence of handicapping conditions associated with childbearing. The Development Disabilities Services and Facilities Construction Amendment of 1970 (PL 91-517), provided assistance to states in developing a plan for the provision of comprehensive services for those affected by mental retardation and other developmental disabilities originating in childhood. This included some funding for construction of facilities. The federal government also passed PL 90-480 which required that all buildings financed with federal funds be designed and constructed so as to be accessible to the physically handicapped. This referred only to those buildings intended for public use.

While Congress in the mid-seventies had many committee meetings and hearings to help determine the extent of legislation for the handicapped, President Nixon also proposed special funds for the handicapped for 1975. Funding for education to help handicapped children was recommended at $50 million, an increase of $2 million over the previous fiscal year. States were to be assisted in providing educational services for handicapped children. It was estimated that more than 285,000 handicapped children would be served directly under this program as a result of the stimulus created by the presence of federal funds and leadership in the area.[7] While a major emphasis at the time was forward funding for educational bills one fiscal year in advance, the President requested exemption of forward funding for the various legislative bills being written in Congress for the handicapped. The President promised a consolidation bill on all acts for the handicapped with a forward funding provision and wanted Congress to wait upon the Administration. (See Appendix H for Summary of *The Education of All Handicapped Children Act.*

NATIONAL CENTERS FOR INSTRUCTIONAL MATERIALS AND MEDIA

In 1962, the Task Force of the President's Panel on Mental Retardation identified a specific problem. The Task Force found that while many specialized fields of general education had devel-

---

[7]George Neill, "Washington Report,"*Phi Delta Kappan*, 55 (April, 1974), p. 580.

oped significant teaching materials, there was a deficit of teaching materials and techniques in the area of special education. It recommended the development of Instructional Materials Centers (IMC's) for the purpose of providing personnel working in the field of special education with ready access to valid instructional materials and information for the education of handicapped children and youth. The USOE took the recommendation and provided the leadership under the Bureau of Education for the Handicapped to initiate IMC's in a three phase plan of development.

The three areas associated with the IMC are: service, research and development, and materials production. The service function included acquisition of commercially and teacher-prepared instructional materials, describing, classifying and organizing these materials for dissemination to educators. The area of research and development fostered the evaluation of instructional materials and the development and production of new materials on a pilot basis to establish their potential effectiveness. In the stimulation phase, the following were included: contacting organizations which had production capacity and encouraging them to produce materials which had been found effective in the research phase, and consulting with producers to assure that ideas believed meritorious were given consideration.[8]

A new component was added to this network in June of 1972, the National Center on Educational Media and Materials for the Handicapped (NCEMMH). This center included the thirteen existing Regional Instructional Materials Centers (IMC's), the four Regional Media Centers for the Deaf (RMC's), the Council for Exceptional Children (CEC) Information Center, and the Instructional Materials Reference Center at the American Printing House for the Blind. All the centers combined to form a unified, national program designed to improve education for handicapped children through the use of instructional technology.

The development of specialized media and materials with the training of personnel in the use of technology was supplemented

---

[8]George M. Olshin, "Special Education Instructional Materials Center Program," *Exceptional Children*, 34 (October, 1967), pp. 137-141.

with the development of an information system. The network functioned as a means of bringing current, relevant information to special education. Besides using media such as newsletters, exhibition booths and displays, brochures and flyers, several centers and the CEC Information Center provided computer printouts about resources in education. The CEC Information Center also published the *Exceptional Child Education Abstracts*. This journal provides a comprehensive set of abstracts of published and unpublished documents in special education. A delivery system of nearly 300 associate special education instructional materials centers were established at state and local levels to get materials to teachers for immediate use with learners.[9] The Special Education IMC/RMC Network can be found in Appendix B.

ORGANIZATIONAL COALITION MOVEMENT

A coalition of some twenty to thirty individual organizations and agencies serving the handicapped was called for by the President of the Council for Exceptional Children (CEC) in the mid-seventies. CEC was then the only one of many national organizations which spoke for all types of handicapped and gifted individuals. Though many of these organizations spoke only for a specific type of handicapped group, it was felt that to some extent, efforts, goals, and resources were being duplicated. An interagency action network designed to coordinate all efforts on behalf of handicapped individuals was called for as opposed to each organization advancing its own views.

Among those organizations which were cited for, but not limited to, inclusion in such a coalition were: Alexander Graham Bell Association for the Deaf, American Association on Mental Deficiency, American Association for the Blind, American Speech and Hearing Association, Association for Children with Learning Disabilities, National Association for Mental Health, National Association for Retarded Citizens, National Epilepsy Foundation, National Society for Crippled Children and Adults, and the

---

[9]Robert MacIntyre, "IMC, RMC Network News and Notes," *Teaching Exceptional Children*, 5 (Fall, 1972), p. 45.

United Cerebral Palsy Association. The prime purpose of such an interagency network was for identifying specific problems, forming a strong advocate group, promoting needed legislation, and initiating or supporting litigation for the handicapped.[10]

Educational Research and Resources

The Council for Exceptional Children (CEC) has the distinction of being the only major professional educational organization in the United States whose concern focuses on the needs of all handicapped and gifted children. In the fifty-two years since its founding in 1922, and particularly in the last twelve years under the leadership of its current Executive Director, William C. Geer, CEC has come to be recognized as a major influence in the improvement of federal, regional, state, and local programs for handicapped and gifted children. With more than 60,000 members located throughout the United States and Canada, it serves the educational community through its publications, governmental relations programs, conventions, special conferences, and related special projects. Two special projects of The Council for Exceptional Children are:

The State-Federal Information Clearinghouse for Exceptional Children (SFICEC)

With the advent of greater opportunities for handicapped children to receive an education in the United States, there was an increased awareness that the degree and quality of special education programs depended on the activities of government at all levels and in all branches — executive, judicial, and legislative. The Council for Exceptional Children, through a grant from the Bureau of Education for the Handicapped, USOE, established the State-Federal Information Clearinghouse for Exceptional Children (SFICEC). The purpose of SFICEC was to identify, acquire,

---

[10]Jack C. Dinger, "President's Page," *Exceptional Children*, 40 (March, 1974), pp. 469-471.

process, selectively retrieve, and disseminate information pertaining to government and the education of handicapped children. A computer-based information system was developed for the retrieval and dissemination of this information. Such information included articles relating to state laws for gifted children, pending and completed litigation regarding the education of the handicapped, descriptions and excerpts of laws relating to exceptional children, legal provisions for state and local planning for delivery of special education services, personnel certification, special education financing, transportation legalities, and summaries of various statistical reports.[11]

The CEC Information Center: An EHIC Clearinghouse on Handicapped and Gifted Children

The convergence of several major developments in education in 1966 led the CEC to compete for and win a grant (OEG-2-6-062473-1717(607) from the USOE Bureau of Research to establish and operate an ERIC Clearinghouse on Handicapped and Gifted Children. A statement of purpose was drafted in CEC's 1966 proposal which specified that the Clearinghouse on Exceptional Children would "serve as a comprehensive information center identifying and collecting all significant literature and materials of value to educators of gifted and handicapped children." From 1966 until the present time, CEC has been the operator of the ERIC Clearinghouse on Handicapped and Gifted Children which is a member of the Network of ERIC Clearinghouses.

Several major objectives have shaped the services and products of the ERIC Clearinghouse on Handicapped and Gifted Children since its inception in 1966:

1. To serve as a comprehensive information center on research, instructional materials, programs, administration, teacher education, methods, curricula, services, and facilities for handicapped and gifted children.

2. To participate in the ERIC Network as the Clearinghouse

---

[11]Alan Abeson, "State-Federal Information Clearinghouse for Exceptional Children," (Virginia: The Council for Exceptional Children, 1974).

on Exceptional Child Education by cataloging, abstracting, and indexing appropriate documents for ERIC products such as *Research in Education* (RIE), and *Current Index to Journal in Education* (CIJE).

3. To survey the research related to the education of handicapped and gifted children and identify results that have implications for classroom teaching.

4. To translate information for classroom use and to develop materials (literature, films, videotapes, etc.) which illustrate desirable educational practices indicated by the research evidence.

5. To provide for a continuous review of research literature identifying that which has relevance for classroom instruction of handicapped and gifted children.

6. To develop a variety of appropriate vehicles for dissemination of information to the field.[12]

The CEC Information Center provides three major information services:

1. Customer Computer Searches (The most current information on a specialized topic.)

2. Topical Bibliographies (More than fifty preselected bibliographies updated annually.)

3. *Exceptional Child Education Abstracts* (Published quarterly; contains citations of all current special education publications stored in the CEC Information Center.)

Another BEH-USOE Effort

In addition to the above efforts, the Education Commission of the States formed the Handicapped Children's Education Program (HACHE). The Education Commission of the States was a nonprofit organization formed by an interstate compact through legislation within forty-six states by 1973. Its goal was to further a working relationship among state governors, legislators, and

---

[12]"Overview of CEC," (Virginia: The Council for Exceptional Children, 1975).

educators for the improvement of education. More specifically, the objectives of HACHE were as follows:

1. Improve state legislation for handicapped children by assisting states in initiating, reviewing, amending, and implementing legislation.

2. Improve the utilization and allocation of each state's resources for providing educational services for the handicapped through study and analysis of legislative issues and administrative procedures.

3. Provide for the formulation and application of state policies for the education of the handicapped through task force activities, staff services to state governments, and the promotion of the value of improved educational opportunities.

The HACHE program was funded by a grant from the BEH-USOE. The focal point was directed towards aiding the 60 percent population in the United States who needed but were not receiving special education services.[13]

STATE ROLE IN SPECIAL EDUCATION

Traditionally, the state over a period of time assumed the responsibility of ensuring a minimum education for its residents. Most state constitutions contained some statement or mandate requiring the legislature to provide an effective system of public instruction, free of tuition charges and equally open to all. Each state determined the basic policies relating to a plan of organization for education within the state.[14]

The citizens of each state relied upon the legislature to enact laws providing for the implementation of educational policies and provisions incorporated in the constitution.[15] Each state

---

[13]Education Commission of the States, *HACHE, Handicapped Children's Education Project*, Brochure, USOE, OEG-0-72-0242 (607), 1973.
[14]Edgar L. Morphet, et al., *Educational Organization and Administration*, 2nd Ed. (New Jersey: Prentice-Hall, Inc., 1967), pp. 233-237.
[15]*Ibid.*

acquired a State Education Agency charged with developing policies, guidelines, and standards for carrying out the law. The agency usually comprised the State Board of Education, the chief state school officer, and the State Department of Education.

Three major types of functions for this agency are classified as leadership, regulatory, and operational responsibilities. Leadership functions include planning, research, advising, consulting, and coordinating activities. The regulatory functions are designed to help protect the welfare of the children, guarantee prudential use of funds, assure efficiency in management, and provide a framework for ensuring a minimal instructional program to all citizenry. Some states have specific operational responsibilities for various local school programs and/or facilities.[16]

Basic Concepts in Special Education

Since state constitutions, and then laws, directed that a public school system for all children be maintained by local boards of education, a commitment was made to the public. In the past, however, many state laws were permissive with respect to handicapped children. These permissive laws gave school districts the option of serving or not serving handicapped children. It was noted that, as of 1972, more than 70 percent of the states had changed to mandatory legislation regarding the education and/or training of handicapped children. These mandatory laws removed the option of local boards of education to serve handicapped children.[17] There were a number of states that broadened this area to speak on behalf of exceptional children and included mandatory programs for the gifted.

In the mid-seventies, the major rulings of attorney generals occurred on the state and federal levels. These rulings established that the handicapped had an inalienable right to free public education. With these rulings came the need and availability of increased funding and attention for the delivery of services to the

[16]*Ibid.*, pp. 243-244.

[17]Alan Abeson, "Movement and Momentum: Government and the Education of Handicapped Children," *Exceptional Children*, 39 (September, 1972), pp. 63-66.

handicapped. These actions further stimulated state mandatory legislation which did more than require the operation of educational programs for the handicapped. Work was begun on new funding formulas, provisions for personnel training, production, and dissemination of special materials and provision for adequate facilities.[18]

The guarantee of the rights of handicapped children also gave rise to other state responses. Research programs in early childhood education were especially designed for the handicapped. The minimum school entrance age for the handicapped was extended by law to birth in many states through parent-infant programs. Similarly, in recognition that some handicapped youth needed prolonged preparation and training, the maximum school age was extended to twenty-one years of age or higher. Traditional services to the handicapped were expanded and became more comprehensive in scope. In some states, transportation obligations were increased for the handicapped to include transport to private schools and institutions as well as public. To accommodate the exceptional student, local school districts were encouraged to and did form regional programs using common facilities.[19]

THE COURTS AND LITIGATION

The movement for the right to education for the handicapped as well as for quality programs was pronounced in the seventies. The passage of both state and federal laws, rulings of attorney generals, and judicial activities were given considerable attention by the media. Present conditions for the handicapped were exposed and critiqued via television specials, radio, and newspapers. Hearings on state and federal levels included testimony by national experts and were given wide media coverage. Political action groups lobbied for increased funding of special education programs. Politicians seeking office as state governors as well as higher positions were quizzed on the position they would take in

---

[18]*Ibid.*
[19]*Ibid.*

regard to the education of the handicapped.[20]

In the past, proponents for state support of programs for exceptional children had resorted to lobbying or appealing to the state's chief executive through negotiations with statewide or local school officials. A thorough review of societal trends indicated another way that advocators of quality programs for the handicapped could achieve their goals. In the 1950's and the 1960's, the courts had played a significant role in determining the constitutionality of decisions made by legislators and executives. Great strides were made in 1954 when segregated schools were declared unconstitutional. Further giant steps resulted when the courts supported the civil rights movement of the 1960's as well as supported the rights for legal advice to be made available to low income citizens, the poor, welfare recipients, public housing tenants, and low income consumers. Movements for women, labor, and the elderly received relief through the courts. The seventies, therefore, became the time of "turning to the courts" for relief for the handicapped.[21]

Relief through litigation began early in the seventies with the landmark case of Mills vs. Board of Education of the District of Columbia (1971). This case emphasized and established the right to an education for all children previously excluded from school. Also in 1971, the Pennsylvania Association for Retarded Children vs. Commonwealth of Pennsylvania filed a class action suit to obtain and guarantee a public supported education program in the state for all mentally retarded children. The Commonwealth of Pennsylvania yielded to the evidence presented in court. This decision guaranteed the educational rights of the mentally retarded child, and required that the child and his family be provided the rights of notice and due process prior to any alterations in the child's educational status. This included schools notifying parents of the right to council, cross examination, presentation of evidence, and appeals. This action suit stimulated other litigation in states throughout the nation.[22]

---

[20]*Ibid.*

[21]Thomas K. Gilhool, "Education: An Inalienable Right," *Exceptional Children*, 39 (May, 1973), pp. 597-609.

[22]Abeson, *loc cit.*

Many of the civil actions were brought to the courts as class actions on behalf of handicapped children rather than referring to a single disability. Implicit in the entire litigation movement was a basic philosophy: Handicapped people are to be treated in as normal an environment as possible. There are always some persons who need institutional services. These people who are institutionalized have the right to a program of full treatment which includes education.[23] In the memorandum from the judge on the court decrees of the Maryland Association for Retarded Children, et al. vs. State of Maryland, et al., 1974 the term "education" was defined as "... any planned or structured program administered by competent persons that is designed to help individuals achieve their full potential.[24]

Attorney Generals' Opinions

The power of the courts to adjudicate the inequities regarding the education of the handicapped was nationally recognized in the seventies. Abeson noted that in that period the power of the attorney generals' opinions had almost been totally unnoticed. He pinpointed two examples: First, in 1969, the Attorney General of North Carolina ruled that the state's permissive special education law was contrary to the state's constitutional requirements that a free education be provided to all children including the handicapped. Secondly, in 1971, the Attorney General of New Mexico ruled that it was the duty of the state to provide education to all children including the handicapped. In addition, it was declared that all mentally retarded children, through public education, must have the opportunity to develop fair skills and abilities necessary in becoming a useful citizen of the state.[25] Evidence mounted that this form of relief might be sought more frequently.

---

[23]*Ibid.*

[24]Judge John E. Raine, Jr. in a memorandum, 77676, Maryland Association for Retarded Children, Inc., et al. vs. State of Maryland, et al. in the Circuit Court for Baltimore County, 1974.

[25]Abeson, *loc. cit.*

STATE PROCEDURES FOR
LEGISLATIVE IMPLEMENTATION

The impact of the needs for handicapped children, public pressures, educators, and advocate associations for the handicapped encouraged the conception and passing of Senate Bill No. 649, Section 106A (effective July 1, 1975), Chapter 7A Special Education Services of the State of Maryland. This bill described and decreed that educational agencies develop standards for the education of the handicapped, and be responsible to the local boards of education, the State Superintendent, and the State Board of Education.

Within the duties of education agencies, it was stated that the Maryland State Board of Education shall, by July 1, 1974, adopt standards in the form of bylaws for the identification, diagnosis, examination, and education of all children in the state through the age of twenty-one years who needed special educational services. Standards were not to be lower than those for regular children. Services designed were not to be limited and were to begin as soon as a child could benefit from such services regardless of age. Standards were to include the following:

1. Qualifications for teachers, administrators, and other professional, paraprofessional, and nonprofessional persons;

2. Procedures for identifying, testing, and diagnosing children in need;

3. Guidelines for curricula, instructional materials, equipment, and the organization, administration, and supervision of the program (including accounting, auditing, and reporting procedures);

4. Encouragement of local, regional, or state day and residential centers (where educationally and financially feasible) for children who cannot reasonably be served in the regular public schools;

5. Coordination of special educational services with other government agencies;

6. Standards for approval of placement in nonpublic schools

or facilities when no suitable public programs were available.

Upon adoption of the above standards, each of Maryland's twenty-four school systems were to plan in accordance with them. The plan was to provide for the education of all handicapped children domiciled in their school district. The local plan could exceed state standards but had to include provisions for full implementation within a five-year period. The local plan was to be submitted to the Maryland State Deaprtment of Education within nine months after the state standards were adopted.

The State Superintendent had the obligation to review each local plan, recommend approval to the State Board of Education or return it to the local board for revisions to be completed in sixty days. All special educational services for children through age twenty-one who were in state institutions had to be developed by the State Superintendent. The State Board of Education was to review all approved plans at least annually.

The overall concept of the bill was most encouraging to the citizenry. It was noted that the financial section of the bill was not voted into law. The Office of Special Education, Maryland State Department of Education, did begin work on meeting the requirements to implement the bill. A task force of 117 persons which comprised fourteen different committees was organized to carry out the task. The task force report was assembled and evaluated. From this report two documents were prepared: a "Proposed Bylaw for Special Educational Services" (To Repeal and Reenact Bylaw 13.04.01.01.A), and a set of regulations to implement the Bylaw. Public hearings were held on the bylaw and changes made in accordance. The regulations were organized within the Office of Special Education, Maryland State Department of Education. This permitted some flexibility at the state level for operational procedures without having to go to the legislature.*

STATE FINANCING

Theoretically, all the children of the state were entitled to have

---

*A copy of the adopted bylaw can be obtained from the Maryland Board of Education, Baltimore, Maryland.

the same educational advantages. In practice, this concept would not have been realized unless monies were equalized for school districts within states and for states within the nation. It was within this dilemma that the nation, states, and local education agencies grappled in funding programs for exceptional children.

R. L. Johns in 1972 stated two major threats to equalization opportunities: efforts on the part of wealthy school systems to retain their privileged funding positions and the advocacy of the use of public funds to support nonpublic schools. Should arguments persuade the adoption of these policies, it was stated, an elite society would be strongly supported despite America's claim to equalitarianism.[26]

There were three major trends in school finance which called for more or full state funding. These were as follows: growth in expenditures for schools, dissatisfaction with the local property tax as a means of financing education, and concern that there was no opportunity for many individual school districts within a state to equalize funding. Full state funding was advocated as an answer to greater equalization of educational opportunity with a greater equity for taxpayers and property tax relief.[27] Other critiques called for more federal funding as a way to meet the national commitment for full educational opportunity. The NEA stated the solution would be one-third federal funding of education.[28]

Education for "exceptional" children was stated as being more costly than programs for "regular" children. Expenditures differed due to the need for more specialized personnel, more personnel due to smaller class sizes, the need for ancillary personnel, special equipment, materials, facilities, and transportation. States and local education agencies were no longer able to use the excuse that there were no funds to supplement the regular funds to provide special education programs because the courts has decreed that money must be found without or within the regular

---

[26]R. L. Johns, "The Coming Revolution in School Finance," *Phi Delta Kappan*, 54 (September, 1972), pp. 18-22.

[27]Richard A. Rossmiller, "The Case for Full State Funding," *Today's Education*, 62 (April, 1973), pp. 30-32.

[28]NEA Government Relations, "The Case for More Federal Funding," *Today's Education*, 62 (April, 1973), pp. 35-36.

education budgets.

To offset the cost of educating exceptional children beyond the programs which local school systems could afford, various state fiscal support procedures were established across the nation. They were classified by Thomas into six categories: (a) unit, (b) weight, (c) percentage, (d) personnel, (e) straight sum or (f) excess cost. The "unit plan" basically reimbursed a local agency a fixed sum to cover expenses for such items as a unit of classroom instruction, administration, transportation, and facilities for special education programs. Units were usually limited to a specific number of pupils and the reimbursement amount seldom, if at any time, paid complete expenses. The "weighted formula plan" reimbursed local agencies for the regular per pupil expenditure allotted multiplied by a factor which sometimes varied with the disability. This system tended to treat all children with a similar disability as alike in needs and discouraged local agencies from initiating programs for disabilities requiring higher expenditure. The "percentage reimbursement plan" consisted of a formula or percent of all costs incurred by school districts in providing programs for handicapped children. This type of plan tempted school districts to place handicapped children in their least expensive program. The reimbursement for personnel gave local agencies assistance but encouraged larger class sizes to decrease per pupil expenditure and added incentive for special class placement in lieu of mainstreaming. In the "straight sum reimbursement plan," specific amounts of money were given local agencies for each handicapped child and usually varied according to the disability. This plan also discouraged mainstreaming and necessitated labeling of children. A formula for the "excess cost reimbursement plan" basically took the total district cost for educating a handicapped child, subtracted the district's cost for educating a regular child, and paid the difference. In some cases this plan was not fully funded and deterred districts from providing handicapped children a full range of services. All the plans contained weaknesses which advocates of exceptional children felt harmful.[29]

---

[29]Sister Marie Angele Thomas, "Finance: Without Which There Is No Special Education," *Exceptional Children*, 39 (March, 1973), pp. 475-478.

In respect to the above state fiscal reimbursement plans for educating exceptional children, Thomas stated that the following questions should be considered:[30]

1. How much visibility does special education have in the process of budget decisions at state and local levels? Is it buried in administrative line relationships to such an extent that the representation of exceptional children's financial realities to the total body politics is minimal?

2. What recourse do school districts have when allocations prorated to them for the state are delinquent or not forthcoming? What adjustment is made for accommodating either forward-funding (for unforeseen expansion programs) or payment at the close of the academic year (for meeting current expenses)? Since expenses during the first year of a newly initiated program are greater than those during succeeding years, what compensation is made for this?

3. Is the fiscal organization of regionalization — intermediate units, joint agreements, and cooperative administrative arrangements — structured so as not to preclude the relationship between special and general education or between local and state governments? Do problems such as ownership of property across districts with different tax rates or staff teaching in districts with incompatible salary schedules inhibit the development of programs for children with handicaps of low prevalence?

4. How adequately does the reimbursement formula support ancillary professional workers and noncertified personnel needed along the continuum of services for complete programming in the life span of handicapped children at the preschool, school, and postschool levels? At both ends of the spectrum, from care to sheltered workshops and adult vocational training, are persons with wide ranges of expertise added to the traditional list of faculty?

5. Since, in the light of the current mandate of zero reject, several facilities, agencies or organizations other than the

---

[30]*Ibid.*, p. 478.

public school system may be in a position to help supply certain aspects of handicapped children's needs, what manner of interagency planning in coordinating the flow of funds provides the prerequisites of comprehensive care services so children are not lost between the cracks or services are not needlessly duplicated?

6. When advancing the cause of general revenue sharing or block grants with the intention of reducing the network of categorical funding and allowing for greater flexibility of application, what mechanics are built in to assure that aid from general funds will actually reach the destination of handicapped children? How can the earmarking of funds be made compatible with the trend toward normalization and the interlocking nature of special education with regular education?

7. What allowances for individualized learning, computer-aided instruction, competency-based curricula, or alternative educational prescriptions are made in planning for the allocation of resources? Are such concepts as the special education contract between parents and educators, with specific goals and a clear time limit, used with the handicapped child?

8. Is the amount of state aid given to a school district dependent upon its local property tax effort? If this be the case, does wealth or a district determine the degree and the quality of intervention a handicapped child receives or whether he is given an education tailored to his needs at all?

9. Does the support system substantially include research and development, personnel training, demonstration activities and evaluation analysis? Does the cost effectiveness parameter consider, in addition to monetary benefits, other goals of human dignity, growth and development, self-fulfillment, and family happiness?

The early and mid-seventies were times when various financial plans for educating exceptional children were explored. The 1971 policy statement of the Council for Exceptional Children recommended that local school districts finance special education in an amount equal to that of nonhandicapped children with supplemental funds from state and federal agencies to cover the excess cost.

Pressures and needs of states for greater financial support promoted the ninety-third Congress to initiate in each house a bill to provide funds to assist in improving educational services for handicapped children. The Senate bill set the federal aid at 75 percent of the states' costs entailed in the educational expenditures for every handicapped pupil aged three to twenty-one years, which was in excess of the educational costs per nonhandicapped pupil aged five to seventeen years in public school. The House bill proposed that federal aid for the handicapped be $600 multiplied by the number of handicapped children in the state aged three to twenty-one plus 75 percent of the excess costs of the program beyond six hundred dollars per pupil. Hearings on both of these bills were held nationally. A joint conference convened to implement input from hearings and to reach common grounds between the Senate and House bills.[31]

The Senate bill was implicit in setting forth eligibility criteria. The following six points were considered essential:

1. The state law must indicate the right to education by all handicapped children.

2. All states must have all handicapped children receiving appropriate services in 1976.

3. All local education agencies must institute a "due process" procedure which involves parents in determining the educational program for their child.

4. States must make provision for special programs for all children.

5. States must implement testing procedures which do not discriminate against handicapped children.

6. Children must be placed in the least restricted environment possible in which to receive the educational program.[32]

---

[31]*Ibid.*, p. 479.
[32]Session 160, "What Is Happening In Washington?" 52nd Annual International Convention, The Council for Exceptional Children, New York City, April 19, 1974.

The Council for Exceptional Children (CEC) endorsed the concepts in both bills. They saw the federal government fulfilling two roles: guaranteeing the equal protection rights to the handicapped as required in the Constitution of the United States, and assisting the states in financing such an education. A major concern held by this organization was that the bill not require a backward step in labeling children but define the handicapped to identify for accounting purposes. The CEC also contended that any bill should begin the education of the handicapped at birth and focus attention on mainstreaming the handicapped; that is, placing the child in the least restrictive environment. The Council supported the idea that aid to the gifted should also be included in any legislation.

Though these bills for the handicapped were in committee for reclarification, there was another attempt to ensure funds for the handicapped. Senator Charles Mathias (R., Md.) proposed an amendment to S.1539 — The Education Amendments of 1974, ESEA. This amendment allotted each school district fifteen dollars for each child enrolled with the stipulation that this money be available only for use in programs for the handicapped. The amendment, providing approximately $630.8 million for the handicapped nationally, was overwhelmingly passed by the Senate but had to be considered in the joint House-Senate Conference. There was every indication that more federal funds for the handicapped would be forthcoming.[33] (See Appendix H for Summary of *The Education of All Handicapped Children Act.*)

FACILITIES FOR THE HANDICAPPED

There was a realization on the part of the public and their selected officials that close to 15 percent of the American population have some permanent physical disability. These handicapped citizens make a valuable contribution to society and represent a significant amount of participation in the economic stability of the nation. It was determined that, throughout the United States, architectural barriers hindered those who are dis-

[33]Larry N. Chamblin (Ed.), *Washington Watch,* Maryland State Department of Education, No. 32, May, 1974.

abled from becoming involved in the ordinary endeavors of education, employment, and recreation.

An example of this concern was reflected in the legislation enacted by the 1968 Maryland General Assembly. This act imposed certain architectural requirements in the construction of public buildings and those buildings constructed either on state land or with the participation of state and/or county, or other governmental funds. The provision also applied to all educational facilities constructed with public funds. The standards formulated included necessary information on the wheelchair from which architects could design necessary spaces; requirements for site development which included grading, walks, and parking spaces; and, specifics for consideration in buildings such as ramps, entrances, doors and doorways, stairs, floors, toilet rooms, water fountains, switches and controls, building identification, warning signals, avoidance of hazards, and spacing in assembly areas.[34]

The impact of the growth of special education classes for handicapped pupils produced innumerable problems and issues. One of the major problems that confronted administrators in the area of special education was the recruitment, selection, retention, and supervision of personnel.[35] Cruickshank and Johnson stated that this was one of the most difficult tasks facing the administrator because the worth of a special education program for exceptional children depended upon the quality of the classroom teacher.[36] The difficulty of obtaining qualified teachers was one of the greatest obstacles in local, county, or state programs for exceptional children.

According to figures obtained from state education agencies by the U. S. Office of Education, Bureau of Education for the Handicapped, six out of ten handicapped children should be, but were not, receiving special education. It was estimated that 10 percent

[34]*Regulations Governing Construction of Facilities for the Handicapped,* Department of Public Improvements, State of Maryland, 1968.

[35]James C. Chalfant and Robert A. Henderson, "Administration," in G. Orville Johnson and Harriet D. Blank (Eds.), *Exceptional Children Research Review* (Washington: The Council for Exceptional Children, 1968), p. 325.

[36]William M. Cruickshank and G. Orville Johnson (Eds.), *Exceptional Children and Youth* (New Jersey: Prentice-Hall, Incorporated, 1958), p. 656.

of the school age population of the nation, or more than 5,000,000 children were handicapped.[37] In reports published by the National Education Association in 1968 and 1969, special education teaching positions were listed as extremely difficult to fill with qualified personnel. Of the students graduated to teach special education, approximately 72 percent actually accepted special education teaching positions. The teachers constituted between 48 percent and 62 percent of the estimated number of teachers needed in special education.[38]

The states held, as their major function, the determination and accreditation of teacher training programs in the institutions of higher education and prescribing certification requirements for teachers in the area of special education. Both the philosophy of the times and the need for teachers had impact on this function. In the area of teacher training programs, there was involvement with competency-based special education teacher training, noncategorical special education teacher training, television instructional programs, training packages, teacher centers, and in-service teacher programs. Special education certification varied from state to state depending on the mode and/or need of programs within that state for the handicapped.

It appeared in the mid-seventies that a number of teacher training programs in special education were moving in the direction of a competency-based program. A major impetus for such activity was financial support from the U. S. Office of Education, Bureau of Education for the Handicapped. Shores, Cegelka, and Nelson reviewed such programs in 1973.[39] They concluded that the specific effects of teacher behavior on the performance of handicapped children were largely unknown. It was also stated that much work was yet needed in establishing, writing, measuring, and validating teacher competencies for training programs. The activity in this field was further stimulated in 1973 by mandated legislation for performance-based teacher education by the

[37]Edwin W. Martin, "Special Education: New Priority, New Money," *Nation's Schools*, 84 (October, 1969), pp. 57-58.
[38]National Teachers' Association, *Teacher Supply and Demand in Public Schools* (Washington, The Association, Research Report, 1967 and 1968).
[39]Shores, Cegelka and Nelson, *loc. cit.*

following ten states: Alabama, California, New York, North Carolina, Oregon, Pennsylvania, South Dakota, Texas, Vermont, and Washington.[40] The terms "performance" and "competency" appeared interchangeable. The institutions of higher education as well as state departments of education were in the midst of vast changes with specific need for a nationwide assessment of these types of programs.

Coinciding with competency-based teacher training programs was the special education concept of noncategorical training. This type of program emphasized that the majority of special education pupils were mildly handicapped and could profit most by being in the mainstream of regular education with supplementary services. These supplementary services required the need of a teacher with training to work with a variety of exceptionalities. The philosophy appeared widely endorsed by educators in the mid-seventies but difficult to translate into a practical and valid teacher education program. Though many states were moving toward a competency-based, noncategorical certification, the majority still awarded teaching certificates on a categorical basis. It appeared that certain content and instructional procedures were specific to some disability areas, especially where severe degrees of handicap existed. Any attempt to completely eliminate categorical certification programs was deemed unwise by some on the basis of the need to develop and validate such programs without reducing the quality presently found in categorical programs.[41] There was an apparent need for better communication between state departments of education, institutions of higher education and local education agencies on determining needs and verifying training methods.

Other methods considered and developed during this period were instructional television, teacher training packages, and protocol materials. Various states developed instructional television series to meet the needs of local education agencies. These series were allotted college credits by institutions of higher education.

---

[40]Alfred P. Wilson and William W. Curtis, "The States Mandate Performance Based Teacher Education," *Phi Delta Kappan*, 55 (September, 1973), p. 73.
[41]A. Edward Blackhurst, et al., "Approximating Noncategorical Teacher Education," *Exceptional Children*, 39 (January, 1973), pp. 284-285.

The instruction was usually via television with opportunity for group encounters under the guidance of a special education expert. For improving or perfecting specific skills in teaching, training packages were developed. The training package was basically conceived as a self-contained instructional unit which contained all the necessary directions and materials. Training teachers to observe, pinpoint, and remediate errors in a specific skill area was illustrative of this approach. Protocol materials were developed as another approach to helping train teachers, enabling them to study behavior that was educationally significant. Concepts and cognitions gained served as a basis for classroom teaching interpretation and decisionmaking. (See Appendix A, "Development of Protocol Materials.")

EDUCATIONAL DEVELOPMENT CENTER

The concept of an Educational Development Center in special education was utilized in the mid-seventies by the State of Maryland. The Board of Education of Baltimore County, Maryland, Department of Personnel and Office of Special Education, developed a project under the Education Professions Development Act to secure and train critically needed special education teachers. The project, initially local, developed into a state program in a four-year span. The main thrust of the program was to provide preservice and in-service training through a blend of theory and practice. A ten-minute colored film "Teach Me" was developed by Hallmark Films of Baltimore to depict the center. The basic organization of the concept is shown on the following page.

TEACHER CERTIFICATION

Certification was an area that had to be coordinated with teacher preparation in the states. Reger, Schroeder, and Uschold in their 1968 review of teacher certification, stated that the teacher certification process was arbitrary and often led to ridiculous contradictions. They commented that the general rules made for the benefit of the group often made individuals with unique talents or backgrounds suffer. There was agreement that guidelines were needed for selecting teachers. Reger, Schroeder, and

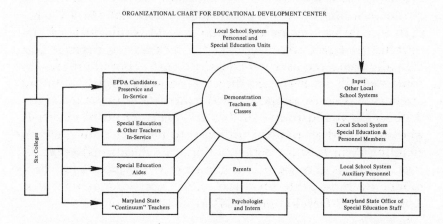

ORGANIZATIONAL CHART FOR EDUCATIONAL DEVELOPMENT CENTER

Figure X-2. This schematic of the Educational Development Center shows the general organization utilized in this teacher training project. A specialist in staff development, under the Coordinator of Special Education and the Director of Personnel, developed the center. Input was obtained from staff members of the Baltimore County Office of Special Education, Department of Personnel, as well as from participating colleges, other local school systems, and the Maryland State Department of Education.

The focal point of the center was the twenty-two classes of pupils and their demonstration teachers working as a school unit. Involved in this focal point were the staff members of the local Special Education office, local auxiliary personnel, and the staff of the Maryland State Office of Special Education. Parents of these children were also included in a program under a psychologist and intern.

Education Professions Development Act candidates, special education teachers, regular teachers, special education aides, and teachers of the State of Maryland Special Education "Continuum" Program were all trainees who received preservice and in-service training at the center through an intricate combination of theory and practice. This was coordinated through the school unit and local colleges during a four to six-week period.

Uschold concluded that only two kinds of special education certificates should be granted: elementary and secondary.[42]

In the 1960's, according to Robinson and Robinson, state requirements for certification of special education teachers ranged from eight hours of special education course work in New Mexico to thirty-six hours in Florida. An average of eighteen hours of special education credits were necessary for certification in most states. This amounted to approximately one semester of special training.[43] The diversity of special education programs and the need for teachers in the mid-seventies broadened the range of the various state requirements for certification. The trend in certain situations appeared to be in training regular school teachers to instruct the mildly handicapped children in regular classrooms.[44]

The state had an enormous task in viewing the total picture of special education, not only within its geographical boundaries but also throughout the entire United States. There was little doubt that the events in other states would have a direct relationship within one's own state. More than ever, leadership from the state departments of education was a major factor in meeting the needs of handicapped children.

LOCAL ROLE IN SPECIAL EDUCATION

Throughout the history of education in the United States, the concept of local control was traditional. Dating back to the early New England pattern of educational organization, the local agency assumed basic responsibility for implementing a school program. There were differences with regard to elementary and secondary education programs as reflected by each local education agency's perception of their needs. Despite the many thousands of local education agencies and their differences, a commonality prevailed across the nation in education.

This book has attempted to acquaint the reader with a

---

[42]Roger Reger, Wendy Schroeder and Kathie Uschold, *Special Education Children with Learning Problems* (New York: Oxford University Press, 1968), pp. 46-47.

[43]Robinson and Robinson, *op. cit.*, p. 460.

[44]Raymond M. Glass and Roy S. Meckler, "Preparing Elementary Teachers To Instruct Mildly Handicapped Children in Regular Classrooms," *Exceptional Children*, 39 (October, 1972), pp. 152-156.

thorough overview of the basic premises for educating exceptional individuals with clear specifics for implementing strategies of teaching. It was the implementation and the development of these strategies that most concerned and involved local school districts. Educators embraced the concept of individualized education as the most proficient means of meeting the needs of exceptional individuals. Literally thousands of schools in America utilized some method of individualized instruction: programmed instruction; computer-assisted education; diagnostic, clinical, and prescriptive teaching; learning stations and centers; instruction through media technology; discovery-learning techniques; perceptual remediation, training packages, and open education. These were only a partial listing of instructional methods or procedures implemented in the mid-seventies.

Continuum of Special Education Services

Many local education agencies initiated on their own, or in conjunction with their state office of special education, a design for a continuum of special education services. The continuum design stressed the concept that special education was a part of the total school program rather than a distinct entity. The major concept of the continuum was to provide an educational program for every child in an environment that was the least prohibiting. The majority of children entering school came into the continuum at the base level, regular education; as handicaps or specific needs of the child demanded more specific attention or programs, the child moved upward from the base. Shown here is a diagram of continuum design implemented by the Montgomery County Public Schools, Maryland.

In the Montgomery County conceptual model, the "Continuum of Educational Services," there was an indication that as the pupils' severity of problems increased the population of that group decreased. The majority of the school age population was served in the regular school program.

The Maryland State Department of Education, Office of Special Education, promoted a similar continuum of special education services. The following were listed by that office in their 1972

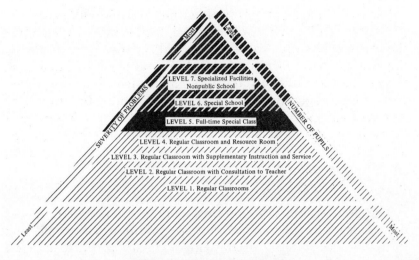

CONTINUUM OF EDUCATIONAL SERVICES

Figure X-3.

brochure *Prescription for Special Education.*

Program I — Consultant Services

Prevention, early identification, and intervention of actual or potential problems which may interfere with learning and adjustment are the primary objectives of this program. Psychologists, pupil personnel workers, nurses, and guidance counselors provide consultative services to parents, teachers, and pupils before the problem becomes a major handicap.

Program II — Diagnostic Prescriptive Services

Children exhibiting a learning problem are referred to the diagnostic/prescriptive teacher for an educational assessment. An educational prescription is developed based on the child's learning profile and appropriate placement is determined in cooperation with other professionals. The diagnostic/prescriptive teacher interprets the learning profile, suggests methodology, prepares and demonstrates materials to be used in the remedial process, and provides continuous follow-up and supportive services.

Program III — Itinerant Services

Included in this program are group and individual services provided to children by itinerant specialists. While they remain in the regular classroom to receive the bulk of their education with the rest of their peers, those children with visual handicaps, speech, hearing, and/or language impairments may receive services such as special instruction, therapy, and counseling. The itinerant specialist serves as a consultant to the teachers in other continuum programs and demonstrates appropriate materials and techniques used in working with children having vision, speech, hearing, and/or language handicaps.

Program IV — Cooperative Services

The child assigned to a resource room spends part of the school day in the resource room receiving special tutorial assistance and the remainder of the day in the regular classroom. He remains on this schedule until the problem is minimized and is then returned full-time to the regular classroom. If progress is not evident, the child is referred back to the diagnostic/prescriptive teaching program (Program II) for reevaluation.

Program V — Special Class Services

Special education classes in the public schools.

Program VI — Nonpublic Special Day Classes

Nonpublic special day classes and home-hospital teaching programs.

Program VII — Residential Services

These three continuum programs (V, VI, and VII) provide for educational programs and services for severely handicapped children who require major modifications in curriculum which cannot be accommodated for even a portion of the day in the regular classroom.

The Maryland continuum design provided for the maintenance of children with mild to moderate handicaps in the mainstream of education rather than in segregated, self-contained special education classes. Increased articulation was encouraged between professional personnel in the regular and special education programs. The focus was on educational programming toward individual learning strengths rather than a categorical label by handicap. Local school systems were provided financial incentive to initiate such a model. Regardless of the state department's guidance, the responsibility to implement programs rested with the local agencies. Many aspects of the continuum are aimed toward total integration of exceptional individuals. A first step in eliminating the negative effects of labels, therefore, is being made by the Maryland State Department of Education in providing equal educational opportunities for the exceptional.

Career Education

Through a comprehensive program of career education, many local education agencies enabled children with special needs to recognize that the ability to earn a livelihood for themselves and for their families was an important requirement of good citizenship. The Council for Exceptional Children selected for publication six exemplary programs in career education for the handicapped.[45] The six programs were as follows:

The Career Development Center, Syosset, New York.

Students, aged fifteen to twenty-one, who had difficulty adjusting to local public schools were offered a transitional program of study aimed at individual needs. In an open campus setting, under careful guidance and through personal contact, students participated in occupational and academic learning activities.

The Mobile Unit for Vocational Evaluation, Towson, Maryland.

Tenth grade special education students in fifteen Baltimore County high schools had their career potential and work behavior assessed. A mobile unit traveled from school to school spending a one-week period testing and evaluating students. Parents, teachers, and counselors shared results with the students to gain a better understanding of the students'

[45]Thomas P. Lake, (Ed.), *Career Education: Exemplary Programs for the Handicapped* (Virginia: Th Council for Exceptional Children, 1974).

potential in the world of work.

Project Serve, St. Paul, Minnesota.

Serving educable mentally retarded students in Grades ten through twelve, Project Serve personnel worked in special high school classrooms to carry out individualized programs in vocational education. Students were scheduled for a half-day of class work and a half-day of work in the community.

Project Worker, Fullerton, California.

The teenaged handicapped job seeker was prepared by Project Worker with the job entry skills needed to enter employment in the community. Extensive use of videotape was used for preemployment instruction as well as on-the-job performance evaluation.

The Technical Vocational Program for Deaf Students, St. Paul, Minnesota.

This project was a postsecondary training program demonstrating the feasibility of using an existing school serving hearing students to train deaf students. Deaf students were helped to pursue advanced vocational training. Supportive services such as counseling, interpreting, and auditory training helped students integrate.

Vocational Village, Portland, Oregon.

Vocational Village was, for most of its students, the last opportunity to overcome a life pattern of chronic failure and underachievement. Young people aged fourteen through twenty-one, learned to understand their worth as individuals through an interdisciplinary curriculum that was basic and career oriented.

Other school systems across the country established policies and procedures for developing community-centered work experience programs for individuals with special needs. These programs were designed to identify areas that needed thorough investigation. Based upon results, programs were developed in order to provide students and employers with a meaningful work experience. The Community-Centered Work Experience Program provided a transition for the student from the school and classroom to the world of work. Proper experiences were needed to enable the students to master work skills and habits essential to the job. Opportunities were presented to the student for evaluating his work potential, interests, abilities, and limitations. Vocational evaluation was considered essential before a student was scheduled for the Community-Centered Work Experience Program. The school system usually employed a job development coordinator to work closely with the employer, the student, and the teacher to ensure that proper relationships and responsibilities were assumed.

Early Intervention

Local school districts, through their own initiative and help from federal funding, experimented with and implemented various programs aimed at early identification and correction of children with learning disabilities. Such programs identified students prior to their usual school entrance date and provided an introductory year to schooling. The teaching strategy was an attempt to answer the full range of children's developmental needs by breaking down each task to ensure that all children were able to achieve success. Free periods were interspersed between structured sessions to encourage the development of independence. Programs involving severely handicapped children, such as the deaf, began educational instruction with the parents and child as soon after birth as the handicapping condition was diagnosed. The general concept that early identification is an important component to a child's future was endorsed nationally.

Referral and Placement Procedures

A major task of local education agencies was to establish policies and procedures for the referral and placement of exceptional children in proper educational programs. This area of responsibility assumed on the local level was one of the most contested by parents in the courts. Most school systems organized their policies to include the following types of procedures: initial referral, written referral, psychological evaluation, screening, placement, and review committee.

The initial referral was usually centered around the observation of a student's problem by his parents, teacher, school administrator, counselor, or nurse. Observation indicated that the situation involved a learning problem, a physical problem, or both. The initial response called for a thorough check of the child's records — health records, as well as school cumulative files. Identification of a problem required a conference with parents to discuss possible ramifications for intervention. A thorough physical examination included a vision and hearing test. Any physical problems found were corrected to their best level, and the child was again observed for his educational progress.

Continuous learning problems due to physical conditions and/or unknown causes were further discussed by the school team consisting of the teacher, counselor, administrator, and other school personnel such as the psychologist, pupil personnel worker, and nurse. If the team concluded that the child might be exceptional and needed services not offered totally in the regular school program, the parents were again contacted. Upon parental agreement, a written referral was initiated at the school level requesting that a full psychological examination be administered to the child.

The psychological evaluation was done in conjunction with a special history prepared by the pupil personnel worker. After the reports of the clinical psychologist and pupil personnel worker were received by the school administrator, another conference was held by the school team. The parents were then informed of the existing conditions, accompanied by the team recommendation. If it were thought that the child needed special services, and the parents consented, the child was referred to the Central Office Screening Committee of the school system.

The screening was accomplished by a group of experts through the Office of Special Education. These experts included supervisors specialized in various areas of exceptionalities, as well as other adjunct personnel employed by the local board of education. The child's records were carefully examined to see first that all steps in the referral procedure had been followed and completed. The various experts and consultants then determined the needs of the child and how the child could best be served. Placement depended on the severity of the handicapping condition, availability of the program, and location of the program. In some cases, the child only needed itinerant services or minor changes in his regular school program. Whether special class placement or some other service (or no special service) was determined by the screening committee, the principal was sent a report. The principal held a conference with the parents, and if special services were decided upon, the parents signed an agreement to that effect. (Some states required parent notification and conferences for any change in a child's program not consistent with the regular school program. Parents were advised of their rights to hearings and procedures for appealing school decisions.)

The school administrator followed up the screening committee's recommendations. If special placement was deemed best to help the child, all arrangements, including any necessary transportation, were made at the appropriate time. The parents were informed and kept posted of these arrangements.

A major component of the referral and placement procedure was the review committee. This committee was usually established within the individual school district. As soon as the child was able to apply himself in any part of the regular school program, arrangements were made to transfer him. To preclude students being placed in a "one-track" special education program, periodical retesting and evaluating were done every several years. All efforts were put forth to determine where each child could best obtain an educational program that would permit him to perform at his optimal level.

PARENT INVOLVEMENT

In the area of special education, the involvement of parents with the school district is an essential need. It is felt that programs for exceptional individuals could be substantially improved when parents are meaningfully involved. The task of the professionals is to continuously seek new and improved ways of involving parents in the educational program.

A good parental program is based on a recognition of individual differences among them and the provision of activities to meet their individual needs. The attitudes of teachers toward parents are prime determinants of the success of the program. The teacher has to convey a feeling of faith in the parent to acquire improved skills in working with his exceptional child.[46]

In some schools, special media presentations and training packages are developed to enable the parent to better understand and work with his child. These packages may be story books, slide presentations, 8mm. films, cassette tapes, videotapes, 16mm. films, games, posters and many other means to interpret the school's program. Parents are able to select those areas of need, and view, listen, or read them at school or at home. This type of procedure will provide an unlimited opportunity for parents to: (1) continue to support the school's efforts in educating their children, and (2) obtain a better understanding of the school's goals and objectives for their children.

CONCLUSION

The mid-seventies were times for cooperative efforts in the field of special education. There was an improved relationship between federal, state, local education agencies, and organizations. The various roles of these agencies and organizations on the different levels did not change as much as the conditions of the services rendered.

The major thrust appeared to be a recognition that special education was a part of a total school program which enabled all individuals to be given appropriate educational services. The laws, the courts, and the attorney generals' opinions combined to necessitate that funding and programs be coordinated on and among federal, state, and local levels. The predominant philosophy of that time encouraged that children should be taught in the least restrictive environment possible. Early identification and programming for children with special needs were deemed essential.

---

[46]Merle B. Karnes and R. Reid Zehrbach, "Flexibility in Getting Parents Involved in the Schools," *Teaching Exceptional Children*, 5 (Fall, 1972), pp. 6-19.

The people of the United States embarked upon a new concept of education: "education of ALL children." There is every indication that this concept is not just a verbal commitment but one of action. Agencies and organizations on the federal, state, and local levels are at work to establish a foundation for implementing this philosophy to its fullest meaning.

A new classification system is needed by states and local school districts which does not stigmatize the exceptional, and it is recommended that this proposed system be employed in developing new budget formulas to fund special education programs. Positive attempts can be seen on the parts of the federal, state, and local governments to adapt the principles set forth in this volume.

REFERENCES

Abeson, Alan: Movement and Momentum: Government and the Education of Handicapped Children. *Exceptional Children, 39:*63-66, 1972.

Abeson, Alan: State-Federal Information Clearinghouse for Exceptional Children. The Council for Exceptional Children, brochure, 1974.

Anderson, B. R.: Mainstreaming Is The Name for A New Idea. *School Management,* pp. 28-30, 1973.

Anderson, Robert N., Hemenway, Robert E., and Anderson, Janet W.: *Instructional Resources for Teachers of the Culturally Disadvantaged and Exceptional.* Springfield, Thomas, 1969.

Aspy, David: *Toward A Technology For Humanizing Education.* Illinois, Research, 1972.

Ausbel, D. P.: *Theory and Problems of Child Development.* New York, Grune, 1970.

Banathy, Bela H.: *Instructional Systems.* Belmont, Fearson, 1968.

Bayley, N.: The Development of Motor Abilities During the First Three Years. *Monograph of Society for Research in Child Development, 1:*1-26, 1935.

Blackhurst, A. Edward, Cross, Donald P., Nelson, C. Michael, and Tawney, James W.: Approximating Noncategorical Teacher Education. *Exceptional Children, 40:*284-285, 1973.

Bradfield, R. H.: Special Child in the Regular Classroom. *Exceptional Children, 40:*384-390, 1973.

Bruininks, R. H.: Social Acceptance of Mildly Retarded Pupils In Resource Rooms and Regular Classes. *American Journal of Mental Deficiency, 78:*377-383, 1974.

Bruner, J. S.: The Course of Cognitive Growth. *American Psychologist, 19:*1-15, 1964.

Bureau of Education for the Handicapped: *Better Education for the Handicapped.* Annual Reports FY 1968 and FY 1969. Washington, D. C., p. 4, 1969; p. 4, 1970.

Budoff, M.: Providing Special Education Without Special Classes. *Journal of School Psychology,* pp. 199-205, 1972.

Bush, Robert N., and Allen, Dwight W.: *A New Design for High School Education Assuming A Flexible Schedule.* New York, McGraw, 1964.

Cameron, S.: Move To Integrate the Handicapped. *Times Educational Supplement,* p. 10, January 26, 1973.

Christopherson, J.: Special Child in the Regular Preschool: Some Administrative Notes. *Childhood Education,* pp. 138-140, December, 1972.

Christoplos, F.: Keeping Exceptional Children in Regular Classes. *Exceptional Children, 39:*569-572, 1973.

Claiborn, W. L.: Expectancy Effects In the Classroom: A Failure to Replicate. *Journal of Educational Psychology, 60:*377-383, 1969.

Coleman, J.: The Children Have Outgrown the Schools. *Psychology Today, 5:*72-75, 82, 1972.

Cormany, R. B.: Returning Special Education Students to Regular Classes. *Personnel and Guidance Journal,* pp. 641-646, April, 1970.

Council for Exceptional Children: Proposed CEC Policy Statement on the Organization and Administration of Special Education. *Exceptional Children, 39:*493-497, 1973.

Cresswell, D.: Integration Is A Two-Way Street. *Education In Canada,* pp. 4-7, September, 1973.

Cronbach, Lee J.: How Can Instruction Be Adapted To Individual Differences? In Gagne, R. (Ed.), *Learning and Individual Differences.* Columbus, Merrill, pp. 23-39, 1967.

Delacato, Carl H.: *Neurological Organization and Reading Problems.* Springfield, Thomas, 1966.

Dinger, Jack C.: President's Page. *Exceptional Children, 40:*469-471, 1974.

Erikson, E.: *Childhood and Society.* New York, Norton, 1963.

Exceptional Children/Regular Classroom. *Instructor, 39:*94-99, 1972.

Farina, A., Allen, J., and Saul, B. B.: The Role of the Stigmatized Person In Affecting Social Relationships. *Journal of Personality, 36:*169-182, 1963.

Fernald, G. M.: *Remedial Techniques In Basic School Subjects.* New York, McGraw, 1943.

Flanders, N. A.: *Teacher Influence, Pupil Attitudes and Achievement.* U. S. Department of Health, Education, and Welfare, Cooperative Research Monograph No. 12, Washington, D. C., 1966.

Gallagher, J. J.: The Future Special Education System. In Meyen (Ed.), *The Missouri Conference on the Categorical/Non-Categorical Issue in Special Education,* University of Missouri, 1971.

Goodman, H., Gottlieb, J., and Harrison, R.: Social Acceptance of EMR's Integration into A Nongraded Elementary School. *American Journal of Mental Deficiency, 76:*412-417, 1972.

Gottlieb, J. and Budoff, M.: Social Acceptability of Retarded Children In Nongraded Schools Differing in Architecture. *American Journal of Mental Deficiency,* 78:15-19, 1973.

Grosvenor-Myer, V.: Ordinary Schools Will Have One Million ESN Children by 1972. *Times Educational Supplement,* p. 10, June 26, 1970.

Hartman, R. K. and Rockhold, A. E.: Case Studies in the Resource Room Approach. *The Journal for Special Educators of the Mentally Retarded,* 9:108-115, 1973.

Harvey, J.: To Fix or To Cope: A Dilemma for Special Education. *Journal of Special Education, 3:*389-392, 1969.

Hill, B.: Over Half the Handicapped Attend Ordinary Schools. *Times Educational Supplement,* p. 5, August 13, 1971.

Hill, F.: Slow Progress in Moves to Integrate the Handicapped. *Times Educational Supplement*, p. 6, July 27, 1973.

Iano, R. P.: Sociometric Status of Retarded Children in an Integrative Program. *Exceptional Children, 40:*267-271, 1974.

Jenkins, J. R.: Another Look at Isolation Effects. *American Journal of Mental Deficiency, 76;*591-593, 1972.

Jones, R. L.: *Problems and Issues in the Education of Exceptional Children.* Boston, Houghton, 1971.

Jones, R. L.: *New Directions in Special Education.* Boston, Allyn, 1970.

Kidd, J. W.: Toward A More Precise Definition of Mental Retardation. *Mental Retardation, 2:*209-212, 1964.

Lake, Thomas P. (Ed.): *Career Education: Exemplary Programs for the Handicapped.* Virginia, The Council for Exceptional Children, 1974.

Lerner, J. W.: *Children with Learning Disabilities: Theories, Diagnoses and Teaching Strategies.* Boston, Houghton, 1971.

Martmer, Edgar E. (Ed.): *The Child With A Handicap.* Springfield, Thomas, 1959.

Maryland: *Regulations Governing Construction of Facilities for the Handicapped.* 1968.

Monroe, J. D. and Howe, C. E.: Effects of Integration and Social Class on the Acceptance of Retarded Adolescents. *Education and Training of the Mentally Retarded,* pp. 20-24, February, 1971.

Morphet, Edgar L., Johns, Roe L., and Reller, Theodore L.: *Educational Organization and Administration,* 2nd ed., Englewood Cliffs, Prentice-Hall, 1967.

McIntyre, B. M., and McWilliams, B. J.: Creative Dramatics in Speech Correction. *Journal of Speech and Hearing Disorders, 24:*227-230, 1959.

Meyen, E. L.: *Developing Units of Instruction for the Mentally Retarded and Other Children with Learning Problems.* Dubuque, Wm. C. Brown, 1972.

Meyerowitz, J. H.: Self-Derogation in Young Retardates and Special Class Placement. *Child Development, 33:*443-451, 1962.

Meyerson, L. and Michael, J. L.: *The Measurement of Sensory Thresholds In Exceptional Children.* Houston, U of Houston, 1960.

National Society for the Study of Education. C. Thorensen (Ed.): *Behavior Modification in Education.* Chicago, U of Chicago Pr, 1972.

Neisworth, J. L.: *Student Motivation and Classroom Management.* Lemont, Behavior Tech, 1973.

O'Leary, K. D., and O'Leary, S. G.: *Class Management: The Successful Use of Behavior Modification.* New York, Pergamon, 1972.

Olsen, H. C.: *The Teaching Clinic: A Team Approach to Improve Teaching.* Washington, D. C., NEA, 1971.

Payne, S.: Where Handicapped Mix With the Rest. *Times Educational Supplement,* p. 1712, May 23, 1969.

Peter, L.: *Prescriptive Teaching.* New York, McGraw, 1967.

Paiget, J.: *The Psychology of Intelligence.* New York, HarBrace J, 1950.

Paiget, J., and Inhelder, B.: *The Psychology of the Child.* New York, Basic, 1969.

Quay, H. C., Morse, W. C., and Cutler, R. L.: Personality Patterns of Pupils In Special Classes for the Emotionally Disturbed. *Exceptional Children, 32:*297-301, 1966.

Rapport, Virginia: *Learning Centers: Children On Their Own.* Washington, D. C., International Association for Children's Education, 1970.

Reger, Roger: What Is A Resource Room Program? *Journal of Learning Disabilities,* pp. 609-613, December, 1973.

Rubington, E., and Weinberg, M.: *Deviances: An Interactionist Perspective.* New York, Macmillan, 1968.

Sawrey, G. M., and Telford, C. W.: *Psychology of Adjustment.* Boston, Allyn, 1967.

Schmidt, B. G.: Changes In Personal, Social and Intellectual Behavior of Children Originally Classified As Feeble-Minded. *Psychological Monograph, 60,* 5:1-14.

Shotel, J. R.: Teacher Attitudes Associated with the Integration of Handicapped Children. *Exceptional Children, 38:*677-683, 1972.

Skinner, B. F.: *Science and Human Behavior.* New York, Macmillan, 1953.

Smith, W. L.: Ending the Isolation of the Handicapped. *American Education,* pp. 29-33, November 1971.

Smith, R. M.: *Teaching Diagnosis of Educational Difficulties.* Columbus, Merrill, 1969.

Stephens, J. M.: *The Psychology of Classroom Learning.* New York, HR & W, 1965.

Taylor, G. R.: Special Education at the Crossroad: Class Placement for the EMR. *Mental Retardation, 11:*30-33, 1973.

Taylor, G. R.: The Radio: An Experiment In Communication Skills. AV Guide — *The Learning Media Magazine, 51:*12-15, 1972.

Thurstone, T. G.: *An Evaluation of Educating Mentally Handicapped Children In Special Classes and In Regular Grades.* U. S. Office of Education Cooperative Research Program, University of North Carolina, 1960.

Vallett, R. E.: *Modifying Children's Behavior: A Guide for Parents and Professionals.* Belmont, Fearson, 1969.

Vallett, R. E.: *Effective Teaching: A Guide to Diagnostic Prescriptive Task Analysis.* Belmont, Fearson, 1970.

Vogel, A. L.: Integration of Nine Severe Learning-Disabled Children in Junior High School Core Program. *Academic Therapy,* pp. 99-104, Fall, 1973.

Weininger, O.: Integrate or Isolate: A Perspective on the Whole Child. *Education,* pp. 139-146, November, 1973.

Wiegerink, R.: Organizational Model for Preparing Future Special Educators. *Journal of Special Education, 10:*135-139, 1972.

Wolfensberger, W.: *The Principles of Normalization In Human Services.* Toronto, Natl Inst Mental Retard, 1972.

DEVELOPMENT OF
PROTOCOL MATERIALS*

STAFF development in teacher education, both pre-service and in-service, has become a prime necessity in our swiftly technologically changing environment. Frequent demands are being made of teachers to change curricula for relevancy, reorganize for vertical or horizontal administrative programs, and utilize specialized new or experimental skills that will individualize instruction. The dissemination of successful practices, skills, or situations for developing cognitions has been, and remains, a difficult process.

In the majority of school systems, the on-site observation of the classroom continues as a prime source of communication to educators. This procedure has proven to be time consuming, costly, a gamble on seeing the desired situation, and dubious as to transferred learnings. There is a need to fix situations which either portray desired skill procedures or significant behavior for cognitive development.

B. Othanel Smith and others in the book *Teachers for the Real World* clearly distinguish the terms: training materials and protocol materials. Basically, training materials provide for the identification of skills, give a description of situations to be practiced, show or describe the performance the skills entail, and are often available to give the performer feedback. Protocol materials enable the teacher to study behavior that is educationally significant. Concepts and cognitions as an outgrowth of the study of this behavior can serve as the basis for interpretation and decision making. Film or videotape, as well as other visual, auditory, or printed materials, may be used as media for preserving training and/or protocol materials.

Under the Education Professions Development Act, and other

---

*Paul J. Arend, Ed.D., Associate Professor, Coppin State College, Baltimore, Maryland.

funding, the Board of Education of Baltimore County has had several experiences in developing both training and protocol materials. The basic medium for this material has been videotape.

FIRST EXPERIENCE

The first experience involved a period of four-week half-day sessions during the summer of 1971. The teacher-training program involved approximately 169 participants working with fifteen special education classes. The major medium for reproducing training and protocol materials was videotape. Specific kinds of lessons were taught as "The Use of Concrete Materials" and "Stimulation Experiences in Problem Thinking." In these situations, the demonstration teachers were videotaped while teaching a specific subject area, concept, and/or skill. In addition, teachers in training were taped while teaching. All materials taped in the mornings within the regular classrooms were critiqued and employed in afternoon college course work sessions. Coordinating sessions were also held with college personnel, demonstration teachers, and administrators for designing day-by-day, videotape needs for the college courses.

The materials developed on specific subject areas, concepts, and/or skills were used in the school system the following school year by helping teachers. These materials provided quick assessment, through the means of videotape, to meet the needs of particular teachers in the field. In general, these tapes were broad presentations. The best approach for their use was in having the classroom teacher view and analyze the situations that had been taped with the helping teacher.

In conjunction with this taping, a thirty-minute videotape was edited to show the many facets of the training program coordinated at the center. The tape was later reproduced as a film to better facilitate dissemination of the procedures and content of the teacher-training center.

THE STUDIO APPROACH

The following summer, plans called for the development of an educational center almost three times as large as the previous one with three different programs. This necessitated another approach to overcome technological problems and yet provide the situation with renewed vigor and thought for the development of training and protocol materials. The Educational Development Center involved approximately 400 participants over a period of four to six weeks, offered more than twenty college courses, a host of supportive staff, a curriculum implementation program, and a statewide in-service program for developing a new philosophical approach with special education children. These preservice and in-service programs for special education teachers were coordinated with twenty-one classes of pupils, kindergarten through junior high school.

The need was to accommodate teachers in training to view educationally significant pupil behavior, view master teachers in action, and videotape (for evaluation) a variety of techniques and new procedures. There was also a need to interpret the entire center as a whole and its use for teacher training.

A studio approach was used for the accomplishment of the majority of these objectives. This approach overcame the majority of technological problems of equipment movement, sound control, lighting control, and time consumed in moving from one classroom to the next and setting up the equipment. Teachers brought their pupils to the studio and taught lessons of their choice. The prime purpose was to permit others to observe the behavior of these special education pupils. From the behavior seen, college classes could discuss the best psychoeducational approach for reaching a particular child or group of children. The approach could be tried, taped, and critiqued as to the degree of success achieved.

The large number of observations necessary to provide a better theory-practice situation was accomplished through closed circuit television. In this situation, teachers taught the pupils in their own classrooms while their cohorts observed via TV. Later the videotapes could be replayed for the college class and permitted candid discussions without any impositions to the pupils. This also helped to alleviate an excessive number of teachers observing in one classroom at any one time.

Master teachers were scheduled to be taped on a regular basis. This permitted each class to be viewed over the entire period of its program. It was anticipated that changes in pupil behavior would be noticeable under this situation. As videotapes were made, a list of them was compiled for dissemination throughout the center. The list included the kind of special education class taped, a statement on the lesson content, the teacher, the videotape number, and the program number. In addition, a format was developed to explain each lesson that could be used at a later date with other teachers.

The training concept of the Educational Development Center was portrayed through a ten-minute professionally produced 16mm. color film. The film, "Teach Me," presented all the various facets of the center. Concentration was given to the center's organization and philosophy. The film was used to motivate change by the Maryland State Department of Education, Board of Education of Baltimore County, and colleges throughout the United States.

"RUN-ON" DEVELOPMENT

Another model for the development of protocol and training materials was begun in the summer of 1972 at the Educational Development Center and carried throughout the 1972-73 school year. This was in the special education area containing children with Behavior and Learning Problems.

The development of these materials began at the center with a curriculum implementation program involving more than twenty-five teachers and ancillary staff members, and six classes of pupils who had behavior and learning problems. Videotapes were made in the mornings in various classrooms and utilized during the afternoon seminars in critiquing a self-analysis of both verbal and nonverbal behaviors communicated to these children. The supervisor also demonstrated with pupils the specific approaches which teachers might use for diagnostic/prescriptive techniques in the educational assessment of these children. The taped pupil behavior became a prime tool in the project. Teachers were able to observe the characteristics of children having neurologic-psychiatric problems and to observe the educational approaches which could be taken in teaching these children. Both group and individualized pupil programming was viewed.

This program was taped throughout a five-week period basically as a "run-on" type. That is, the camera "ran on" the pupils as an observer of their actions and that of their teachers. After their initial use in the afternoon seminar sessions, and during the 1972-73 school year, the tapes were to be edited and added to for the creation of an overall view of the program and particular specifics which could be utilized by teachers presently within the system and by those educators who might need orientation to the program.

SUMMARY AND CONCLUSIONS

These experiences in the development of training and protocol materials in the area of special education have been invaluable and have some specific implications for school systems. They supplied supplementary training as aids and appeared to have contributed significantly to understandings of the teachers in training. Their future value, however, under the present school setting is problematic.

The development of these materials was only one goal of many, and of a lesser priority in the Educational Development Center. The use of these materials were basically only temporal. The experiences encountered with developing training and protocol materials lead to the evaluation that this area of education is too important to see as only another goal of some other project.

Administrative and organizational procedures need to be established for the development of such materials. This goal should be the major objective of some one individual staff member. Prior to this development, a committee is needed to explore this area, and write the philosophy, goals, and specific objectives for the use of such materials in the school system. A flow chart of the administrative and organizational plan developed would be conducive for a clear understanding of the procedures. The general mechanics of how and who will carry out the dissemination of such materials should also be included in the flow chart. Necessary equipment and other technological considerations should be discussed with knowledgeable media specialists and planned well in advance of need.

Some general considerations which were concluded through the above experiences are as follows.

1. Videotapes of pupil and teacher behaviors may best be acquired by working with them in their own classroom. Despite the technological problems, the outcomes are superior to those tapes produced through the studio approach.

2. The specific behavior desired should be planned well in advance. It may or may not be extemporaneous.

3. Short, ten to fifteen-minute tapes, are of most use and value. Longer or drawn out episodes tend to lose their significance in the taping as well as in the usage.

4. The run-on type of videotaping program can produce excess amounts of tapes that become a paramount task to edit. This procedure also is most costly and takes a chance on obtaining desired materials.

5. Editing videotapes and working over a complete school year to produce a view of one program may dissolve itself in interest, usage, and outdated procedures and/or techniques.

6. All training and protocol materials should be self-contained packages that can be used independently by teachers or in groups. Materials which must be shown and interpreted by a supervisor for the teachers can lose many of the possible advantages originally cited.

7. Once the specifics of the behavior, skill, technique, or observation desired have been established by the supervisors of a particular office, the materials should then be produced through the administrative/organizational procedures set up by the committee. The supervisors or office should then act in the capacity of consultants.

8. All packaged materials should contain written matter which will aid the viewers in understanding the objectives of the materials and the understandings they should acquire through the use of them.

9. Materials should be of a professional quality. If the need

arises, videotape should be changed to 16mm. film, a slide presentation, or some other media.

In today's society, one must seek to provide the very best education to every child. Educators must not only be vigilant in finding the most appropriate means in helping teachers, but must take the initiative to explore and try conceivable methods that have promise. The use of training and protocol materials have promise; however, the development of such materials can only occur through persistent efforts.

ERIC AS A RESOURCE*

THE Educational Resources Information Center (ERIC) is a national information system, sponsored by the National Institute of Education to serve the educational community. Through a network of sixteen specialized centers or clearinghouses, each of which is responsible for a particular educational area, information is monitored, acquired, evaluated, abstracted, indexed, and listed in ERIC reference products. The CEC Information Center (ERIC Clearinghouse on Handicapped and Gifted Children) participates in this network.

ERIC Tools and Products

Research in Education. A monthly publication listing resumes of research and resource documents as well as newly funded research projects. Subscription is $38 per year ($47.50 foreign); single issues are $3.25.

Pacesetters in Innovation — Cumulative Issue — (Fiscal Years 1966-1969). Cumulative volume of all ESEA Title III projects in operation as of February 1969. OE 2-20103-69, $5.00.

Office of Education Research Reports, 1956-1965. Research reports received before the publication of *Research in Education.* Two volumes are available: *Resumes* (OE 12029) $1.75, and *Indexes* (OE 12028) $2.00.

Manpower Research Inventory for Fiscal Years 1966 and 1967 (OE 12036) $2.75.

Manpower Research Inventory for Fiscal Year 1968 (OW 12036-68) $1.75.

Manpower Research Inventory for Fiscal Year 1969 (OE 12036-69) $1.75.

HOW TO USE ERIC (OE 12037-B) 35 cents.

The above items are available at the prices indicated from Super-

---

*Source: *Exceptional Child Education Abstracts,* CEC Information Center, Vol. 7, No. 2, Summer 1975.

intendent of Documents, US Government Printing Office, Washington, D.C. 20402.

Thesaurus of ERIC Descriptors, New Edition, $8.95 (PB $6.96.) Macmillan Information, 866 Third Avenue, New York, New York 10022.

ERIC Educational Documents Index, 1966-1969, 2 Volumes, $34.50. Macmillan Information, 866 Third Avenue, New York, New York 10022.

Complete Guide and Index to ERIC Reports through December 1969, $35.00. Prentice-Hall, Inc., Englewood Cliffs, New Jersey 07632.

A Directory of Educational Information Resources, $3.50. Macmillan Information, 866 Third Avenue, New York, New York 10022.

ERIC Current Index to Journals in Education

Articles from over 560 education journals are announced and indexed by subject and author in ERIC's monthly *Current Index to Journals in Education (CIJE)*. Indexing began with January 1969 journal publications. Order from Macmillan Information, 866 Third Avenue, New York, New York 10022.

CIJE Annual Subscription	$44.00
Semiannual and Annual Indexes	95.00
Monthly Subscription plus Semiannual and Annual Indexes	83.00

ERIC Clearinghouses

Clearinghouses produce newsletters, bulletins, bibliographies, research reviews, etc., and thus serve as information sources in particular educational areas.

Career Education
204 Gurler School
Northern Illinois University
Dekalb, Illinois 60115

Counseling and Personnel Services
University of Michigan
Ann Arbor, Michigan 48104

Early Childhood Education
University of Illinois
Urbana, Illinois 61801

Educational Management
University of Oregon
Eugene, Oregon 97403

Handicapped and Gifted Children
1920 Association Drive
Reston, Virginia 22091

Higher Education
One Dupont Circle Suite 630
Washington, D. C. 20036

Information Resources
Stanford University
Stanford, California 94305

Junior Colleges
University of California at Los Angeles
Los Angeles, California 90024

Languages and Linguistics
Center for Applied Linguistics
1611 North Kent Street
Arlington, Virginia 22209

Reading and Communication Skills
National Council of Teachers of English
1111 Kenyon Road
Urbana, Illinois 61801

Rural Education and Small Schools
New Mexico State University
Las Cruces, New Mexico 88001

Science, Mathematics, and Environmental Education
Ohio State University
Columbus, Ohio 43210

Social Studies/Social Science Education
855 Broadway
Boulder, Colorado 80302

Teacher Education
One Dupont Circle Suite 616
Washington, D. C. 20036

Tests, Measurement, and Evaluation
Educational Testing Service
Princeton, New Jersey 08540

Urban Education
Teachers College
Columbia University
New York, New York 10027

THE SPECIAL EDUCATOR'S INDEX OF FREE MATERIALS*

1. *About Jobs and Retarded People*
   38 pages — a booklet that explains to parents, counselors, teachers, social workers, and prospective employers of the retarded how to prepare for the working world and how to find a job
   The President's Committee on Mental Retardation
   Att: Mrs. Mattie Smith
   Washington, D. C. 20201

2. *An Activity Curriculum for the Residential Retarded Child*
   39 pages — lists and describes crafts activities, physical activities, social activities, and music activities for various levels of retardates
   Southern Wisconsin Colony and Training School
   Union Grove, Wisconsin 53182

3. *AFB Publications Catalog No. 362-F229*
   lists various publications of the American Foundation for the Blind; up to 200 copies
   American Foundation for the Blind
   15 West 16th Street
   New York City, New York 10036
   Note: Enclose self-addressed stamped no. 10 envelope

4. *Amblyopia — Lazy Eye*
   a pamphlet which explains amblyopia and provides a series of pictures to use to test for its presence

---

*Source: *The Journal for Special Educators of the Mentally Retarded*, Fall, 1973.

American Association of Ophthalmology
1100 17th Street, N.W.
Washington, D. C. 20036

5. *Arthritis — The Basic Facts*
21 pages — a discussion of what arthritis is and what it is not;
also discusses treatment available for victims
The Arthritis Foundation
1212 Avenue of the Americas
New York City, New York 10036

6. *Arthritis Quackery*
4 pages — a brochure that discusses fraudulent schemes used
on the public in the name of medicine
The Arthritis Foundation
1212 Avenue of the Americas
New York City, New York 10036

7. *Attitudes Towards the Retarded*
a summary of studies evaluating attitudes towards the re-
tarded
The President's Committee on Mental Retardation
Att: Mrs. Mattie Smith
Washington, D. C. 20201
President's Committee on Employment of the Handicapped
Washington, D. C.

8. *Be Good To Your Baby Before It Is Born*
a booklet that explains what every mother-to-be needs to
know for her baby's health
Public Education Division
The National Foundation/March of Dimes
Box 2000
White Plains, New York 10602

9. *Biochemical and Genetic Aspects of Mental Retardation*

No. RS-84
Professional Education Department
The National Foundation/March of Dimes
Box 2000
White Plains, New York 10602

10. *Canadian Association for the Mentally Retarded* (G-1)

outlines the history, function, and goals of CAMR at various levels.

National Reference Service
National Institute on Mental Retardation
Kinsmen NIMR Building, York University Campus
4700 Keele Street, Downsview (Toronto)
Ontario, Canada

11. *CAMR Athletic Program* (G-69)

two manuals containing teaching aids, lesson plans, etc. for physical educators of the mentally retarded.

National Institute on Mental Retardation Reference Service
Kinsmen NIMR Building, York University Campus
4700 Keele Street, Downsview (Toronto)
Ontario, Canada

12. *Causes of Blindness in School Children* — P609

National Society for the Prevention of Blindness, Inc.
79 Madison Avenue
New York City, New York 10016

13. *Challenge: Youth Volunteers With The Retarded: CAMR* (G-13)

answers questions about the retarded and outlines the role of volunteers in recreation, home care, public education, etc.

National Reference Service
National Institute on Mental Retardation
Kinsmen NIMR Building, York University Campus
4700 Keele Street, Downsview (Toronto)
Ontario, Canada

14. *Changing Patterns in Residential Services for the Mentally Retarded*
    No. 72-25033
    SRS Publications Distribution Unit
    Room G-115B
    330 C Street, S.W.
    Washington, D. C. 20201

15. *Chromosome 21 and Its Association With Down's Syndrome,*
    No 59-100
    Public Education Division
    The National Foundation/March of Dimes
    Box 2000
    White Plains, New York 10602

16. *Classroom Lighting* — G301
    National Society for the Prevention of Blindness, Inc.
    79 Madison Avenue
    New York City, New York 10016

17. *Clinical Programs for Mentally Retarded Children*
    lists names, addresses, areas served, and ages accepted
    Maternal and Child Health Service
    5600 Fishers Lane, Room 12A-17
    Rockville, Maryland 20852

18. *The Clinical Team Looks at Phenylketonuria*
    56 pages — six papers reflecting viewpoints of the bio-chemist, pediatrician, medical social worker, public health nurse, psychologist, and nutritionist,
    Maternal and Child Health Service
    5600 Fishers Lane, Room 12A-17
    Rockville, Maryland 20852

COMMERCIAL PRODUCERS OF SEATWORK ACTIVITIES*

THE following companies produce duplicating masters for seatwork exercises or for exercises accompanying prescribed material produced by them.

1. Charles E. Merrill Publishing Co.   Has duplicating masters for:
   1300 Alumcreek Drive
   Columbus, Ohio 43216
   their Linguistic Readers
   Diagnostic Reading Workbook Series
   Language Mastery Speller Series
   Grammar for English Sentences
   Universal Practice Worksheets (Math)
   American Government in Action
   Homeland Series
   Maps
   Universal Using the Library

2. Continental Press, Inc.
   P. O. Box 554
   Elgin, Illinois 60120

3. Gel-Sten   New math, reading, language, music,
   911-913 South Hill Street   social studies, writing, arithmetic,
   Los Angeles, California 90015   health, nature, phonics.

4. Hayes School Publishing Co.   Music, art, math, social studies,
   321 Pennwood Avenue   reading, writing, science, phonics,
   Wilkinsburg, Pennsylvania 15221   language, health.

5. Houghton-Mifflin Co.   Has duplicating masters and records
   110 Tremont Street   for "Listen and Do."
   Boston, Massachusetts 02107

6. Ideal   Has duplicator masters for their
   11000 South Lavergne Avenue   reading tapes:

---

*Source: *Developing Units of Instruction,* by L. Meyen, Wm. C. Brown, 1972.

Oak Lawn, Illinois 60453

vowel
vowel enrichment
initial and final consonants
blends and digraphs
syllable rule — accent clue

7. Milliken Publishing Company
611 Olive Street
St. Louis, Missouri 63101

Arithmetic, reading, phonics, science,
health, safety, citizenship, holidays,
seasons, language, social studies,
English.

STAGES OF OPEN SPACE MOVEMENT*

STAGES	*CHARACTERISTICS*
Movable Walls between Classrooms	Combinations limited to two or occasionally three classrooms Cooperative teaching optional Cooperative teaching part-time Exchange of home groups for occasional specialist teaching Possible regrouping for basic skills teaching Occasional large group teaching or common experiences Homeroom remains dominant
Pods, clusters, and the like	Combination of larger number of home groups — three to six Expectation of cooperative teaching Cooperative teaching in several fields Homeroom time less than before More use of grouping to meet individual needs Teams made up of specialist teachers Resource rooms or instructional materials centers
Communities or subschools	Absence of partitions within teaching space Large number of children — 125, 150 or more Units seem as a whole rather than as comprised of several home groups Augmented staff with aides and student participants and apprentices

*Source: Alexander Frazier, *Open Schools for Children,* Association for Supervision and Curriculum Development, 1972, p. 18.

Likelihood of interage or intergrade
 population
Heavy emphasis on individualized
 instruction and independent study
Less time used in group instruction
Instructional materials center as part
 of teaching space

THE DIAGNOSTIC TEACHING MODEL*

THE diagnostic teaching model is applicable both to preservice and in-service training of special education and regular elementary teachers. The following eight objectives delineate the basic act of global competencies that are required to carry out the diagnostic teaching model:

1. Identify characteristics of individual children that indicate the need for special teaching or management procedures.

2. Specify relevant educational objectives for individual children.

3. Select techniques for effective classroom management.

4. Choose and use specialized teaching strategies for reaching specific objectives for children with varying behavioral and learning characteristics.

5. Choose and use special materials in association with specific strategies.

6. Identify and use appropriate evaluation procedures.

7. Draw upon existing sources of information regarding specialized strategies and materials.

8. Consult with available resource persons for assistance.

---

*Source: Rae Jones, Ph. D., Paper presented in lecture series, Coppin State College, 1973.

Decision Model for Diagnostic Teaching

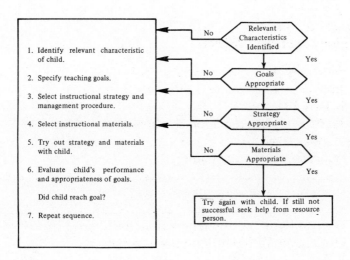

Figure X-4.

LEARNING STATIONS

Learning Station I
"Learning about the Alphabet"

    I. Jane and Jean like to play school.
   II. Jane prints her name on the board.
      It look like this:
  III. Jean writes her name on the board.
      It looks like this:
  IV. Can you print your name?

_____

      Can your write your name?

_____

   V. Do you know all the letters that are in your name?
  VI. How many different letters are in your name?

_____   _____

                                           Letters
 VII. Do you know all the letters of the alphabet?
VIII. There are 26 letters in the alphabet.
  IX. Let us learn them in order.
   X. Here are the printed capital letters. Copy them neatly in the blocks below.

A	B	C	D	E	F	G	H	I	J	K	L	M
N	O	P	Q	R	S	T	U	V	W	X	Y	Z

Figure X-5a.

Learning Station II.
"Learning About the Alphabet"

I.   These are the printed small letters. Make them neatly in the blocks below.

a	b	c	d	e	f	g	h	i	j	k	l	m

n	o	p	q	r	s	t	u	v	w	x	y	z

II.   This is the way the capital letters are written. Write them in the blocks.

A	B	C	D	E	F	G	H	I	J	K	L	M

N	O	P	Q	R	S	T	U	V	W	X	Y	Z

III.   The small letters are written this way. Write them carefully.

a	b	c	d	e	f	g	h	i	j	k	l	m

n	o	p	q	r	s	t	u	v	w	x	y	z

Figure X-5b, c, d.

Learning Station III
"Learning About the Alphabet"

I. Let's see what you have learned about this alphabet.
    Print all the letters in the alphabet by yourself. Try not to
    look at a copy of the alphabet.

    — — — — — — — — — — — — —

    — — — — — — — — — — — — —

II. There are ____ letters in the alphabet.
    Write the letter that comes before.
    __c __f__h__s__l__r__b__j__t__z__k
    Write the letter that comes after.
    j__l__o__m__a__d__r__i__g__u__x__
    Write the letter that comes between.
    a__c f__h l__n r__t w__y t__v j__l m__o e__g

Learning Station IV
"Learning About the Alphabet"

I. Look at the list of words below.
    See how each word begins.
    Write a word beside the right letter below.

boy	moon	hill	jump
egg	apple	one	tree
letter	nut	vase	puppy
umbrella	queen	sled	kite
xylophone	coat	wagon	girl
yellow	fish	ice cream	rabbit
zebra	doll		

a_____   j_____   s_____

b_____   k_____   t_____

c_____   l_____   u_____

d_____   m_____   v_____

e_____   n_____   w_____

f_____   o_____   x_____

g_____   p_____   y_____

h_____   q_____   z_____

i_____   r_____

SUMMARY — THE EDUCATION OF ALL HANDICAPPED CHILDREN ACT, PUBLIC LAW 94-142*

ON November 29, 1975, President Ford signed into law S.6, the "Education for All Handicapped Children Act." The President's approval followed overwhelming endorsement of the House-Senate conference agreement in the Congress, with the House giving its approval to the conference report on November 18 by a vote of 404 to 7. On the following day the Senate gave its approval by a margin of 87 to 7. S.6 is now Public Law 94-142.

Formula

P. L. 94-142 establishes a formula in which the Federal government makes a commitment to pay a gradually-escalating percentage of the National average expenditure per public school child times the number of handicapped children being served in the school districts of each State in the Nation. That percentage will escalate on a yearly basis until 1982 when it will become a permanent 40 percent for that year and all subsequent years.

Here is the scale:

Fiscal 1978, five percent.

Fiscal 1979, ten percent.

Fiscal 1980, twenty percent.

Fiscal 1981, thirty percent.

Fiscal 1982, forty percent.

It should be carefully noted that such a formula carries an inflation factor, i.e. the actual money figure fluctuates with inflationary-deflationary adjustments in the National average per pupil expenditure.

Formula "Kick-in"

As obviously indicated in the preceding heading, the new formula will not go into operation until fiscal 1978.

It will be recalled that existing law was already moving toward a permanent, significant increase in the Federal commitment. Public Law 93-380, the Education Amendments of 1974 (signed August 21 of 1974), created the first entitlement for handicapped children, based upon factors of the number of *all* children aged three to twenty-one within each State times $8.75. This formula (called the "Mathias formula" after its originator), amounting to a total annual authorization of $680 million, was authorized for fiscal 1975 only — with a view toward permitting an emergency infusion of money into the states while at the same time deferring to final determination of a permanent new funding formula as now contained in P. L. 94-142. This "Mathias formula" would be retained in both bills until "kick-in" of the new formula.

Ceilings

For the two years of fiscal 1976 and 1977 when the formula remains under the "Mathias entitlement," the conferees set authorization ceilings of $100 million for fiscal 1976 and $200 million for fiscal 1977. On the basis of the current national average per pupil expenditure, the following authorization ceilings are generated for the first years on the new formula:

Fiscal 1978: $387 million (on the five-percent factor).
Fiscal 1979: $775 million (on the ten-percent factor).
Fiscal 1980: $1.2 billion (on the twenty-percent factor).
Fiscal 1981: $2.32 billion (on the thirty-percent factor).
Fiscal 1982: $3.16 billion (on the forty-percent factor).

Counting Limitation

P. L. 94-142 addresses the potential threat of "overcounting" children as handicapped in order to generate the largest possible Federal allocation. The measure prohibits counting more than 12 percent as handicapped served within the total school-age population of the state between the ages of five and seventeen.

Learning Disabilities

P. L. 94-142 retains, with minor alterations, the existing Federal definition of handicapped children (EHA Section 602(I) and (15) of extant law), and this definition includes children with specific learning disabilities. However, it would appear at this point of interpretation of conference action that the Commissioner *may*, within one year, provide detailed regulations relative to SLD, including the development of a more precise definition, the prescription of comprehensive diagnostic criteria and procedures, and the prescription of procedures for monitoring of said regulations by the Commissioner. If the authorizing committees of the House and Senate disapprove the Commissioner's regulations, then a ceiling on the number of children with learning disabilities who may be counted by the State for purposes of the formula will be included when the new formula takes effect. The ceiling would provide that not more than one-sixth of the 12 percent of school-age children aged five to seventeen who may be counted as handicapped children served may be children with specific learning disabilities.

Priorities

Existing law (P.L. 93-380), in conformance with the overall goal of ending exclusion, orders a priority in the use of Federal funds for children "still unserved." P. L. 94-142 maintains and broadens that priority in the following manner:

First priority to children "unserved."

Second priority to children inadequately served when they are severely handicapped (within each disability).

Beneficiaries

P. L. 94-142 stipulates that all handicapped children, aged three to twenty-one years, may enjoy the special education and related services provided through this measure. There is also provision for the use of Federal monies for programs of early identification and screening.

Pass-Through

As finalized, P. L. 94-142 contains a substantial pass-through to the local school districts. In the first year of the new formula, 50 percent of the monies going to each state would be allocated to the local education agencies. In the following year, fiscal 1979, the LEA entitlement would be enlarged to 75 percent of the total allocation to a given State with the SEA retaining 25 percent. This 75-25 arrangement commencing in fiscal '79 becomes the permanent distribution arrangement. The current State-control of all funds is retained for the remainder of fiscal 1976 and fiscal 1977.

Constraints upon Localities

Though P. L. 94-142 authorizes a substantial local entitlement, there are numerous "strings attached." Initially, the state education agency will act as the clearinghouse of all data from the localities gathered in order to determine local entitlement, and the state will transmit that information to the commissioner. Furthermore, the state education agency may refuse to pass-through Federal monies generated when:

The school district does not conform to the overall state-plan requirements contained in this Act and in existing law (such as "full service" goal, confidentiality, etc.);

The school district fails to meet the local application requirements:

The state deems the local district unable to make effective use of its entitlement unless it consolidates its entitlement with the entitlement of one or more other school districts (this apparently allows great flexibility in funding arrangements — intermediate districts, special districts, etc.);

When the program for handicapped children within the school district is of insufficient size and scope;

When the school district is maintaining "full service" for all its handicapped children with state and local funds. (This provision will end when all districts within the states have reached "full service," at which time a degree of supplanting will in effect be permitted.)

Most significantly, P. L. 94-142 sets a flat monetary minimum. If a school district, after counting all of its handicapped children served, cannot generate an allocation for itself of at least $7,500, a pass-through to that school district does not occur. This provision is, of course, also aimed at encouraging various sorts of special education consortia in order to make a meaningful use of the Federal dollars.

State and Local Requirements

P. L. 94-142 makes a number of critical stipulations which must be adhered to by both the State and its localities. These stipulations include:

Assurance of extensive child identification procedures;

Assurance of "full service" goal and detailed timetable;

A guarantee of complete due process procedures;

The assurance of regular parent or guardian consultation;

Maintenance of programs and procedures for comprehensive personnel development;

Assurance of special education being provided to all handicapped children in the "least restrictive" environment;

Assurance of nondiscriminatory testing and evaluation;

A guarantee of policies and procedures to protect the confidentiality of data and information;

Assurance of the maintenance of an individualized program for all handicapped children;

Assurance of an effective policy guaranteeing the right of all handicapped children to a free, appropriate public education, *at no cost* to parents or guardian.

It is most important to observe that an official, written document containing all of these assurances is now required (in the form of an application) of *every* school district receiving its Federal entitlement under P. L. 94-142.

Hold Harmless

P. L. 94-142 stipulates that every State will be "held harmless" at its actual allocation for fiscal 1977 (the last year of appropriations under the "Mathias formula").

Excess Cost

P. L. 94-142 provides that Federal monies must be spent only for those "excess cost" factors attendant to the higher costs of educating handicapped children. A given school district must determine its average annual per pupil expenditure for all children being served, and then apply the Federal dollars only to those additional cost factors for handicapped children beyond the average annual per pupil expenditure. Such a requirement does not obtain for the state education agency in the utilization of its allocation under this Act.

Individualized Instruction

P. L. 94-142 requires the development of an individualized written education program for each and every handicapped child served, to be designed initially in consultation with parents or guardian, and to be reviewed and revised as necessary at least annually. This provision takes effect in the first year under the new formula, fiscal 1978.

Each child requires an educational blueprint custom-tailored to achieve his/her maximum potential.

All principles in the child's educational environment, including the child, should have the opportunity for input in the development of an individualized program of instruction.

Individualization means specifics and timetables for those

specifics, and the need for periodic review of those specifics — all of which produces greatly enhanced fiscal and educational accountability.

Date Certain

It is generally agreed that the Congress ought to fix a chronological date, however, innately arbitrary, beyond which no state or locality may be failing without penalty to guarantee against outright exclusion from the public educational systems. Also, it is felt that the states ought to be given a reasonable, but not lengthy, time period in which to reach "full service."

P. L. 94-142 therefore requires that every state and its localities, if they are to continue to receive funds under this Act, must be affording a free public education for all handicapped children aged three to eighteen by the beginning of the school year (September 1) in 1978, and further orders the availability of such education to all children aged three to twenty-one by September 1, 1980. However, these mandates carry a "big 'if' " in the area of preschool, apparently in the age range of three to five. Under P. L. 94-142, such mandate for children in that group would apply only when there is a similar mandate in State law or practice.

Due Process

The vital provisions of existing law (P.L. 93-380, the "Stafford guarantees") toward the guarantee of due process rights with respect to the identification, evaluation, and educational placement of handicapped children are constructively refined on P. L. 94-142 to ward at least the following objectives:

To strengthen the rights of all involved;

To conform more precisely to court decrees;

To clarify certain aspects of existing law;

To guarantee the rights of all parties relative to potential court review:

To insure maximum flexibility in order to conform to the varying due process procedures among the States.

Federal Sanction

If the commissioner finds substantial non-compliance with the various provisions of this Act, with emphasis upon the guarantees for children and their parents, he shall terminate the funding to a given locality or State under this Act, as well as the funding of those programs specifically designed for handicapped children under the following titles:

Part A of Title I of the Elementary and Secondary Education Act

Title III of the Elementary and Secondary Education Act (innovative programs) and its successor, Part C. Educational Innovation and Support, Section 431 of P.L. 93-380

The Vocational Education Act

Sea Authority

P. L. 94-142 requires that the state educational agency be responsible for ensuring that all requirements of the Act are carried out, and that all education programs within the state for all handicapped children, including all such programs administered by any other state or local agency, must meet state educational agency standards and be under the general supervision of persons responsible for the education of handicapped children. This provision establishes a single line of authority within one state agency for the education of all handicapped children within each state.

This provision is included in the Act for at least the following reasons:

To centralize accountability, both for the state itself and from the standpoint of the Federal government as a participant in the educational mission;

To encourage the best utilization of education resources;

To guarantee complete and thoughtful implementation of the comprehensive state plan for the education of all handicapped children within the state as already required in P.L. 93-380, the Education Amendments of 1974, with the further planning provisions of this Act;

To ensure day-by-day coordination of efforts among involved agencies;

To terminate the all too frequent practice of the bureaucratic "bumping" of children from agency to agency with the net result of no one taking substantive charge of the child's educational well-being;

To squarely direct public responsibility where the child is totally excluded from an educational opportunity;

To guarantee that the state agency which typically houses the greatest educational expertise has the responsibility for at least supervising the educational mission of all handicapped children;

To insure a responsible public agency to which parents and guardians may turn when their children are not receiving the educational services to which they are entitled.

Special Evaluations

P. L. 94-142 orders a statistically valid survey of the effectiveness of individualized instruction as mandated in the legislation. P. L. 94-142 also orders the U.S. Commissioner to conduct an evaluation of the effectiveness of educating handicapped children in the least restrictive environment and orders the Commissioner to evaluate the effectiveness of procedures to prevent erroneous classification of children.

Supplanting

P. L. 94-142 carries a stipulation which permits the U.S. Commissioner to waive the provision against supplanting of state and local funds with Federal dollars when a state presents clear and convincing evidence that all handicapped children within said state do in fact have available to them a free, appropriate public education.

Employment

P. L. 94-142 stipulates that recipients of Federal assistance under this Act shall make positive efforts to employ and advance in employment qualified handicapped individuals.

Architectual Barriers

P. L. 94-142 authorizes such sums as may be necessary for the U.S. Commissioner to award grants to pay all or part of the cost of altering existing buildings and equipment to eliminate architectural barriers in educational facilities. Such provision is aimed at assuring certain handicapped children an appropriate public education in the least restrictive environment.

Lifetime

P. L. 94-142 establishes a permanent authorization with no expiration date.

Preschool Incentive

P. L. 94-142 carries a special incentive grant aimed at encouraging the states to provide special education and related services to its preschool handicapped children. Each handicapped child in the state aged three to five who is counted as served will generate a special $300 entitlement. It should be noted that this incentive entitlement goes to the state education agency and must be used by the SEA to provide preschool services. Additionally, this entitlement is a separate "line item" appropriation, independent of the larger P. L. 94-142 entitlement.

Advisory

P. L. 94-142 provides that each State shall have a planning and advisory panel with the following duties:

Advise the state education on unmet needs and general policies for educating handicapped children;

Comment publicly on rules and regulations issued by the state and procedures proposed by the state for distribution of funds;

Assist the state in developing and reporting such data and evaluations as may assist the U.S. Commissioner.

Legislative Format

P. L. 94-142 amends the existing Education of the Handicapped Act and rewrites Part B of that Act. In that context, it is important to observe that all of the important advances made in Part B through P.L. 93-380 (Education Amendments of 1974) are retained in P. L. 94-142, and, in many instances, are considerably improved upon.

Impact

P. L. 94-142 provides for an annual evaluation of the effectiveness of this legislation toward assistance in the achievement of a free, appropriate public education for all of the Nation's handicapped children.

INSIGHT, The Government Report of The Council for Exceptional Children, December 1975, pp. 1-6.

AUTHOR INDEX

243

SUBJECT INDEX

A

Agencies, federal, 161-173, 200-201
Bureau of Education for the Handicapped
(BEH), 163-165
centers for instructional materials, 167-
168
information system and, establishment
of, 169
coalition movement, organizational, 169
organizations included in, 169-170
purpose of, 170
Congress, measures of, 161-162
Council for Exceptional Children (CEC),
168, 169, 170-172
Elementary and Secondary Education Act
Amendments of, 162
"handicapped", definition of, 162-163
Handicapped Children's Education Program (HACHE), 172-173
legislation for special education, 162, 163-
165, 165-167
NEA 1973 program objectives for, 161
role of, traditional, 162
Agencies, local, 191-200, 200-201
career education program of, 195-197
concern of, 192
continuum of special education services
by, implementation of, 192-193
Fig. X-3, 193
see also Special Education services, continuum of,
intervention programs of, 197
parent involvement and, 199-200
referral and placement procedures of, 197-
199
role of, traditional, 191
Agencies, state, 173-191, 200-201
courts and litigation, 175-177
action suits, 176-177
Attorney Generals' opinion, power of,
177

landmark case, 176
Educational Development Center, 189
facilities for the handicapped, 185-189
construction of, standards for, 186
Maryland General Assembly Act on, 186
personnel, 186-187
teacher-training programs, 187-189
financing, *see* Financing, state
legislation of, mandatory, 174-175
legislation of, permissive, 174
implementation, legislative, procedures
for, 178-179
State Education Agency, functions of, 174
teacher certification, 187, 188, 189-191
see also Teacher certification
role of, traditional, 173-174
American Printing House for the Blind,
165, 168
Audio recordings, 111-113
cassette tapes, materials for use with, 111
steps for successful taping, 112
studies with retardates using, 112-113
teacher-made tapes, 111-112
use of, 112
videotapes, value of, 113
Audiometry, electrodermal, (E.D.R.), 75
Auditory perception, *see* Perception and
Remediation, perceptual
Automated programmed instruction, *see*
Instruction and Devices and Materials

B

Baltimore City Schools' Special Learning
Conference, 151-153
Behavior, perceptual, mechanisms of, 6
see also Remediation, perceptual
Behavior modification strategies, xii, 6, 48-
62
adaptation and design of, 48
advantages of, 56-58, 61, 62
educational, 57-58